THE BASIC VOLUMES:

Gropp, Arthur E. A Bibliography of Latin American Bibliographies. 1968. (Includes monographs only, through 1964.)

Gropp, Arthur E. A Bibliography of Latin American Bibliographies Published in Periodicals. Vol. I: A-D; Vol. II: E-Z, Index. 1976. (Includes periodical literature only, through 1965.)

THE SUPPLEMENTS:

Gropp, Arthur E. A Bibliography of Latin American Bibliographies. 1971. (Includes monographs only, 1965-1969.)

Cordeiro, Daniel Raposo. A Bibliography of Latin American Bibliographies: Social Sciences & Humanities. 1979. (Includes monographs, 1969-1974, and periodical literature, 1966-1974.)

Piedracueva, Haydée. A Bibliography of Latin American Bibliographies, 1975-1979: Social Sciences and Humanities. 1982. (Includes monographs and periodical literature.)

Loroña, Lionel V. A Bibliography of Latin American Bibliographies, 1980-1984: Social Sciences and Humanities. 1987. (Includes monographs and periodical literature.)

All of these works have been published by Scarecrow Press, Inc., Metuchen, N.J.

A Bibliography of Latin American Bibliographies, 1980-1984:

Social Sciences and Humanities

LIONEL V. LOROÑA
Editor

(Supplement No. 4 to
Arthur E. Gropp's
*A Bibliography of
Latin American Bibliographies*)

THE SCARECROW PRESS, INC.
METUCHEN, N.J., & LONDON
1987

Library of Congress Cataloging-in-Publication Data

A Bibliography of Latin American bibliographies, 1980-
1984.

"Supplement no. 4 to Arthur E. Gropp's A bibliography
of Latin American bibliographies."
Includes indexes.
1. Bibliography--Bibliography--Latin America.
2. Latin America--Bibliography. I. Loroña, Lionel V.
II. Gropp, Arthur Eric, 1902- . Bibliography of
Latin American bibliographies.
Z1601.A2G76 1968 Suppl. 4 016.98 86-22093
[F1408]
ISBN 0-8108-1941-4

Manufactured in the United States of America

This volume is dedicated

to

DANIEL RAPOSO CORDEIRO

(1940-1986)

CONTENTS

Preface	vii
List of Serial Titles Cited/Examined	ix
General Works	1
Agriculture	18
Anthropology	24
Archaeology	27
Art and Architecture	29
Bibliographies of Bibliographies	32
Bibliography--National	34
Biography (Collective)	38
Biography (Individual)	41
Dissertations	53
Economics	56
Education	63
Folklore	70
Geography, Cartography	71
History	72
Indexes	84
International Relations	95
Language and Literature	97
Law	112
Libraries and Archives	114
Library Science	128
Manuscripts and Rare Books	129
Mass Media	131
Microforms	132
Minority Groups	133
Music	136
Periodicals	138
Philosophy	144
Political Science	144
Publishers	148
Religion	149
Social Sciences	151
Statistics	162
Urbanization	163
Subject Index	165
Author Index	205

PREFACE

With this volume, we are now up to the fourth supplement to Arthur E. Gropp's Bibliography of Latin American Bibliographies published in 1968. Successive supplements have been compiled by Mr. Gropp, Daniel Raposo Cordeiro and Haydée Piedracueva. These have been published in 1976, 1979 and 1982; the coverage to this point has been extended through 1979. The present volume hopes to encompass material for the period 1980-1984, though, as in previous volumes, we are including relevant items not previously noted regardless of their publication dates.

As in previous compilations, the impetus behind this project has been the work of the Committee on Bibliography of the Seminar on the Acquisition of Latin American Library Materials (SALALM). This volume consolidates the entries submitted by committee members that appeared in the SALALM Annual Report for the years 1980-1982 and for the years 1983-1985 when it appeared as a separate publication (Bibliography of Latin American Bibliographies), as part of the SALALM Bibliography and Reference Series. The volumes for 1980-1982 were edited by Haydée Piedracueva. The others were edited by me. Committee members were given the assignment of checking specific journals for bibliographies, as well as for reporting bibliographies in monographic form. Beginning with journals published in 1979, we have also had, through the assistance of committee member Barbara G. Valk, Editor of the Hispanic American Periodicals Index (HAPI), contributions made by HAPI indexers which have provided an additional and welcome flow of information.

The geographical area covered in this bibliography is Latin America and the Caribbean. Bibliographies published in or about these areas in subjects pertaining to the humanities and social sciences are included. Bibliographies in the pure sciences and technology are generally excluded unless the bibliography is sufficiently broad in perspective to contain material of interest to those working in other fields.

As mentioned in earlier editions, we include bibliographies that appear as articles in periodicals or as monographs. Bibliographies appended to articles or monographs are generally excluded. However, I have seen fit to make a few exceptions where a bibliography, substantial in volume and interest, has been included within a body of another work. In the majority of cases, bibliographies listed are new works. The exceptions are reprints of important works which have made this material available once more, or continuing national bibliographies wherein the latest volume or issue examined has been cited.

This volume is arranged in subject categories subdivided by countries within each category (unless unwarranted by the small number of entries). The section on individual bibliographies and the section on specific indexes are arranged alphabetically by subject (i.e., the name of the biographee, or the title of the work indexed). The number and type of subject categories remain the same as in the expanded list first used in the previous compilation. Author and subject indexes and a list of the serial publications examined complete the work.

In addition to my deep thanks to Barbara Valk and the indexers of HAPI, I should also like to express my gratitude to the following members of the Bibliography Committee for their contributions: Linda Alexander, Ana María Cobos, Russ Davidson, Danilo Figueredo, Donald C. Henderson, María Segura Hoopes, Sara de Mundo Lo, César Rodríguez, Iliana Sonntag, Olga Torres-Seda, Carole Travis, Lourdes Vásquez, Gayle Williams, and Richard D. Woods. A particular note of thanks goes to Paula Covington, who served as Chair of the Bibliography Committee during the years I was putting together the annual cumulations and supplied me with many contributions as well as guidance and counsel.

Lastly, my unending gratitude to my colleague at New York Public Library, Gary Gisondi, who introduced me to the mysteries of computer technology and helped me bring the whole thing together in truly wondrous fashion.

Lionel V. Loroña

LIST OF SERIAL TITLES CITED/EXAMINED

A: revista de ciencias sociales y humanidades
Academia (Santiago, Chile)
Academia chilena de la historia. Boletîn
Academia colombiana. Boletîn
Academia de artes y ciencias de Puerto Rico. Boletîn
Academia hondureña de la lengua. Boletîn
Academia nacional de la historia. Boletîn (Argentina)
Academia nacional de la historia. Boletîn (Bolivia)
Academia nacional de la historia. Boletîn (Venezuela)
Academia paulista de letras. Revista (São Paulo)
Academia puertorriqueña de la historia. Boletîn
Academia venezolana. Boletîn
Actualidades (Caracas)
Afro-Asia (Bahia)
Agenda (Washington, D.C.)
Aisthesis
Amazonia peruana
America latina (USSR)
American anthropologist
American antiquity
American book publishing record
The Americas; a quarterly review of inter-American cultural history
Americas (OAS)
Anales de antropología (Mexico)
Anales de investigación histórica
Anales de la literatura española contemporánea
Anales de la literatura hispanoamericana (Madrid)
Anales del Instituto de Investigaciones Estéticas (UNAM Mexico)
Antropología e Historia
Antropológica (Venezuela)
Anuario antropológico (Brazil)
Anuario científico
Anuario colombiano de historia social y la cultura
Anuario de estudios americanos
Anuario de estudios centroamericanos
Anuario de geografía (Mexico)
Anuario de letras (Mexico)
Anuario indigenista
Apuntes
Araucaria de Chile
Archivo ibero-americano
Archivos de historia potosina
Areito
Arizona and the West
Artes de México
Atenea (Chile)
Aula
Aztlán

Bibliografía económica de México
Bibliografia folclorica (Brazil)
Bibliografía histórica mexicana
Bibliografía mexicana
Bibliografía teológica
Bibliography of the English speaking Caribbean
Biblioteca Municipal Mario de Andrade. Boletim bibliográfico
Bilingual review
Biography: an interdisciplinary

quarterly
Boletín americanista
Boletin bibliográfico CERLAL
Boletín bibliográfico de antropología americana
Bolctín bibliográfico mexicano
Boletín cultural y bibliográfico
Boletín de educación (Chile)
Boletín de estudios latinoamericanos y del Caribe
Boletín de historia y antigüedades
Boletín del Instituto de Investigaciones Bibliográficas (UNAM Mexico)
Boletín del Museo del Hombre Dominicano
Boletín interamericano de archivos
Boletín nicaragüense de bibliografía y documentación
Borderlands journal
Brazil. Biblioteca Nacional. Anais
Brazil. Biblioteca Nacional. Boletim bibliográfico
Brazil. Biblioteca Nacional. Revista
Brazilian economic studies
Bulletin hispanique
Bulletin of bibliography and magazine notes
Bulletin of Eastern Caribbean affairs
Bulletin of Hispanic studies
Bulletin of Latin American research

CEPAL Review
Cahiers des amériques latines
Cambio (Mexico)
Caravelle
Caribbean monthly bulletin (Puerto Rico)
Caribbean quarterly
Caribbean review
Caribbean studies
El Caribe contemporáneo
Casa de las Américas
Chasqui
Chile. Congreso. Biblioteca. Boletín bibliográfico
Círculo militar
Comercio exterior
Comercio y desarrollo
Comunicación (Caracas)
Conjonction
Conjunto
Convivium
Correo de los Andes
Creación y crítica
Crítica (Mexico)
Crítica y utopia
Cuadernos americanos
Cuadernos de bibliografía nicaragüense
Cuadernos de economía
Cuadernos hispanoamericanos
Cuadernos políticos
Cuba. Biblioteca Nacional. Revista
Cuban studies. Estudios cubanos
Cultura (Ecuador)
Cultura de Guatemala
Cultures et développement

Dados
De Colores
Debate (Peru)
Demografía y economía
Derecho y reforma agraria; revista
Desarrollo económico
Desarrollo indoamericano
Desarrollo y sociedad
Diálogos (Mexico)
Diálogos (Puerto Rico)
Dianoia
Discurso literario
Docencia post-secundaria

EURE
ECA; estudios centroamericanos
Eco
Economía y desarrollo
Economic development and cultural change
Ecuador; bibliografía analítica
La educación
Educación hoy
Eme-eme; estudios dominicanos

Encuentro (Nicaragua)
Los ensayistas
Ensayos ECIEL
Escandalar
Escritos de teoría
Escritura (Venezuela)
Estrategía (Argentina)
Estudios andinos
Estudios de Asia y Africa
Estudios de cultura maya (UNAM Mexico)
Estudios de cultura nahuatl (UNAM Mexico)
Estudios de historia moderna y contemporánea de México (UNAM Mexico)
Estudios internacionales
Estudios latinoamericanos (Poland)
Estudios paraguayos
Estudios rurales latinoamericanos
Estudios sociales (Chile)
Estudios sociales (Dominican Republic)
Estudios sociales centro-americanos
Estudos afro-asiaticos (Brazil)
Estudios brasileiros (Paraná, Brazil)
Estudos económicos
Estudos iberoamericanos
Ethnos (Sweden)
Explicación de textos literarios

Fem
Fichero
Folklore americano
Foro internacional
Foro literario

Government publications review
Grassroots development
El grito del sol
Guatemala indígena

Hispamérica
Hispania
Hispanofila
Historia (Chile)
Historia mexicana
Historia obrera
Historia y cultura (Peru)
Historiografía y bibliografía americanistas
History teacher
Horizontes (Puerto Rico)
Hueso húmero
Human rights quarterly
Humboldt (Spanish ed.)

Ibero-Americana; nordic journal of Latin American studies
Ibero-Amerikanisches Archiv
Ideologies and literature
Institut français d'études andines. Bulletin
Instituto de cultura puerto-rriqueña. Revista
Instituto do estudos brasileiros. Revista
Instituto histórico e geográfico brasileiro. Revista
Integración latinoamericana
Inter-American economic affairs
Inter-American music review
Interciencia
International bibliography
International journal of American linguistics
International migration review
Inti
Investigación económica (Mexico)
Investigaciones y ensayos
Islas (Cuba)
Iztapalapa; revista de ciencias sociales y humanidades

Jahrbuch für Geschichte von Staat, Wirtschaft und Gesellschaft Lateinamerikas
Jamaica journal
Journal de la Société des Américanistes
Journal of Caribbean studies
Journal of commonwealth literature
Journal of developing areas
Journal of inter-american studies and world affairs
Journal of international affairs
Journal of Latin American lore
Journal of Latin American studies

Journal of reading

Lateinamerika (E. Germany)
Latin American Indian literature
Latin American literary review
Latin American music review
Latin American perspectives
Latin American research review
Latinoamerica; anuario de estudios latinoamericanos
Lenguaje (Colombia)
Lenguaje y ciencias
Lenguas modernas
Letras de Buenos Aires
Letras de hoje
Lingua e literatura
Literatura chilena: creación y crîtica
Logos (Mexico)
Lotería
Luso-Brazilian review

Maldoror
Mercado de valores
Mesoamerica (Guatemala)
Mester
Mexico. Archivo General de la Nación. Boletîn
Mexico en el arte
Modern drama
Modern Language Association. Publications
Modern language journal
Montalban
Mundo nuevo (Venezuela)
Mundus
Museo Nacional (Peru). Revista

NACLA Report on the Americas
NS/North-South
Nawpa pacha
New Mexico historical review
New scholar
New voices (Trinidad and Tobago)
Nexos
Nicarahuac
Nova americana
Nuestra historia
Nueva antropología
Nueva polîtica
Nueva revista de filología hispánica
Nueva sociedad (Costa Rica)

La palabra y el hombre
Pensamiento iberoamericano
Peru. Museo Nacional. Revista
Pesquisa e planejamento económico
Phaedrus: an international annual of children's literature
Pluma (Colombia)
Plural
Polîtica (Brazil)
Pontificia Universidad Católica del Ecuador. Revista
Problemas de desarrollo
Punto de contacto

Quimera

RLA; revista de lingüîstica aplicada
Reading teacher
Relaciones internacionales
Reportorio americano
Repertorio latinoamericano
Review. (Ctr. for Interamerican Relations)
Revista andina
Revista brasileira de biblioteconomia e documentaçao
Revista brasileira de economia
Revista brasileira de estadistica
Revista brasileira de estudos pedagogicos
Revista brasileira de estudos polîticos
Revista brasileira de filosofia
Revista brasileira de geografia
Revista brasileira de mercado de capitais
Revista canadiense de estudios hispánicos
Revista chicano-riqueña
Revista chilena de historia y geografía
Revista chilena de literatura
Revista colombiana de antropología
Revista de antropologia. (São

Paulo)
Revista de ciencia política (Brazil)
Revista de ciencias sociales (Puerto Rico)
Revista de ciencias sociais
Revista de crítica literaria latinoamericana
Revista de cultura brasileña
Revista de economía rural
Revista de estudios hispánicos
Revista de extensión cultural
Revista de filosofía de la Universidad de Costa Rica
Revista de historia de América
Revista de historia de las ideas
Revista de Indias
Revista de legislación y documentación en derecho y ciencias sociales
Revista de letras (Brazil)
Revista de literatura
Revista de planeación y desarrollo
Revista de teatro
Revista del pensamiento centroamericano
Revista española de antropología americana
Revista geográfica (Mexico)
Revista hispánica moderna
Revista histórica (Argentina)
Revista histórica (Uruguay)
Revista iberoamericana
Revista interamericana de bibliografía
Revista jurídica de la Universidad de Puerto Rico
Revista latinoamericana de estudios educativos
Revista letras (Brazil)
Revista mexicana de ciencias políticas y sociales (UNAM)
Revista mexicana de sociología
Revista musical chilena
Revista musical de Venezuela
Revista nacional de cultura
Revista paraguaya de sociología
Revista/Review interamericana
Revolución y cultura
Revue des deux mondes
Revue tiers mondes

SALALM Final report and working papers
SALALM Newsletter
Santiago (Cuba)
Sapientia
Serials librarian
Shupihui
Signo; cuadernos bolivianos de cultura
Sillages
Sin nombre
Socialismo y participación
Stromata
Studi di letteratura ispanoamericana
Studies in comparative international development
Studies in Latin American popular literature
Sur

Terra Ameriga
Texto crítico
Thesaurus
Tradición popular
El trimestre económico

UNESCO journal of information science, librarianship and archives administration
U.S. Library of Congress. Accessions List. Brazil
Union (Cuba)
Universidad Autónoma de México. Revista
Universidad de la Habana
Universidad de San Carlos
Universidades (Mexico)
Universitas (Argentina)
Universitas 2000

Venezuela. Archivo General de la Nación. Boletín
Veritas
Vínculos
Vozes
Vuelta

World literature today

World literature written in
English

Yucatan. Universidad. Revista

Zeitschrift für Lateinamerika
Wein

Zona franca

GENERAL WORKS

GENERAL

1. Albonico, Aldo. Bibliografia della storiografia e pubblicistica italiana sull' America (1940-1980). Milano: Cisalpino-Goliardica, 1981. 146 p.

2. Amaya, José Antonio. Bibliografía de la Real Expedición Botánica del Nuevo Reyno de Granada. Bogotá: Instituto Colombiano de Cultura Hispánica, 1983. 184 p. Note: 9 leaves of plates.

3. "América en la bibliografía española (Reseñas informativas)." Historiografía y bibliografía americanistas, 1980, 24, 263-305.

4. Becco, Horacio Jorge. Contribución para una bibliografía de las ideas latinoamericanas. Paris: Unesco, 1981. 230 p. (América Latina en su cultura)

5. Becker, Félix, and Klaus Müller. "Instituciones de investigación y estudios latinoamericanistas en la República Federal Alemana." Historiografía y bibliografía americanistas, 1984, 28, 129-150.

6. Behar, D., and R. Behar, compilers. "Bibliografía hispanoamericana: libros antiguos y modernos referentes a América y España." Reprint of 1947 ed. London: H. Pordes, 1982. 372 p.

7. Bellini, Giuseppe. Bibliografia dell ispanoamericanismo italiano; contributi critici. Milano: Cisalpino-Goliardica, 1981. 100 p.

8. Bellini, Giuseppe. Bibliografia dell' ispanoamericanismo italiano. Milano: Cisalpino-Goliardica, 1982. 144 p. (Letterature e culture dell' America Latina, 3).

9. "Bibliografía amazónia." Amazonia peruana, Jul 1983, 5 (9), 137.

10. "Bibliografía de ['Estudios latinoamericanos'], tomos 1-5." Estudios latinoamericanos (Poland), 1981, 8, 221-229.

11. Bibliographic guide to Latin American studies. Boston: G. K. Hall, 1983. 3 vols. Note: Published annually.

12. "Bibliographie der in der DDR vom 1 April bis 30 September, 1981 erschienenen Zeitschriftenaufsätze und Ganzschriften." Lateinamerika, Fall 1981, 199-209.

13. Butler, Erwin. "Spanish American books." Booklist, Apr 15, 1981, 77 (16), 1144-1146.

14. Butler, Erwin. "Spanish reference books." Booklist, Jul 14/Aug 1981, 77 (22-23), 1438-1441.

15. Foster, David William, editor. Sourcebook of Hispanic culture in the United States. Chicago: American Library Association, 1982. 532 p.

16. Goodman, Edward Julius. The exploration of South America: an annotated bibliography. New York: Garland Publishing Company, 1983. 174 p. (Garland reference library of social science, 48).

17. Gormly, Mary. "Latin America: a selected list of recent reference materials." SALALM Newsletter, June 1983, 10 (4), 3-4.

18. Gormly, Mary. "Latin America: a selected list of recent reference materials." SALALM Newsletter, Mar 1982, 9 (3), 11-13.

19. Goslinga, Marian. "Recent books: an informative listing of books about the Caribbean, Latin America, and their emigrant groups." Caribbean Review, 1983, 12 (1). Note: Appears as a regular feature.

20. Granmer, Jan, et al. Latinamerikana i svensk bibliografi, 1977-1980 (América Latina en la bibliografía sueca, 1977-1980). Stockholm: [n.p.], 1982. 80 p.

21. Griffith, William J. "Some Latin American bibliographies." Latin American Research Review, 1980, 15 (1), 256-261.

22. Grothey, Mina Jane. "Tools of the trade: recent reference works for Latin Americanists." Latin American Research Review, 1984, 19 (3), 248-262.

23. Grover, Mark L. Latin America: a reference guide to the Brigham Young University Library, 1984. Provo: Harold B. Lee Library, Brigham Young University, 1984. 139 p.

24. "Guía bibliográfica para una historia de la cultura en Hispanoamérica." Nuestra América, Jun 1982, 1, 115-134.

25. Hallewell, Laurence. "Charting the middle passage: recent reference books on the African diaspora." Latin American Research Review, 1984, 19 (3), 217-222.

26. Hartmann, Roswith. "Estudios americanistas de Bonn." Revista andina, Jul 1984, 2 (1), 299-307.

27. Hartness Graham, Ann, and Richard D. Woods. Latin American in English-language reference books: a selected, annotated bibliography. New York: Special Libraries Association, c1981. 49 p.

28. Hartness-Kane, Ann. "Governments as publishers of reference materials: Mexico and Brazil, 1970-1980." Latin American Research Review, 1982, 17 (2), 142-155.

29. Hébert, John R. "Bibliography and general works." In: Handbook of Latin American Studies, 1982, 44: 3-31. Note: This section of the Handbook appears in all volumes.

30. Hilton, Sylvia L. "El americanismo en España, 1982-1983." Revista de Indias, Jul-Dic 1983, 43 (172), 847-914.

31. Hilton, Sylvia L. "El americanismo en España, 1983-1984." Revista de Indias, Jul-Dic 1984, 44 (174), 573-680.

32. Huneeus, Carlos. "Eppur si muove: visiones alemanas sobre la politica latinoamericana." Latin American Research Review, 1984, 19 (1), 243-260.

33. Jenkins Company. Latin America and the southwestern United States. Austin, TX: Jenkins Co., [1982?]. 228 p.

34. Klementeva, N.M. Otnosheniia mezhdu KNR i stranami Latinskoi Ameriki: ekonomika, politika, ideologiia: bibliograficheskii ukazatel. Moskva: Vsesoiuznaia Gosudarstrennaia Biblioteka Inostrannoi Literatury, 1981. 163 p.

35. León Pinelo, Antonio de. Epítome de la biblioteca oriental, occidental, náutica y geográfica. Barcelona: Ediciones de la Universidad de Barcelona y Horacio Capel Sáez, 1982. Note: Facsimile of second edition, rev. and aug. by Andrés González de Barcia.

36. Libros en venta en Hispanoamérica y España; por autor, por título, por materia. Suplemento: 1982. San Juan, PR: Ediciones Melcher, 1983. Note: First vol. published in 1964 by R. R. Bowker.

37. Lowder, Stella. "Latin America. An introduction to the region." Cultures et développement, 1983, 15 (1), 79-83.

38. Martin, Dolores Moyano, editor. Handbook of Latin American Studies: Humanities. Austin: University of Texas Press, 1982, c1983, 24. Note: v. 1, 1935-.

39. Matos, Antonio. Guía a las reseñas de y sobre Hispanoamérica. 1981. A guide to reviews of books from and about Hispanic America. 1981. Detroit: Blaine Ethridge books, 1983. Note: Published annually. v.1 (1960-64)-.

40. Méndez-Domínguez, Alfredo. Mesoamérica: directorio y bibliografia, 1950-1980. Guatemala: Universidad del Valle de Guatemala, 1982. 313 p.

41. Miller, Eugene Willard, and Ruby M. Miller. Latin America: a bibliography on the third world. Monticello, IL: Vance Bibliographies, 1982. 33 p.

42. Miller, Eugene Willard, and Ruby M. Miller. Middle America and the Caribbean: a bibliography on the third world. Monticello, IL: Vance Bibliographies, 1982. 98 p.

43. Miller, Eugene Willard, and Ruby M. Miller. South America: a bibliography on the third world. Monticello, IL: Vance Bibliographies, 1982. 81 p.

44. Moss, Alan, editor. "Current bibliography." Caribbean Studies, 1980, 20. Note: Appears as a regular feature.

45. Nef, J. "Latin American and Caribbean studies in Canada--A developmental perspective." Canadian journal of development studies, 1982, 3 (1), 177-197.

46. "New resources." NACLA report on the Americas, 1981, 15 (1). Note: Appears as a regular feature.

47. Podestá, Bruno. "Estudios latinoamericanos en Italia: el caso peruano, 1960-1979." Apuntes, 1981, 6 (11), 79-91.

48. Rolland, Denis. Guide des organisations internationales et de leurs publications: Amérique Latine. Paris: Harmattan, 1983. 221 p.

49. Tóth, Agnes. "Hispanoamérica en la historiografía húngara: bibliografía selecta, 1945-1982." Historiografía y bibliografía americanistas, 1983, 27, 95-110.

50. Turner, Mary C., compiler. Libros de los Estados Unidos traducidos al idioma español tomados de catálogos vigentes hasta enero [1983]. Buenos Aires-México, D.F.: Centro Regional del Libro, 1983, 320 p.

51. University of California, Berkeley. Library. Source materials of Latin America. Supplement. Gaston Somoshegyi-Szokol, compiler. [Berkeley], 1983. 35 p.

52. Vorobeva, Z G. Latinskaia Amerika v sovetskoi pechati, 1979-1980: Ukazatel knig i statei na russkom iazyke o sovremennom polozhennii, ekonimike, kulture, geografii i istorii stran latinsko Ameriki. Moskva: Institut Nauchnoi Informatsii po Obschchestvennym, Akademiia Nauk SSSR, 1981. 214 p.

53. Welch, Thomas L., and Myriam Figueras. Travel accounts and descriptions of Latin America and the Caribbean, 1800-1920; a selected bibliography. Washington, DC: Organization of American States, 1982. 293 p.

AMAZON VALLEY

54. Guimarães, Anarcila Ma. C.; Francisca Dantas de Lima; and Isete Cordeiro Franco. Indice bibliográfico dos trabalhos realizados pelo CODEAMA [Centro de Desenvolvimento, Pesquisa e Tecnologia do Estado do Amazonas]. Manaus: Setor de Documentação e Sistemas de Informação, 1982. 44 leaves.

55. Hernández de Caldas, Angela; Martha Helena Giraldo Isaza; and Gloria Chapetón de Ortiz. Recursos naturales de la Amazonia a través de su documentación. Bogotá: Servicio Andino de Información Forestal de CONIF y Centro de Documentación, 1983.

56. Levistre de Ruiz, Jeanine. "Visión bibliográfica de los paises amazónicos." Shupihui, Ene-Mar 1984, 9 (29), 71-111.

57. Porras Barrenechea, Paúl. "Esquema para una bibliografía amazónica." Shupihui, Ene-Mar 1984, 9 (29), 15-23.

ANDES REGION

58. "Bibliografía." Bulletin de l'Institut Français d'Etudes Andines, 1981, 10 (3-4), 177-185.

59. Cardich, Augusto. "A propósito del 25 aniversario Lauricocha," Revista andina, 1983, 1 (1), 151-173.

60. Fernández Baca L, José, and Lorena Masias Q. "La región andina vista desde fuera: bibliografía." Estudios andinos, 1983, 19, 85-109.

ARGENTINA

61. Argentina, Estado Mayor Conjunto. Biblioteca y Centro de Documentación. Islas Malvinas: artículos contenidos en publicaciones periódicas existentes en la biblioteca y centro de

documentación del E.M.C: enero-junio de 1983. [Argentina]: La Biblioteca, [1983?]. 21 leaves.

62. Bagu, Sergio. Argentina, 1875-1975: población, economía, sociedad: estudio temático y bibliográfico. 2 ed. México: Universidad Nacional Autónoma de México, 1983. 159 p. (Serie bibliografías--Centro de Estudios Latinoamericanos, 3).

63. Bibliografía Bahía Blanca. Bahía Blanca, Argentina: Biblioteca Central, Universidad Nacional del Sur, 1979.

64. Bibliografía sobre las Islas Malvinas. Buenos Aires: Ministerio de Educación, Centro Nacional de Documentación e Información Educativa, 1982. 14 p.

65. Bryant, Melrose M. Falklands-Malvinas conflict: selected references. Maxwell Air Force Base, AL: Air University Library, 1982 65 p. (Special bibliography, 266).

66. "Buenos Aires en sus libros." Revista nacional de cultura, 1980. (6), 49-127.

67. Daus, Federico A., and Raúl C. Rey Balmaceda. Islas Malvinas: reseña geográfica. Bibliografía. Buenos Aires: OIKOS Asociación para la Promoción de los Estudios Territoriales y Ambientes, 1982. 242 p. Note: Bibliography compiled by R.C. Rey Balmaceda.

68. Girbal de Blacha, Noemí. "Aportes bibliográficos para el estudio del gran Chaco argentino y la explotación forestal (1880-1914)." Revista interamericana de bibliografía, 1983, 33 (3), 331-354.

69. Library of Congress. Hispanic Division. Everette E. Larson, compiler. A selective listing of monographs and government documents on the Falkland/Malvinas Islands in the Library of Congress. Washington, DC: Library of Congress, 1982. 28 p.

70. Merubia, Sonia. Argentina. Austin: University of Texas at Austin, The General Libraries, 1981. 36 p. (Selected reference sources, 64).

71. Mundo Lo, Sara de. The Falkland/Malvinas Islands: A bibliography of books (1619-1982). Urbana, IL: Albatross, 1983. 65 p.

72. Pellitero, Antonio. Contribución a la bibliografía sobre el Tandil. [Tandil, Argentina]: Universidad Nacional del Centro de la Provincia de Buenos Aires, 1980. 154 p.

73. Santos Gómez, Susana. Bibliografía de viajeros a la Argentina. Buenos Aires: Fundación para la Educación, la Ciencia y la Cultura, 1983. 2 vols.

74. Solveira de Báez, Beatriz Rosario, and Noemí M. Girbal de Blacha. "El Museo Social Argentino: su origen, acción y proyección; informe bibliográfico." Historiografia y bibliografia americanistas, 1984, 28, 95.

75. Tesler, Mario, et al. Temas de Buenos Aires: contribución bibliográfica y hemerográfica. Buenos Aires: Empresa Nacional de Telecomunicaciones, 1981. 419 p.

76. Vinci, Liliana F.; María E. Rios; and Martha Valdez Escalera. Contribución para una bibliografia sobre Córdoba II. Córdoba, Argentina: Biblioteca Mayor, 1981. 156 leaves. (Publicaciones de la Biblioteca Mayor, 15).

BARBADOS

77. Callender, Jean A.; Loraine Jackson; and Carlyle Best. Barbadian society, past and present: a select bibliography compiled in celebration of the 14th anniversary of the independence of Barbados. Cave Hill, Barbados: Main Library, University of the West Indies, 1980. 63 p.

78. Handler, Jerome, and Samuel Hough. "Addenda to 'A guide to source material for the study of Barbados history' Part IV." Journal of the Barbados Museum and Historical Society, 1983, 37 (1), 82-92.

79. Handler, Jerome, and Samuel Hough. "Addenda to 'A guide to source material for the study of Barbados history, 1627-1834' Part III." Journal of the Barbados Museum and Historical Society, 1982, 36 (4), 385-397.

BELIZE

80. Woodward, Ralph Lee. Belize. Santa Barbara, CA: American Bibliographical Center, Clio Press, 1980. 229 p. (World bibliographical series, 21).

BOLIVIA

81. Aramayo Santa Cruz, Carlos, and Rosa María Sensano Zárate. Catálogo de documentos nacionales. La Paz: CEBIAE, 1984.

82. Centro Nacional de Documentación Científica y Tecnológica. Artículos sobre aspectos bolivianos en publicaciones periodicas del exterior, 1977-1979. La Paz: Universidad Mayor de San Andrés, 1980. 30 p. (Serie bibliográfica, 4).

83. Inch, Marcela, and René Poppe. Catálogo de bibliografia

boliviana. La Paz: Editorial Piedra Libre, 1980. 71, 62, 53 p.

BRAZIL

84. Augel, Johannes. A pesquisa alemã sobre o Brasil de inicios de 1970 a maio de 1981: (Levantamento provisario). Salvador, Brazil; Bielefeld, [W. Germany]: Pro Reitoria de Posgraduação e Pesquisa, Universidade Federal de Bahia; Universität Bielefeld, 1981. 64 p.

85. Bercht, Domitila María. Lazer e turismo; bibliografia. São Paulo: Graf. Tiradentes, 1982. 246 p.

86. Berger, Paulo. Bibliografia de Rio de Janeiro de viajantes e autores estrangeiros, 1531-1900. 2a aum. y rev. ed. Rio de Janeiro: SEEC-RJ, 1980. 478 p.

87. Biava, Marian de Lourdes. Bibliografia de Acre. Brasília: EMBRAPA, Unidade de Execução de Pesquisa de Ambito Estadual do Rio Branco, 1981. 521 p.

88. Bibliografia de publicações oficiais brasileiras. Brasília: Camara de Deputados, Coordenação de Biblioteca, Seção de Recebimento e Controle de Publicações Nacionais, 1981-83. 3 vols. Note: v. 1 (1975-77), v. 2 (1978-1980), v. 3 (1981-1982).

89. "Bibliografia sobre a Baixaida Fluminense e Grande Rio." Revista brasileira de geografia, Oct-Dez 1981, 43 (4), 631-634.

90. Brazil. Congresso. Senado Federal. Catalogo de documentos historicos. Brasilia: DF Brasil, 1982. 130 p.

91. Levine, Robert M. Brazil, 1822-1930: An annotated bibliography. New York: Garland Publishing Company, 1983. 487 p.

92. Nodal, Roberto. "La presencia africana en Cuba y Brasil: una bibliografía general." Anuario científico, 1978, 3, 221-248.

CARIBBEAN AREA

93. Baptiste, Fitzroy André. "Caribbean studies at the University of the West Indies, 1963 to the present: from chaos towards order." In: Windward, leeward and main: Caribbean studies and library resources: University of California, Los Angeles, California, June 17-22, 1979. Madison, WI: SALALM Secretariat, 1980: 235-262. (Seminar on the Acquisition of Latin American Library Materials, 24).

94. Best, Carlyle, and Jenipher Carnegie. CARICOM; a select bibliography. Materials available in the Main Library, University of the West Indies. Cave Hill: Library, University of the West Indies, 1983. 21 p.

95. Bibliography of the English-speaking Caribbean. v. 1-. Robert J. Neymeyer, editor. [Parkersburg, IA]: R.J. Neymeyer, 1979-. Note: Semiannual (some issues combined).

96. Bloomfield, Valerie. "The bibliography of the English-speaking Caribbean islands." In: Windward, leeward and main: Caribbean studies and library resources: University of California, Los Angeles, California, June 17-22, 1979. Madison, WI: SALALM Secretariat, 1980, 285-311. (Seminar on the Acquisition of Latin American Library Materials, 24).

97. Caribbean Archives Conference (2nd: 1975: Guadeloupe and Martinique). Actes de la Seconde Conférence des archives antillaises (Guadeloupe and Martinique, 27-31 october 1975): Proceedings of the Second Caribbean Archives Conference. München; New York: K.G. Saur, 1980. 160 p. Note: French or English.

98. "Caribbean studies in the Netherlands." Boletín de estudios latinoamericanos y del Caribe, Dec 1980, 29, 99-103. Note: Appears as a regular feature.

99. Der Karibische Raum: El area del Caribe. Hamburg: Institut für Iberoamericka-Kunde, Dokumentations-Leitstelle Lateinamerika, 1980. [37] leaves. (Dokumentationsdienst Lateinamerika. Kurzbibliographie)

100. Hall-Alleyne, Beverley; Garth White; and Michael Cook. Towards a bibliography of African-Caribbean studies. Kingston: African Caribbean Institute of Jamaica, 1982. 37 p.

101. Nilsen, Kirsti. "Commonwealth Caribbean government publications: bibliographies and acquisition aids." Government Publications Review, 1980, 7A (4), 489-503.

102. Quamina, Lynda, and Kaye Larbi. East Indians in the Caribbean: a select bibliography. St. Augustine, Trinidad: The Library, University of the West Indies, 1979. 48 leaves.

103. Serbín, Andrés. "¿Que pasa en el Caribe?: libros sobre una región emergente." Nueva sociedad, Sept-Oct 1983. (68), 153-156.

104. Wilkinson, Audine. "A select bibliography: Anguilla and St. Kitts-Nevis." Bulletin of Eastern Caribbean Affairs, Sept-Oct 1982, 8 (4), 71-78.

CENTRAL AMERICA

105. Central America, a bibliography. 2d rev ed. Los Angeles: Latin American Studies, California State University, c1981. 146 p. (Latin America bibliography series, 2).

106. Hoy, Don R., and Samuel Macfie, compilers. Central America: a bibliography of economic, political and cultural conditions. Athens: University of Georgia, 1982. 134 p. (Aids to Geographic Research series, 4).

107. Rosenberg, Mark B. "Central America: towards a new research agenda." Journal of Interamerican Studies and World Affairs, Feb 1984, 26 (1), 145-153.

108. University of Kansas. Libraries. Central American accessions at the University of Kansas Libraries. Lawrence, KS: The Libraries, 1981--. (No. 1, Nov. 1981)

CHILE

109. Bibliografía de la Junta de Gobierno de Chile, 1973-1976. [Santiago]: Servicio de Extensión de Cultura Chilena, [between 1976 and 1982]. 6 leaves.

COLOMBIA

110. Hernández de Caldas, Angela; María Magdalena Hernández, and Emperatriz Llanos de Ramírez. El Valle del Cauca a través de su documentación: un catálogo colectivo. Cali: Corporación Autónoma Regional del Cauca, 1981. 133 p.

COSTA RICA

111. Bibliografía costarricense, 1937-1945. San José: Dirección General de Bibliotecas y Biblioteca Nacional, Centro de Documentación y Bibliografía, 1984. 75 leaves.

112. Instituto Costarricense de Electricidad. Bibliografía general sobre el canton de Buenos Aires, Provincia de Puntarenas: proyecto--Instituto Costarricense de Electricidad, Universidad de Costa Rica. [San José]: El Instituto, 1980. [22] p.

CUBA

113. Braem, Martin. Selective bibliografie van de Cubaanse Revolutie (1953-1978). Brussels: Vrienden van Cuba, 1979. 109 p. (Cuba doc, 8).

114. León, René. "Fernando Ortiz: bibliografía sobre el tema negro." Explicación de textos literarios, 1983-84, 12 (1), 19-25.

DOMINICAN REPUBLIC

115. "Bibliografía sobre pueblos." Estudios sociales (Dom. Rep.), Jul-Sept 1984, 17 (57), 73-76.

116. Butler, Erwin. "Dominican books." Booklist, Nov. 15, 1981, 78 (6), 431-432.

ECUADOR

117. Guía para investigadores del Ecuador. Quito: Instituto Geográfico Militar; Pan American Institute of Geography and History, 1982. 150, 23, 117 p.

118. Handelman, Howard. "Development and misdevelopment in Ecuador." Journal of Interamerican Studies and World Affairs, Feb 1982, 24 (1), 115-122.

EL SALVADOR

119. "El Salvador en la prensa europea, octubre de 1982." Estudios centroamericanos, Dic 1982, 37 (410), 1124-1129.

120. "El Salvador en la prensa europea, diciembre 1982." Estudios centroamericanos, Feb 1983, 38 (412), 174-179.

121. Kruse, David Samuel. El Salvador bibliography and research guide. Cambridge, MA: Central American Information Office, 1982. 233 p.

122. Likins, John R. El Salvador-History-Civil War, 1977-. Bibliography: books, cassettes, clipping services, films, magazines, posters, slides etc.. Wellesley, MA: Wellesley Free Library, 1982. 9 leaves.

123. Marín, Lucas. "El Salvador en la prensa europea en agosto-septiembre de 1982." Estudios centroamericanos, Sept-Oct 1982, 37 (407-408), 930-935.

124. Marín, Lucas. "El Salvador en la prensa europea en noviembre de 1982." Estudios centroamericanos, Ene 1983, 38 (411), 68-73.

GRENADA

125. Goslinga, Marian. "U.S. press coverage of Grenada: a listing of articles published in the 'New York Times' October, 1983." Caribbean Review, 1983, 12 (4), 66-68.

GUATEMALA

126. Franklin, Woodman B. Guatemala. Santa Barbara, CA: Clio, 1981. 109 p.

GUYANA

127. The Guyana-Venezuela territorial issue: a select list of newspaper articles available at the National Library, Guyana. Georgetown: The Library, 1982. 46 p.

HAITI

128. Bellegarde-Smith, Patrick. "Haitian social thought: a bibliographical survey." Revista interamericana de bibliografía, 1982, 32 (3-4), 330-337.

129. Chambers, Frances. Haiti. Santa Barbara, CA: Clio, 1983. 177 p.

130. Gladden, Earle M. "Haitian books." Booklist, Jan 15, 1981, 77 (10), 681-682.

131. Gladden, Earle M. "Haitian books." Booklist, Feb 1980, 76 (11), 762-763.

132. Laguerre, Michel S. The complete Haitiana: a bibliographic guide to the scholarly literature, 1900-1980. Millwood, NY: Kraus International Publications, 1982. 2 vols.

133. Manigat, Max. Haitiana 1971-1975: bibliographie haïtienne. La Salle, Que.: Collectif paroles, 1980. 83 p.

134. Tardieu, Patrick D. "Tesis de doctorado y otras memorias sobre Haití presentados en Canadá, USA y Francia, 1960-1980." Caribe contemporáneo, El, Jun 1982. (6), 195-203.

HONDURAS

135. Danby, Colin, and Richard Swedberg. Honduras bibliography and research guide. Cambridge, MA: Central America Information Office, 1984. 333 p.

136. Valle, Rafael Heliodoro. "Bibliografía histórica de Honduras." Boletín de la Academia Hondureña de la Lengua, Jun 1982, 24 (6), 205-214.

JAMAICA

137. Ingram, Kenneth E., compiler. Jamaica. Santa Barbara, CA: Clio Press, c1984. 369 p. (World bibliographical series, 45).

MEXICO

138. Butler, Erwin. "Mexican books." Booklist, May 15, 1981, 77 (18), 1245-1246.

139. Careaga Viliesid, Lorena. Bibliografía general de Quintana Roo. Quintana Roo: Fondo de Fomento Editorial del Estado de Quintana Roo, 1979. 184 p.

140. Center for U.S.-Mexican Studies, University of California, San Diego. International inventory of current Mexico-related research. Vol. 2. Los Angeles: University of California Consortium on Mexico and the United States, [1982?-]. Note: Continues: Current research inventory.

141. Centro de Investigaciones Históricas UNAM-UABC. Bibliografía de Baja California. Tijuana: Centro de Investigaciones Históricas UNAM-UABC, 1980. 20 p.

142. Florescano, Enrique, et al. México en 500 libros. México: Editorial Nueva Imagen, 1980. 187 p. (Serie historia)

143. Gómez Pérez, Griselda, and Rosa María F. de Zamora. "Bibliografía y fuentes de información sobre Azcapotzalco." A; revista de ciencias sociales y humanidades, May-Dic 1982, 3 (6-7), 267-290.

144. Mead, Robert G., Jr. "Libros, artículos y revistas recientes en inglés sobre México." Hispania, Mar 1981, 64 (1), 132-134.

145. Pérez Martinez, Hector, editor. Yucatan: an annotated bibliography of documents and manuscripts on the archaeology and history of Yucatan in archives and libraries of Mexico, North America and Europe. Salisbury, NC: Documentary Publications, 1980. 133 p. Note: Reprint. Originally published: Campeche, México: Museo Arqueológico Histórico y Etnográfico de Campeche, Gobierno Constitucional del Estado de Campeche, 1943.

146. "Recent publications on Mexico." The Mexican forum, Jul 1981, 1 (3), 14-15.

147. Robbins. Naomi C., compiler; Sheila R. Herstein, editor. Mexico. Santa Barbara, CA: Clio Press, c1984. 165 p. (World bibliographical series, 48).

148. Schon, Isabel. "Recent notorious and noteworthy books about Mexico, Mexicans and Mexican-Americans." Journal of reading, Jan 1981, 24 (4), 293-299.

149. Stoddard, Ellwyn R.; Richard L. Nostrand; and Jonathan P. West, editors. Borderlands sourcebook: a guide to the literature on northern Mexico and the American Southwest. Norman: University of Oklahoma Press, c1983. 445 p.

150. Tesoros bibliográficos mexicanos. México: primera imprenta de América, siglos XVI al XIX. México: Universidad Nacional Autónoma de México, 1984. 127 p.

151. Villalobos Vázquez, Miguel Angel. Catálogo de la exposición bibliográfica de Jalisco: 1970-1981. Guadalajara: Primer Encuentro de Investigación Jaliscience (Economía y sociedad), 1981. 11 p.

152. Villaseñor y Villaseñor, Ramiro. Bibliografía general de Jalisco, Guadalajara. Vol. 2. Guadalajara: Gobierno de Jalisco, Secretaría General, Unidad Editorial, 1983. (Publicaciones del Gobierno del Estado. Serie bibliografías y catálogos, 5). Note: Vol. 1 published in 1958.

NICARAGUA

153. Arellano, Jorge Eduardo. "Historia y literatura de la costa atlántica." Boletín nicaragüense de bibliografía y documentación, Ene-Feb 1983. (51), 179-183.

154. Arellano, Jorge Eduardo. "Una bibliografía de la Costa Atlántica de Nicaragua." Nicaráuac, Oct 1982. (8), 193-199.

155. Banco Central de Nicaragua. Biblioteca y Servicios de Información. La costa atlántica de Nicaragua. Managua, 1980. 6 p. (Bibliografías cortas, 18).

156. Nicaragua revolucionaria. Bibliografía 1979-1984. Managua: Centro de Documentación, Instituto de investigaciones económicas y sociales, 1984. 140 p. (Serie Bibliografía, 1).

157. Woodward, Ralph Lee. Nicaragua. Sheila Herstein, editor. Santa Barbara, CA: Clio, c1983. 254 p.

PANAMA

158. Langstaff, Eleanor De Selms, compiler. Panama. Santa Barbara, CA: Clio, c1982. 184 p.

PARAGUAY

159. Biblioteca Roosevelt. Obras paraguayas. Asunción: Biblioteca Roosevelt, Centro Cultural Paraguayo Americano, [1980]. 61 p. Note: Citations in English and Spanish.

160. Centro Paraguayo de Estudios Sociológicos. "Documentación Paraguaya." Revista paraguaya de sociología, 1982. Note: Appears as a regular feature.

161. Díaz Pérez, Viriato. Polibiblia paraguaya: bibliografía. Palma de Mallorca: Ripoll, 1984-. Rev. ed. Revision and notes, Raúl Amaral. (Archivo Familia Díaz Pérez, 25).

162. González Petit, Elena Richer, and Rubén E. Morel Solaeche, compilers. Bibliografías de obras paraguayas: homenaje de la Biblioteca Central en el cincuentenario de la defensa del Chaco. Asunción: Universidad Nacional, Biblioteca Central, 1982. 32 p.

163. Seiferhels, Alfredo M. El Paraguay visto a través del idioma alemán: un intento en alemán sobre el Paraguay. Asunción: [n.p.], 1981. 95 p.

164. Vidaurreta, Alicia. "El Paraguay a través de viajeros, 1843-1917." Estudios paraguayos, Jun 1983, 11 (1), 51-99.

PERU

165. Cavanagh, Jonathan. Peru bibliography 1968-1977. Lima: Peruvian Times, dist., [1981?]. 53 p.

166. Kuczynski, Pedro Pablo. "Recent studies of Peru." Latin American Research Review, 1981, 16 (1), 225-228.

167. Peru, a bibliography of books in English. Washington, DC: Anaquel Press, c1980. 42 p.

168. Phillips, Beverly, and Barbara Saupe, compilers. Peru, land and people: a bibliography; a supplement to the bibliography of materials dealing with Peru in the Land Tenure Center Library. Madison: University of Wisconsin, Land Tenure Library, 1980. 73 p. (Training and methods series, no. 15) Supplement 2.

PUERTO RICO

169. Anderson, Victor D. Bibliografía municipal geográfica puertorriqueña. Rio Piedras: Editorial Universitaria, Universidad de Puerto Rico, 1980. 147 p.

170. Bibliografía de Puerto Rico. La Habana: Casa de las Américas, Biblioteca "José A. Echeverría," 1979. 81 p.

171. Cardona, Luis Antonio. An annotated bibliography on Puerto Rican materials and other sundry matters. Bethesda, MD: Carreta Press, 1983. 156 p.

172. Castro, María de los Angeles; María Dolores Luque de Sánchez; and Gervasio Luis García. Los primeros pasos: una bibligrafía para empezar a investigar la historia de Puerto Rico. Guía descriptiva de los fondos documentales existentes en el Centro de Investigaciones Históricas. Rio Piedras: Oficina de Publicaciones, Facultad de Humanidades, Universidad de Puerto Rico, 1984. 111 p.

173. Olazagasti, Ignacio, editor. Catálogo de documentos históricos de Bayamón. [Bayamón]: Instituto de Historia y Cultura de Bayamón, 1979-, [1982?]. Note: Based on documents held in the Archivo General de Puerto Rico.

174. Ramírez, Rafael L. "Puerto Rico." Latin American Research Review, 1980, 15 (3), 256-260.

SURINAM

175. Nagelkerke, Gerard A. Suriname. A bibliography, 1940-1980. Leiden: Royal Institute of Linguistics and Anthropology, Department of Caribbean Studies, 1980. 336 p.

UNITED STATES

176. Foote, Cheryl J. "The history of women in New Mexico: a selective guide to published sources." New Mexico Historical Review, Oct 1982, 58 (4), 387-394.

177. Jenkins, John H. Basic Texas books: an annotated bibliography of selected works for a research library. Austin, TX: Jenkins Publishing Company, 1983. 648 p.

178. Ortal, José Casimiro. "Cuba views the United States, 1959-1980." Los ensayistas; boletín informativo, Mar 1982. (12-13), 198-214.

179. Roy, Joaquín. "La imagen de los Estados Unidos en América Latina y España: bibliografía selectiva." Los ensayistas; boletín informativo, Mar 1982. (12-13), 87-197.

180. Streeter, Thomas Winthrop. Bibliography of Texas, 1795-1845. Woodbridge, CT: Research Publications, 1983. 576 p. Note: Second edition revised and enlarged by Archibald Hanna with a guide to the microfilm collection, "Texas as a province and republic, 1795-1845."

URUGUAY

181. Arteaga Sáenz, Juan José; Silvia Reyes; and Sergio Silva. Constitución de 1830: bibliografía. Montevideo: Instituto de Filosofía, Ciencia y Letras, Departamento de Investigación y Estudios Superiores de Historia Americana, 1981. 82 p.

182. Di Genio de Carlomagno, Ana M., and Elis Duarte de Bogadjian, compilers. Bibliografía municipal del Departamento de Montevideo, 1830-1980. Montevideo: Junta de Vecinos de Montevideo, Biblioteca "José Artigas," 1980. 68 p.

VENEZUELA

183. Azocar, Jesús Napoleón. Bibliografía del estado Monagas. Maturín, Venezuela: Gobernación del Estado de Monagas, 1982. 262 p.

184. Bueno, Luis Alfonso. Bibliografía del estado Falcón. Coro, Venezuela: Universidad Francisco de Miranda, 1980.

185. Cardozo, Lubio. "La bibliografía mayor de la cultura humanística venezolana." Boletín de la Academia Nacional de la Historia (Caracas), Abr-Jun 1980, 63 (250), 464-466.

186. Cardozo, Lubio. "Los repertorios bibliográficos venezolanos del siglo XIX." Boletín de la Academia Nacional de la Historia (Caracas), Oct-Dic 1981, 64 (256), 887-907.

187. Delepiani, Oscar E. Venezuela. Austin: University of Texas at Austin, The General Libraries, 1980. 22 p. (Selected reference sources, 49).

188. Kozhjevnikov, Emil. "Estudios soviéticos sobre Venezuela." América Latina (USSR), 1980, 12, 114-124.

189. Paz, Miguel Angel. Bibliografía del estado Falcón. v. 2. Coro, Venezuela: Instituto Autónomo de Biblioteca Nacional.

Coordinación de la Red de Servicios de Biblioteca del Estado Falcón, 1983.

190. Ramos Guédez, José Marcial. Bibliografía afrovenezolana. Caracas: Instituto Autónomo Biblioteca Nacional y de Servicios de Bibliotecas, 1980. 125 p. (Serie bibliográfica, 2).

191. Ramos Guédez, José Marcial. Bibliografía del estado Miranda. Caracas: Coedición de la Gobernación del Estado Miranda y del Instituto Autónomo Biblioteca Nacional y de Servicios de Bibliotecas, 1981. 286 p. (Biblioteca de autores y temas mirandinos. Colección Cristóbal Rojas, 1).

WEST INDIES

192. Ingram, Kenneth E. Sources for West Indian studies: a supplementary listing, with particular reference to manuscript sources. Zug, Switzerland: Inter Documentation Company, 1983. 412 p.

193. University of the West Indies. Library. Grenada: a list of references to the literature held in the library. St. Augustine: The Library, 1983. 30 p.

WEST INDIES, FRENCH

194. Archives de Martinique. Bibliographie relative aux Antilles: ouvrages appartenant aux cotes C et D, selon l'ancien cadre de classement des Archives départementales. Fort-de-France: Archives départamentales de la Martinique, 1978-.

195. Nodal, Roberto. The French West Indies; a mini-bibliography. Milwaukee: University of Wisconsin, Dept. of Afro-American Studies, 1978. 30 leaves.

AGRICULTURE

GENERAL

196. Bibliografía sobre café. San José, Costa Rica: Instituto Interamericano de Ciencias Agrícolas, 1982. 547 p.

197. Dyal, Donald H., and David L. Chapman. "Periodical literature of Hispanic American agricultural history: a bibliographical research problem." Revista interamericana de bibliografía, 1981, 31 (2), 215-226.

198. "Informaciones periódicas sobre el henequén." Yucatán; historia y economia, May-Jun 1981, 5 (25), 64-70.

199. Martín de Acuña, Carmen, and Carmen Villegas. Moho azul del tabaco (Peronospora tabacina Adam): una bibliografía parcialmente anotada. San José, Costa Rica: Instituto Interamericano de Ciencias Agrícolas, 1982. 108 p.

200. Nassar, Nazira Leite. Bibliografia de juta: corchorus capsularis l. c. olitorius l. Brasília: EMBRAPA, Departamento de Documentaçao, 1980. 113 p.

201. Ortega, Emiliano. "Enfoques sobre la cuestión agraria." Pensamiento iberoamericano; revista de economía política, Ene-Jun 1982 (1), 209-215.

202. Rodríguez Chaurnet, Dinah. "Estructura agraria y desarrollo agrícola." Problemas de desarrollo, Nov 1980-Ene 1981, 9 (44).

203. Santos, Walda Corréa dos; Palmira Costa Novo; and Newton Bueno. Bibliografia de fertilidade de solos e nutrição da seringueira. Brasília: EMBRAPA, Centro Nacional de Pesquisa de Seringueira e Dendé, Departamento de Informação e Documentação, 1982 [i.e., 1983]. 238 p.

204. Vieira, Dirceu Justiniano, and Elisabeth de Oliveira Serrano. Bibliografia sinalética sobre a cultura do algodão arbóreo.... Brasília: EMBRAPA, 1980. 54 p.

ARGENTINA

205. Bibliografía forestal. Chaco, Argentina: Universidad Nacional del Nordeste, 1980. 68 p.

BOLIVIA

206. Blanes Jiménez, José, and Gonzalo Flores. Bibliografía referida al trópico cochabambino. La Paz: Ediciones CERES, [1982]. 163 p. (Serie estudios regionales, 4).

207. Pozo, Melvin, and Simón Maxwell. Bibliografía agro-económica anotada de Santa Cruz. Centro de Investigación Agrícola Tropical, 1979. 139 p. (Documento de trabajo, 3).

BRAZIL

208. Andrade Aguiar, Paulo Anselmo, et al. Bibliografia sinaletica sobre agricultura em regiões aridas e semi-aridas. Brasília:

Petrolina: EMBRAPA, DID; Centro de Pesquisa Agropecuaria do Tropico Semi-Arido, 1981. 221 p.

209. Banco de bibliografias. v. 1-. Brasília: EMBRAPA, Departamento de Informação e Documentaçao, 1981-. Note: "Boletim bibliográfico."

210. Catálogo de publicações em ciências agrícolas do Rio de Janeiro. Rio de Janeiro: Instituto do Açucar e do Alcool, 1981. 160 p.

211. Guimarães, Pedro Jose. Bibliografia sinaletica matogrossense: agropecuaria, recursos naturais, diagnostico, planejamento e pesquisa. [Brasília]: EMBRAPA, DID, 1981. 565 p.

212. Machado, Nadia Dorian, and Jose Aires Ventura. Bibliografia internacional de doenças do abacaxizeiro. Brasília: Departamento de Informação e Documentação da EMBRAPA, 1983. 311 p.

213. Martins, Miriam Dalva Lima. Catálogo de publicações da EMBRAPA e empresas estaduais de pesquisa agropecuaria: 1974-1979. Brasília: EMBRAPA, Departamento de Informação de Documentação, c1981. 5 vols.

214. Nassar, Nazira Leite. Bibliografia de malva. Brasília: EMBRAPA, DID, Centro de Pesquisa Agropecuária do Trópico Umido, 1980. 64 p.

215. Nassar, Nazira Leite, and Fernando Carneiro Albuquerque. Bibliografia sobre pimenta-do-reino (Piper nigrum L.). Brasília: EMBRAPA, DID, 1981. 147 p.

216. Oliveira, Edilson Batista de, and María de Lourdes Biava. Bibliografia sobre tamanho e forma de parcelas experimentais. Brasília: EMBRAPA, DID, 1982. 201 p.

217. Oliveira, Silas Marques de, and Lujan N. Chagas, compiler. Bibliografia de macadamia. Vicosa: Universidade Federal de Vicosa, Biblioteca Central, 1982. 82 p. (Serie Bibliografia especializada, 30).

218. Pereira, Isanira Coutinho Vaz, and Silvio Leopldo Lima Costa. Bibliografia de castanha-do-Brasil: Bertholletia excelsa H.B.K. Brasília: EMBRAPA, DID, 1981. 92 p.

219. Porto, Everaldo Rocha; Maria Cira Padilha de Luz; and Aderaldo de Souza Silva. Bibliografia sinaletica sobre a pequena irrigação não convencional no tropico semi-arido. Brasília: EMBRAPA, DID: Petrolina: Centro de Pesquisa Agropecuaria do Tropico Semi-Arido, 1980. 122 p.

220. Post, Edite E. Bibliografia brasileira de cevada, Hordeum vulgare L. Brasília: EMBRAPA, DID, 1980. 48 p.

221. Post, Edite E., and Maria Salete Wiggers. Bibliografia internacional de colza, Brassica campestris L. e Brassica napus. Passo Fundo, Brazil: EMBRAPA, Centro Nacional de Pesquisa de Trigo, Setor de Informação e Documentação, 1981. 296 p.

222. Serrano, Elisabete de Oliveira, and Ronaldo Torres Soarez. Bibliografia sinaletica sobre a cultura do algodoeiro herbaceo (Gossypium hirsutum L.). Brasília: EMBRAPA, DID: Lagoa Seca: EMEPA-PB, Coordenadoria Regional de Lagoa Seca, 1980. 181 p.

223. Souza, Maria da P.N. de, Herbene M.V.R. Fernández, and Maria Helene de Souza, compilers. Bibliografia brasileira de mandioca. Brasília: EMBRAPA, DID, Centro Nacional de Pesquisa de Mandioca e Fruticultura, 1981. 266 p.

224. Sperry, Suzana. Bibliografias brasileiras do pessego e de outras frutas de clima temperado. Brasília: EMBRAPA, DID, Unidade Execução de Pesquisa de Ambito Estadual de CASCATA, 1981. 239 p.

225. Teixeira, João Batista; Eugénia Maranhao Bettiol; and Eliezita Romcy de Carvalho. Bibliografia internacional de cultura de tecidos em plantas cultivadas. Brasília: EMBRAPA, Centro Nacional de Recursos Genéticos, DID, 1981. 2 vols.

226. Valois, Eliana Candeira, and Franklin Riet Correa. Bibliografia brasileira sobre plantas toxicas na alimentação animal. Brasília: EMBRAPA, DID, 1982. 228 p.

227. Fieira, Francisca Terezinha Batista. Repertorio bibliográfico dos técnicos da CEPLAC. Ilheus, Brazil: CEPLAC-CEPEC, Divisão de Bibliografia e Documentação, 1981. 111 p.

228. Wiggers, Maria Salete; Edite E. Post; and Ottoni de Sousa Rosa. Bibliografia brasileira de trigo: Triticum aestivum L. v. 1. Passo Fundo: EMBRAPA, Centro Nacional de Pesquisa de Trigo, Setor de Informação e Documentação, 1981-.

229. Wiggers, Maria Salete. Bibliografia brasileira de linho: Linum usitatissimum L. Brasilia: EMBRAPA, DID, 1983. 55 p.

CARIBBEAN AREA

230. Barker, G.H. Bibliography of literature relating to research and development in the agricultural sector of Jamaica, 1959-

1979. Kingston: Inter-American Institute of Agricultural Science, 1980. 201 leaves.

231. Chandler, Michael J. Agriculture, science and technology: resources of information in Barbados: A survey prepared for the National Council for Science and Technology. [Culloden Road, Barbados?]: National Council for Science and Technology, 1980. 75 p.

CENTRAL AMERICA

232. Commonwealth Agricultural Bureau, Slough. Latin America; agricultural situation and development: Central America. Slough: The Bureau, 1979. 28 p.

CHILE

233. Elso G., Sonia, and Veronica Bravo M. Bibliografía agrícola chilena, v. 5 (1960-1982). Santiago de Chile: Instituto de Investigaciones Agropecuarias. Programa de documentación e información, 1983. 269 p. Note: v. 1 published in 1977.

COLOMBIA

234. Bibliografía agropecuaria de Colombia, 1977-1978. Bogotá: Ministerio de Agricultura, Instituto Colombiano Agropecuario, 1980. 208 p.

235. Bibliografía nacional de suelos, 1930-1980. Bogotá: Instituto Geográfico "Agustín Codazzi," Ministerio de Hacienda y Crédito Público, 1981. 376 p.

236. Federación Nacional de Cafeteros de Colombia. Centro de Documentación. 50 años de investigación en la Federación Nacional de Cafeteros de Colombia: bibliografía, 1929-1979. Bogotá: Impr. Banco Cafetero, 1980. 304 p.

237. Gómez V., Stella. Bibliografía de trabajos publicados por el CIAT y su personal científico: 1969-1983. Cali: Central Internacional de Agricultura Tropical, 1984. 233 p.

238. Hernández de Caldas, Angela. Hacia un servicio andino de información forestal ubicado en Colombia. Bogotá: Universidad Distrital Francisco José de Caldas, 1981. 8 p.

239. Ramírez de Díaz, María Teresa, and Sundary de Bahamón. El fique y otras fibras de empaque y amarre: bibliografía. [Bogotá]: Fundación Mariano Ospina Pérez, 1981. 95 p.

240. Rojas Gutiérrez, Angel M., et al. Estudios forestales del Tolima y el Valle del Cauca realizados a través de la Facultad de Ingeniería Forestal (Una bibliografía anotada 1968-1980). Ibagué, Colombia: Universidad del Tolima, 1981. 33 p. (Cuadernos de investigación, Serie A: Ciencias forestales, 1, no. 1).

241. Uribe, Maruja. Bibliografía latinoamericana de desarrollo rural, 1979-1983. Bogotá: Instituto Interamericano de Cooperación para la Agricultura, Oficina en Colombia; Centro Interamericano de Documentación e Información Agrícola, 1984. 104 p.

CUBA

242. Méndez, M.A. Reseña bibliográfica sobre el drenaje agrícola. La Habana: Centro de Información y Divulgación Agropecuario, 1983. 65 p. (Boletín de reseñas. Riego y drenaje, 2).

243. Mesa Nápoles, Angel; Mayda Hernández Díaz; and Osvaldo Suárez Díaz. Compilación bibliográfica acerca de evaluación de tierra y clasificación agroproductiva con referencia particular a la caña de azúcar. La Habana: Centro de Información y Divulgación Agropecuario, 1982. 162 p.

ECUADOR

244. Ibarra, Hernán. Ecuador, bibliografía analítica agraria, 1900-1982. [Quito?]: Ediciones CIESE, assisted by ILDIS, 1982. 419 p.

HONDURAS

245. Centro de Documentación e Información Agrícola (Honduras). Bibliografía agrícola de Honduras, 1977-1979. Tegucigalpa: Secretaría de Recursos Naturales, Centro de Documentación e Información Agrícola, 1980. 105 p.

MEXICO

246. Wessman, James W. "The agrarian question in Mexico." Latin American Research Review, 1984, 19 (2), 243-259.

PERU

247. Castro Rodríguez, Napoleón. Bibliografía forestal del Peru. Lima: Ministerio de Agricultura, 1983 n.p.

248. Eguren, Fernando. "La cuestión agraria en el Perú desde la perspectiva de las ciencias sociales." Pensamiento iberoamericano; revista de economía política, Jul-Dic 1983 (4), 256-261.

249. Matos Mar, José, and José M. Mejía. Bibliografia agraria peruana (1957-1977). Lima: Instituto de Estudios Peruanos, 1980.

250. Painter, Michael. "Agricultural policy, food production and multi-national corporations in Peru." Latin American Research Review, 1983, 18 (2), 201-218.

VENEZUELA

251. Haddad G., Oscar, et al. Bibliografía venezolana de fruticultura. Maracay: Fondo Nacional de Investigaciones Agropecuarias, 1979. 180 p.

ANTHROPOLOGY

252. Arriaga Weiss, David. "Grupos étnicos y cuestión nacional." Revista mexicana de ciencias políticas y sociales, Ene-Mar 1981, 27, (103), 223-260.

253. Azevedo, Thales de. "Variações sobre o caráter nacional brasileiro." Revista de antropologia, 1981, 24, 51-62.

254. Bastarrachea Mansano, Juan Ramón. Bibliografía antropológica de Yucatán. México: Centro Regional del Sureste, Instituto Nacional de Antropología e Historia, 1984. 648 p.

255. Bastien, Joseph W. "Los Aymará: notas bibliográficas." Revista andina, Jul-Dic 1983, 1 (2), 545-578.

256. Berberian, Eduardo E. Bibliografía antropológica de la provincia de Tucumán. Córdoba: [n.p.], 1980. 102 p.

257. Berg, Hans van den. Material bibliográfico para el estudio de los Aymaras, Callawayas, Chipayas, Urus. Cochabamba: Universidad Católica Boliviana, Facultad de Filosofía y Ciencias Religiosas, 1980. 3 vols.

258. Bozzoli de Willie, María; Anita Murchie; and Imelda Leiva. Bibliografía antropológica de Costa Rica. San José: Universidad de Costa Rica, Departamento de Antropología, 1982. 63 p. (Cuadernos de antropología, 1).

259. Caillavet, Chantal. "Ethno-histoire équatorienne: un testament indien inédit du XVIe siecle." Caravelle, 1983, 41, 6-22.

260. Centro de Documentación Antropológica. Catálogo--materiales del Instituto Lingüístico de Verano sobre grupos étnicos de Bolivia, 1944-1980: microfichas existentes en el C.D.A. Luis Oporto, editor. La Paz: Instituto Boliviano de Cultura, Instituto Nacional de Antropología, Centro de Documentación Antropológica, 1981. 47 p.

261. Equipo del Centro de Información y Documentación (CIDOC). "Bibliografía sobre los indígenas guaymíes de Panamá." Lotería, Mar-Abr 1983. (324-325), 79-122.

262. Flores Ochoa, Jorge A. "Pastoreo de llamas y alpacas en los Andes: balance bibliográfico." Revista andina, 1983, 1 (1), 175-218.

263. Foster, David William. "Bibliografía del indigenismo hispanoamericano." Revista iberoamericana, Abr-Jun 1984, 50 (127), 587-620.

264. Glazier, Stephen. "An annotated ethnographic bibliography of Trinidad." Behavior Science Research, 1982, 17 (1-2), 31-58.

265. Gutiérrez Solana, Nelly, and Daniel G. Schavelzon. Corpus bibliográfico de la cultura olmeca. México: Universidad Nacional Autónoma de México, 1980. 135 p.

266. Guyot, Mireille, and Susana Monzon. "Bibliographie américaniste." Journal de la Société des Américanistes, 69, 209-236.

267. Hartmann, Thekla. Bibliografia crítica da etnologia brasileira. Berlin: Dietrich Reimer Verlag, 1984. 3. 724 p. (Völkerkundliche Abhandlungen, Band IX).

268. Holm, Olaf. "Bibliografía antropológica ecuatoriana." Miscelánea antropológica ecuatoriana, 1981, 1 (1), 174-186.

269. Hux, Meinrado. Guía bibliográfica: el indio en la Llanura del Plata. La Plata: Provincia de Buenos Aires, Dirección General de Escuelas, Archivo Histórico Ricardo Levene, 1984. 262 p. Note: "Cartografía de la Llanura del Plata," p. 238-262.

270. Litvak King, Jaime, and Bernd Fahmel Beyer. "Informaciones." Anales de antropología: I) Arqueología y antropología física, 1981, 18, 329-332.

271. Lugan Muñoz, Jorge. "Investigaciones recientes en etnohistoria de Guatemala." Mesoamérica, Jun 1983, 4 (5), 244-252.

272. Marino Flores, Anselmo. "Bibliografía de antropología americana." Boletín bibliográfico de antropología americana, 1979, 40 (50), 179-260.

273. México. Instituto Nacional de Antropología e Historia. Informe 1979: 5 años de vida: evaluación 1975-1979. Proyectos especiales de investigación. México: INAH, 1980. 62 p.

274. Morley, Sylvanus Griswold. The ancient Maya. 4th ed. Stanford, CA: Stanford University Press, 1983, 708 p. Note: This edition revised by Robert J. Sharer.

275. Niles, Susan A. South American Indian narrative, theoretical and analytical approaches: an annotated bibliography. New York: Garland Publishing Co., 1981. 183 p. (Garland refference library of the humanities, 276).

276. Ojeda Díaz, María de los Angeles. Indice de los trabajos sobre Mesoamérica de Eduard Seler. [México, D.F.]: Biblioteca Nacional de Antropología e Historia, [1978]. 26 p. (Cuadernos de la Biblioteca. Serie bibliografía, 5).

277. Oporto, Luis, and Miriam Cuevas. Bibliografía sobre culturas de tradición oral. La Paz: Instituto Nacional de Antropología, 1982. 104 p.

278. Palen, Roberta R. "Weaving and traditional costume in Guatemala: a selective bibliography." Revista interamericana de bibliografía, 1981, 31 (1), 17-26.

279. Pardo, Mauricio. "Bibliografía sobre indígenas chocó." Revista colombiana de antropología, 1980-81, 23, 463-528.

280. Pollak-Eltz, Angelina. Bibliografía antropológica venezolana, 1983. Caracas: Instituto de Lenguas Indígenas y Centro de Estudios Comparados de Religión, Universidad Católica Andrés Bello, 1983. 66 p.

281. Pollak-Eltz, Angelina. Nuevos aportes a la bibliografía afrovenezolana. Caracas: Centro de Religiones Comparadas, Universidad Católica Andrés Bello, 1983. 16 p.

282. Ramírez, Axel. Bibliografía comentada de la medicina tradicional mexicana (1900-1978). México: IMEPLAN, 1978 [i.e. 1979]. 147 p. (Monografías científicas. Instituto Mexicano para el Estudio de las Plantas Medicinales, 3).

283. Salomon, Frank. "Andean ethnology in the 1970's: a retrospective." Latin American Research Review, 1982, 17 (2), 75-128.

284. Santley, Robert S. "Recent works on Aztec history." Latin American Research Review, 1984, 19 (1), 261-269.

285. Topete, María de la Luz. Bibliografía antropológica del Estado de Oaxaca, 1974-1979. [México]: Centro Regional de Oaxaca, Instituto Nacional de Antropología e Historia, 1980. 168 p. (Estudios de antropología e historia, 22).

286. Valle Prieto, María Eugenia. "Guía de antropólogos." Nueva antropología, Dic 1980, 4 (15-16), 287-290.

287. Véliz, Vito. Bibliografía antropológica histórica. Tegucigalpa: Editorial Universitaria, 1982. 71 p.

288. Vickers, William T. "Ethnological methods, results and the question of advocacy in Andean research." Latin American Research Review, 1980, 15 (3), 229-239.

289. Wagner, Erika, and Walter Coppens. "Décima bibliografía antropológica reciente sobre Venezuela." Antropológica, 1982, (57), 55-64.

290. Wagner, Erika, and Walter Coppens. "Novena bibliografía antropológica reciente sobre Venezuela." Antropológica, 1981. (55), 73-92. Note: Includes a thematic index by Mireya Viloria.

291. Wagner, Erika, and Walter Coppens. "Octava bibliografía antropológica reciente sobre Venezuela." Antropológica, 1980. (54), 167-194.

292. Zanutto, Juan Carlos (Karus Watink), and Juan Botasso. Bibliografía general de la nación jivaro. [Sucua, Ecuador?]: Editorial "Mundo Shuar," 1983. 192 p.

ARCHAEOLOGY

293. Anderson, Frank G. Southwestern archaeology: a bibliography. New York: Garland Publishing Co., 1982. 539 p. (Garland reference library of social science, 69).

294. Barrera Vázquez, Alfredo. "Four centuries of archaeology in Yucatan: a bibliographical essay." In: Yucatan; a world apart. Edward H. Moseley and Edward D. Terry, editors. University: University of Alabama Press, 1980: 306-309.

295. Camino, Alejandro, and Carlos Dávila. "Bibliografía de la

arqueología de la Amazona peruana." Amazonia peruana, Ene 1983, 4 (8), 103-112.

296. Diehl, Richard A. "Current directions and perspectives in Mesoamerican cognitive archaeology." Latin American Research Review, 1984, 19 (2), 171-181.

297. Itzstein, Gertraud, and Heiko Prümers. Einführende Bibliographie zur Archäologie Ecuadors. Bibliografía básica sobre la arqueología del Ecuador. Bonn: Seminar für Völkerkunde der Universität Bonn, 1981. 110 p. (Bonner amerikanistische Studien. Estudios americanistas de Bonn, 8).

298. Laporte Molina, Juan Pedro. Bibliografía de la arqueología guatemalteca. Vol. 1. Guatemala: Ediciones de la Dirección General de Antropología e Historia, 1981-.

299. Lee, Thomas A. New World Archaeological Foundation: Obra, 1952-1982. Provo, UT: NWAF, College of Family, Home and Social Sciences, Brigham Young University, 1981. 142 p.

300. López Cervantes, Gonzalo. Bibliografía sumaria para el estudio del vidrio. México: SEP, INAH, Museo Nacional de Antropología, Sección de Arqueología, 1980. 183 p. (Colección científica, 93).

301. Magee, Susan Fortson. Mesoamerican archaeology: a guide to the literature and other information sources. Austin: Institute of Latin American Studies, University of Texas at Austin, c1981. 71 p. (Guides and bibliographies series, 12).

302. Moe, Annette T. Archaeology in New Mexico. Monticello, IL: Vance Bibliographies, 1980. 7 p. (Architecture series--bibliography, A-392).

303. Oberti R, Italo. "Cusco arqueológico y etnohistórico: una introducción bibliográfica." Revista andina, Jul-Dic 1983, 1 (2), 443-474.

304. Rivera, Mario A. "Acerca de la arqueología andina del norte de Chile: comentarios y referencias bibliográficas publicadas entre 1980-1983." Revista andina, Jul 1984, 2 (1), 283-298.

305. Sisson, Edward B., and Modeena Stultz. Postclassic central Mexico: a preliminary bibliography. [University]: University of Mississippi, c1982. 143 p.

ART AND ARCHITECTURE

306. Acevedo, Esther, et al. Bibliografía comentada sobre arte del siglo XIX. [México?]: Seminario de Estudios de Historia del Arte, Dirección de Estudios Históricos, Instituto Nacional de Antropología e Historia, 1978. 210 leaves. (Cuadernos de trabajo, Dirección de Estudios Históricos, INAH, 6).

307. African-Caribbean Institute of Jamaica. Photograph catalogue: general collection 1972-1978. Kingston: ACIJ, 1983. 14 p.

308. Arellano, Jorge Eduardo. "Bibliografía de la pintura y la escultura en Nicaragua." Boletín nicaragüense de bibliografía y documentación, Ene-Feb 1981. (39), 82-87.

309. Bailey, Joyce Waddell, general editor. Handbook of Latin American art; Manual de arte latinoamericano: a bibliographic compilation. 1st ed. Santa Barbara, CA: ABC-Clio Information Services, c1984-.

310. Barnitz, Jacqueline. Latin American artists in the U.S. before 1950: Catalog. Godwin-Ternbach Museum at Queens College, Mattis Room, Paul Klapper Library, Queens College, Flushing, New York, April 28-May 14, 1981. [New York]: [n.p.], [1981]. 36 p.

311. "Bibliografía de la escultura en Nicaragua." Boletín nicaragüense de bibliografía y documentación, Mar-Abr 1980. (34), 99.

312. Britto Pereira, Cecilia Duprat de. "Giovanni Battista Piranesi. Catálogo de estampas existentes na coleção." Brazil. Biblioteca Nacional. Anais, 1979. (99), 187-238.

313. Buntinx, Gustavo. "Contribución a una bibliografía del arte joven peruano." Hueso húmero, Jul-Sept 1983. (18), 184-201.

314. Catálogo bibliográfico de teoría e historia de la arquitectura en México. México: Secretaría de Educación Pública, Instituto Nacional de Bellas Artes. 165 p. (Cuadernos de arquitectura y conservación del patrimonio artístico, 24-25).

315. Catálogo de investigaciones inéditas; patrimonio arquitectónico y urbano: 1950-1980. Santiago de Chile: Universidad de Chile, Facultad de arquitectura y urbanismo, 1980. 94 p.

316. Coloquio Latinoamericano de Fotografía (2nd: 1981: Mexico City, Mexico). Libros fotográficos de autores latinoamericanos: II Coloquio Latinoamericano de Fotografía. México: Instituto

Nacional de Bellas Artes, Dirección de Artes Plásticas, Consejo Mexicano de Fotografía, 1981. 50 p.

317. Coppa & Avery Consultants. Architecture and preservation in New Mexico: a guide to historic sites, churches and homes. Monticello, IL: Vance Bibliographies, 1981. 6 p. (Architecture series bibliography, A-407).

318. Cordero Iñíguez, Juan. Bibliografía ecuatoriana de artesanías y artes populares. Cuenca: Centro Interamericano de Artesanías y Artes Populares, 1982. 373 p.

319. Cueto, Emilio C. "A short guide to old Cuban prints." Cuban Studies, Winter 1984, 14 (1), 27-42.

320. Dannemann Rothstein, Manuel, and Joyce Fuhrmann. Bibliografía de la artesanía tradicional chilena. Santiago: Comisión Nacional Chilena del Instituto Andino de Artes Populares del Convenio Andrés Bello, 1983. 96 p.

321. Fernández, Antonio A. Architecture and urban planning in revolutionary Cuba: an annotated bibliography. Monticello, IL: Vance Bibliographies, 1980. 11 p.

322. Findlay, James A. Modern Latin American art: a bibliography. Westport, CT: Greenwood Press, 1983. 301 p.

323. Gutiérrez-Witt, Laura. Latin American art. Austin: University of Texas at Austin, The General Libraries, 1980. 7 p. (Selected reference sources, 48).

324. Harmon, Robert Bartlett. Architectural splendor in the sun--Mexico's Luis Barragán: a selected bibliography. Monticello, IL: Vance Bibliographies, 1980. 13 p.

325. Hogan, James E. "The contemporaries of Antônio Francisco Lisboa: an annotated bibliography." Latin American Research Review, 1981, 16 (3), 138-145.

326. Kupfer, Monica E., compiler. A bibliography of contemporary art in Latin America: books, articles and exhibition catalogs in the Tulane University Library, 1950-1980. New Orleans: Center for Latin American Studies and Howard-Tilton Memorial Library, Tulane University, 1983. 97 leaves.

327. Lombardo de Ruiz, Sonia. Bibliografía básica comentada sobre la pintura mural prehispánica de Mesoamérica. México: Dirección de Estudio Históricos, Instituto Nacional de Antropología e Historia, 1979. 131 p. (Cuaderno de trabajo. Seminario de Estudios de Historia de Arte, 2).

328. Louie de Irizarry, Florita Z. Architecture in the Caribbean-West Indies: a bibliography. Monticello, IL: Vance Bibliographies, 1982. 15 p.

329. Louie de Irizarry, Florita Z. Architecture in Mexico: A bibliography. Monticello, IL: Vance Bibliographies, 1982. 31 p.

330. Louie de Irizarry, Florita Z. Architecture in South America; a bibliography. Monticello, IL: Vance Bibliographies, 1982. 36 p.

331. Lozano, Eduardo. "Bibliography. Art of the Maya." Latin American Indian literatures, Spring 1982, 6 (1), 49-65.

332. Lozano, Eduardo. "Bibliography. Indian art of Middle America and the Caribbean." Latin American Indian literatures, Fall 1981, 5 (2), 92-102.

333. Lozano, Eduardo. "Bibliography, Indian art of Peru, Part II." Latin American Indian literatures, Spring 1981, 5 (1), 26-32.

334. Lozano, Eduardo. "Indian art of the Andean region." Latin American Indian literatures, Fall 1980, 4 (2), 112-121.

335. Lozano, Eduardo. "Indian art of South America." Latin American Indian literatures, Spring 1980, 4 (1), 52-63.

336. Lozano, Eduardo. "Indian Art of Mexico: Bibliography (Part II)." Latin American Indian literatures, Spring 1983, 7 (1), 68-80.

337. Moe, Christine. Preservation of the regional architecture and historic buildings of New Mexico. Monticello, IL: Vance Bibliographies, 1981. 28 p. (Architecture series bibliography, A-415).

338. National Library (Guyana). Caribbean art and craft: a select list on Caribbean art and craft, with emphasis on Guyana. [Georgetown: The Library], 1981. 39 p.

339. Pagán Perdomo, Dato. "Bibliografía sumaria del arte rupestre del área del Caribe." Boletín (Museo del Hombre Dominicano), Sept 1978, 11, 107-130.

340. "Revert Henrique Klumb, fotógrafo da familia imperial brasileira." Brazil. Biblioteca Nacional. Anais, 1982. (102), 221-234.

341. Rivera de Figueroa, Carmen A. Architecture for the tropics: a bibliographical synthesis (from the beginnings to 1972): con

una versión castellana resumida. Río Piedras: Editorial Universitaria, University of Puerto Rico, 1980. 203 p.

342. Salles, Vicente. Bibliografia analítica do artesanato brasileiro. Rio de Janeiro: FUNARTE, Instituto Nacional do Folclore, 1984. 96 p. (Serie referência, 1).

343. Sánchez, Efraín. "Bibliografía básica del arte colombiano." Trópicos, Nov 1981-Ene 1982, 10, 55-67.

344. Silvestre, Inalda Monteiro, and Sylvia Pereira de Holanda Cavalcanti. Artesanato brasileiro: uma contribuição a sua bibliografia. Recife: Fundação Joaquim Nabuco, Instituto de Documentação, Biblioteca Central Blanche Knopf: Editora Massangana, 1981. 114 p. (Serie obras de consulta, 2).

345. White, Anthony G. Mayan architecture: a selected bibliography. Monticello, IL: Vance Bibliographies, c1984. 5 p. (Architecture series--bibliography, A-1306).

BIBLIOGRAPHIES OF BIBLIOGRAPHIES

346. Bandara, Samuel B. "A survey of bibliographies of Caribbean literature in English." Revista interamericana de bibliografía, 1982, 32 (1), 3-27.

347. Castro, Manuel de. "Bibliografía de las bibliografías franciscanas españolas e hispanoamericanas." Archivo iberoamericano, Ene-Jun 1981, 41 (161-162), 3-222.

348. Centro de Pesquisas e Desenvolvimento. Catalogo de bibliografias. Centro de Pesquisas e Desenvolvimento, Setor de Documentação e Informação. 2a rev e aum ed. Brasília: EMBRAPA, DID, 1981. 169 p.

349. Cunha, Isabel María Ferin. Catálogo de bibliografias existentes no Centro de Estudos Africanos. São Paulo: Universidade, Faculdade de Filosofia, Letras e Ciências Humanas, Centro de Estudos Africanos, 1982. 101 p.

350. Hilton, Sylvia L. Bibliografía hispanoamericana y filipina: manual de repertorios bibliográficos para la investigación de la historia y la literatura hispanoamericanas y filipinas. Madrid: Fundación Universitaria Española, 1983. (Biblioteca histórica hispanoamericana, 6).

351. Johnson, Peter T. "Bibliography: current practices and future trends.' Latin American Research Review, 1983, 18 (1), 254-262.

352. Jordan, Alma, and Barbara Comissiong. *The English-speaking Caribbean: a bibliography of bibliographies*. Boston: G.K. Hall, 1984. 411 p.

353. Loroña, Lionel V., compiler. *Bibliography of Latin American bibliographies: annual report 1982-1983*. Madison, WI: SALALM Secretariat, 1984. 33 p. (SALALM Bibliography and Reference Series, 10).

354. Loroña, Lionel V., compiler. *Bibliography of Latin American bibliographies: annual report 1983-1984*. Madison, WI: SALALM Secretariat, 1984. 34 p. (SALALM Bibliography and Reference Series, 11).

355. Lostaunau Rubio, Gabriel. *Fuentes para el estudio del Perú: bibliografía de bibliografías*. Miguel Angel Rodríguez Rea, editor. Lima: [n.p.], 1980. 500 p.

356. Martínez, Julio A., and Ada Burns. *Mexican Americans: an annotated bibliography of bibliographies*. Saratoga, CA: R&E Publishers, c1984. 132 p.

357. Mesa, Rosa Q., and Robert Howe. "Annotated bibliography of bibliographies of Latin American official publications." In: *Library resources on Latin America: new perspectives for the 1980's: University of New Mexico, Albuquerque, N.M., June 1-6, 1980 (Seminar on the Acquisition of Latin American Library Materials; 25)*. Madison: University of Wisconsin-Madison, SALALM Secretariat, 1981: 255-272.

358. Perú. Instituto Nacional de Cultura, Biblioteca Nacional. *Bibliografía de bibliografías. Segunda parte*. Lima, 1980. 10 p.

359. Piedracueva, Haydée. "Annual report on Latin American and Caribbean bibliographic activities 1979." In: *Windward, leeward and main: Caribbean studies and library resources: Papers of the twenty-fourth annual meeting of the Seminar on the Acquisition of Latin American Library Materials, University of California, June 17-22, 1979*. Madison, WI: SALALM Secretariat, 1980: 61-109.

360. Piedracueva, Haydée. "Annual report on Latin American and Caribbean bibliographic activities 1980." In: *Library resources on Latin America: New perspectives for the 1980's: Papers of the twenty-fifth annual meeting of the Seminar on the Acquisition of Latin American Library Materials, University of New Mexico, Albuquerque, N.M., June 1-4, 1980*. Madison: SALALM Secretariat, University of Wisconsin-Madison, 1981: 123-162.

361. Piedracueva, Haydée. *A bibliography of Latin American*

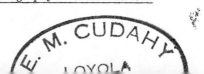

bibliographies, 1975-1979: Social Sciences and the Humanities. Metuchen, NJ: Scarecrow Press, 1982. 313 p.

362. Piedracueva, Haydée. "Bibliography of bibliographies, 1981 Supplement [1981]." In: *Latin American economic issues: information needs and sources: papers of the twenty-sixth annual meeting of the Seminar on the Acquisition of Latin American Library Materials, Tulane University, New Orleans, La., April 1-4, 1981.* Madison; Los Angeles: SALALM Secretariat, University of Wisconsin; UCLA Latin American Center Publications, University of California, Los Angeles, c1984: 304-344.

363. Piedracueva, Haydée. "Bibliography of bibliographies, 1982 Supplement [1982]." In: *Public policy issues and Latin American library resources: papers of the twenty-seventh annual meeting of the Seminar on the Acquisition of Latin American Library Materials, Washington,D.C., March 2-5, 1982.* Madison; Los Angeles: SALALM Secretariat; UCLA Latin American Center Publications, University of California, Los Angeles, c1984: 179-208.

364. Shaw, Bradley A. "Recent bibliographies on Latin American literature." *Latin American Research Review*, 1984, 19 (1), 190-197.

365. Siles Guevara, Juan. *Bibliografía de bibliografías bolivianas.* La Paz: Universidad Mayor de San Andrés, 1983. 104 p.

366. Woodbridge, Hensley Charles. *Spanish and Spanish-American literature: an annotated guide to selected bibliographies.* New York: Modern Language Association of America, 1983. 74 p.

BIBLIOGRAPHY--National

ARGENTINA

367. *Libros argentinos: ISBN 1982.* Buenos Aires: Cámara Argentina del Libro, 1984. 350 p.

BARBADOS

368. *National Bibliography of Barbados, January-December 1982.* Bridgetown: Public Library, 1984. 110 p.

BOLIVIA

369. Castañon Barrientos, Carlos. "Libros bolivianos del año 1983." Signo; cuadernos bolivianos de cultura, Mar 1984 (11), 163-181.

370. Guttentag Tichauer, Werner, compiler. Bio-bibliografia boliviana, 1982. La Paz-Cochabamba: Editorial Los Amigos del Libro, 1984. 143 p.

371. Guttentag Tichauer, Werner, compiler. Bio-bibliografia boliviana, 1981, with 1962-1980 supplement. La Paz-Cochabamba: Editorial Los Amigos del Libro, 1983. 434 p.

BRAZIL

372. Biblioteca Nacional (Brazil). Bibliografia brasileira. Vol. 1, No. 1-2 (Jan-Jun 1983). Rio de Janeiro: Biblioteca Nacional, 1984. Note: Continues Boletim bibliográfico da Biblioteca Nacional.

CARIBBEAN AREA

373. CARICOM Bibliography: a cumulated subject list of current national imprints of the Caribbean Community member countries.... 6:2 (1982). Georgetown, Guyana: Caribbean Community Secretariat, Information and Documentation Section, 1983.

CHILE

374. Bibliografia chilena, 1980. Santiago: Biblioteca Nacional, 1982. 216 p.

COLOMBIA

375. Romero Rojas, Francisco José. Anuario bibliográfico colombiano Rubén Ortiz 1981. Bogotá: Instituto Caro y Cuervo, 1983. 441 p.

CUBA

376. Biblioteca Nacional José Martí. Departamento de Investigaciones Bibliográficas. Bibliografia cubana 1983: enero-diciembre. La Habana: Biblioteca Nacional, 1984.

DOMINICAN REPUBLIC

377. Anuario bibliográfico dominicano, 1980-1982; de contenido retrospectivo al año 1979 y anteriores. Santo Domingo: Biblioteca Nacional, 1984. 263 p.

ECUADOR

378. Ecuador: bibliografía analítica. v. 3. Cuenca: Centro de Investigación y Cultura del Banco Central del Ecuador, 1982.

GUATEMALA

379. Cerezo Dardón, Hugo. A la luz de los libros. Bibliografía guatemalteca comentada (1980-1981). Guatemala: Editorial Universitaria, 1984. 221 p. (Colección creación literaria, 16).

GUYANA

380. Guyanese National Bibliography. Apr-Jun 1984. Georgetown: National Library, 1984.

HAITI

381. Bertrand, Jean Wilfrid, and Patrick Tardieu. "Bibliographie haitienne en 1981." Conjonction, Jun 1982 (154), 91-94. Note: Appears as annual feature.

HONDURAS

382. Anuario bibliográfico hondureño, 1980. Mario Argueta, compiler. Tegucigalpa: Ciudad Universitaria, 1982.

383. Durón, Jorge Fidel. "El libro hondureño en 1981." Boletín de la Academia Hondureña de la Lengua, Jun 1982, 24 (26), 143-160. Note: Appears as annual feature.

JAMAICA

384. Jamaican National Bibliography, 1984. Kingston: The Institute of Jamaica, 1984.

MEXICO

385. Bibliografia mexicana: 4-6 Apr-Jun 1982. México: Universidad Nacional Autónoma de México, 1982.

NICARAGUA

386. Arellano, Jorge Eduardo. "Bibliografía general de Nicaragua. Primera entrega: 1674-1900." Cuadernos de bibliografía nicaragüense, Ene-Jun 1981, 1, 1-87.

PERU

387. Perú. Biblioteca Nacional. Bibliografía nacional: 5:1-12 (Jan-Dec 1982). Lima: Biblioteca Nacional; Instituto Nacional de Cultura, 1983.

PUERTO RICO

388. Anuario bibliográfico puertorriqueño, 1973 and 1974. Gonzalo Velázquez, compiler. San Juan: Biblioteca General, Universidad de Puerto Rico, 1982.

TRINIDAD AND TOBAGO

389. Trinidad and Tobago National Bibliography: 8:2 (1982). St. Augustine, Trinidad: Central Library of Trinidad and Tobago and the University of the West Indies, 1982.

URUGUAY

390. Anuario bibliográfico uruguayo, 1982. Montevideo: Biblioteca Nacional, 1983. 171 p.

VENEZUELA

391. Anuario bibliográfico venezolano, 1977. Caracas: Biblioteca Nacional, 1978.

392. Bibliografía venezolana, I-II, 1982. Caracas: Instituto Autónomo Biblioteca Nacional y de Servicios de Bibliotecas, 1982-. Note: Replaces Anuario bibliográfico venezolano. Includes material cataloged from January 1980 to March 1981. The next volume will include material from 1978-1979.

BIOGRAPHY (Collective)

393. Agraz García de Alba, Gabriel. Biobibliografía de los escritores de Jalisco. México: Universidad Nacional Autónoma de México, 1980-. (Serie bibliografías. Instituto de Investigaciones Bibliográficas, UNAM, 9).

394. Annuario degli iberisti italiani. Milano: Cisalpino-Goliardica, 1980. 103 p.

395. Ardilla, Hector M. Hombres y letras de Colombia; 435 años de suceder literario. Bogotá: Gráficas Herpin Ltda., 1984. 621 p.

396. Arizmendi Posada, Ignacio. Gobernantes colombianos, 1819-1980. [Medellín]: Interprit Editores, 1980. 263 p.

397. Arze, José Roberto. Ensayo de una bibliografía biográfica boliviana. La Paz: Editorial "Los Amigos del Libro," 1981. 71 p.

398. Autores paraguayos: bibliografía. Asunción: Comité Regional de Educación Saturio Ríos, 1982. 62 p.

399. "Bio-bibliografía de los colaboradores del presente número." Revista histórica (Buenos Aires), Ene-Jun 1980, 2 (6), 219-220. Note: Includes bio-bibliographies of Abelardo Levaggi, Alicia Vidaurreta, and Mark D. Szuchman.

400. Carnegie, Jenipher. "Select bibliography on the works of Professor Elsa Goveia, Dr. Walter Rodney and Dr. Eric Williams." Bulletin of Eastern Caribbean Affairs, May-Jun 1982, 8 (2), 47-62.

401. Carrizosa Argaez, Enrique. Linajes y bibliografías de nuestros gobernantes: 1830-1982. Bogotá: Banco de la República, 1983. 623 p.

402. Cordero, Luis Agustín. Nicolás Antonio, bibliógrafo americanista. Lima: Universidad Nacional Mayor de San Marcos, Seminario de Historia Rural Andina, 1980. 118 p. Note: Lists of Peruvian and other Latin American authors taken from "Bibliotheca Hispana Nova."

403. Cortina, Lynn, and Ellen Rice. Spanish-American women writers: a bibliographical research checklist. New York: Garland Publishing Co., 1983. 292 p.

404. Costilla, María Isabel. Biobibliografía de escritores de Tucumán. Tucumán, Argentina: Dirección General de Cultura, 1983. 115 p.

405. Cotera, Martha P., compiler. Latina sourcebook: bibliography of Mexican, Cuban, Puerto Rican and other Hispanic women materials in the U.S. Austin, TX: Information Systems Development, 1982. 39 p.

406. Daumas de Poncho, Ana María. "Indice de estudiantes de la Universidad de Córdoba [Argentina], Vol. 2, 1767-1807." Cuadernos republicanos, 1982, 20, 175-227.

407. Diccionario de autores iberoamericanos. Pedro Shimose, editor. Madrid: Instituto de Cooperación Iberoamericana, Dirección General de Relaciones Culturales, Ministerio de Asuntos Exteriores, 1982. 459 p.

408. Durango de Martínez Almudever, Norma, and Doris Gonzalo de Giles. Indice biobibliográfico de autores pampeanos. [n.p.]: Dirección General de Cultura, Subsecretaría de Educación y Cultura de la Pampa: Facultad de Ciencias Humanas, Universidad de la Pampa, 1982. 163 leaves.

409. Faraco, Sergio. Quen é quem nas letras rio-grandenses: dicionário de autores contemporáneos. 2a ed. [Porto Alegre, Brasil]: Prefeitura Municipal de Porto Alegre, Secretaria Municipal de Educação e Cultura, Divisão de Cultura, 1983. 270 p.

410. Fernández, José B. Indice bibliográfico de autores cubanos (diáspora 1959-1979). Bibliographic index of Cuban authors (diaspora 1959-1979). Miami: Ediciones Universal, 1983. 106 p.

411. Foster, David William, and Roberto Reis. A dictionary of contemporary Brazilian authors. Tempe: Arizona State University, Center for Latin American Studies, 1981. 151 p.

412. Fustinoni, Osvaldo, and Federico Pergola. Médicos en las letras argentinas. Buenos Aires: Prensa Médica Argentina S.R.L., c1981. 108 p.

413. Guide to Latin Americanists in Northern California and the Pacific Northwest. Stanford, CA: Stanford-Berkeley Joint Center for Latin American Studies, 1982. 73 p.

414. Guzmán, Augusto. Biografías de la literatura boliviana: biografía, evaluación, bibliografía. Cochabamba: Editorial Los Amigos del Libro, 1982. 307 p. Note: Illustrations by Carlos Rimassa.

415. "Indice bio-bibliográfico del exilio español en México." In: El exilio español en México 1939-1982. México: Salvat, c1982, 717-878.

416. Moore, Wenceslao. Ayer y hoy en las letras goyanas: 1850--ciento treinta años. Goya, Argentina: Editorial Nuevos Cauces, 1981. 190 p. (Colección historia de la cultura goyana, 1).

417. Mundo Lo, Sara de. Index to Spanish American collective biography. Boston: G.K. Hall, c1981--.

418. Oliveira, Américo Lópes de. Escritoras brasileiras, galegas e portuguesas. Braga: Tip. S. Pereira, [1983?]. 215 p.

419. Page, James Allen, and Jae Min Roh, compilers. Selected black American, African and Caribbean authors: a bio-bibliography. Littleton, CO: Libraries Unlimited, 1985. 388 p.

420. Puentes de Oyenard, Sylvia. Tacuarembo, historia de su gente. [Tacuarembo, Uruguay]: Intendencia Municipal de Tacuarembo, [1981]. 231 p.

421. Quiénes son los escritores argentinos. Buenos Aires: Ediciones Crisol, 1980. 206 p.

422. Sánchez López, Luis María. Diccionario de escritores colombianos. Bogotá: Plaza & Janes, 1982. 826 p. Note: 2d ed., new format.

423. Sosa de Newton, Lily. Diccionario biográfico de mujeres argentinas. Buenos Aires: Plus Ultra, 1980. 533 p. Note: 2a ed. aum. y actualizada.

424. Souza, Maria de Conceição. Autor cearense; índice de bio-bibliografias. Fortaleza: Edições UFC, 1982. 104 p.

425. Suárez, Ida L, and Esther Sánchez M. Latinoamericanistas en Europa, 1981, registro bio-bibliográfico. 3d rev. ed. Amsterdam: Centro de Estudios y Documentación, 1981. 263 p. Note: The register is published every three years.

426. Vieira, Nelson H. "A Brazilian biographical bibliography." Biography: an interdisciplinary quarterly, 1982, 4, 351-364.

427. Villaseñor y Villaseñor, Ramiro. Los primeros federalistas de Jalisco, 1821-1834. Guadalajara: Gobierno de Jalisco, Secretaría General, Unidad Editorial, 1981. 129 p. (Colección textos Jalisco. Serie bibliografías y catálogos, 4).

428. Zayas de Lima, Perla. Diccionario de autores teatrales argentinos, 1950-1980. Buenos Aires: Editorial R. Alonso, 1981. 188 p.

BIOGRAPHY (Individual)

ALEGRIA, FERNANDO

429. Reeves, Rosa E. "Bibliografía de Fernando Alegría." Texto crítico, Jul-Dic 1981, 7 (22-23), 31-58.

ARCE ARAYA, GUILLERMO

430. Epple, Juan Armando. "Cronología biográfica y académica y bibliografía de Guillermo Arce Araya." Literatura chilena; creación y crítica, Abr-Jun 1983 (24), 14-16.

BARLOW, R H

431. Abrams, H. Leon, Jr. Robert Hayward Barlow, an annotated bibliography with commentary. Greeley: Museum of Anthropology, University of Northern Colorado, 1981. 32 p. (Katunob, occasional publication in Mesoamerican anthropology, 16).

BARRETO, PAULO (JOAO DE RIO)

432. Paulo Barreto, 1881-1921: catálogo de exposição comemorativa do centenário de nascimento. Organizado pela Seção de Promoções Culturais. Rio de Janeiro: Biblioteca Nacional, 1981. 47 p.

BATRES MONTUFAR, JOSÉ

433. Castillo López, Victor, compiler. Bibliografía de José Batres Montufar. Guatemala: Biblioteca "César Brañas," 1982. 11 p.

BELLO, ANDRÉS

434. Hanisch Espíndola, Walter. "Bello, historiador sin historia." Academia Chilena de Historia. Boletín, 1981, 48 (92), 29-51.

435. Lovera De Sola, R.J. "Guía elemental para el estudio de Bello." Academia nacional de la historia (Bogotá). Boletín, Oct-Dic 1983, 66 (264), 1119-1128.

436. Rivas Dugarte, Rafael Angel. "Andrés Bello en publicaciones periódicas del exterior: una bibliografía." Letras (Caracas), 1982, 37.

BOLIVAR, SIMON

437. Aljure Chalela, Simón. Bibliografía bolivariana: bicentenario del natalicio del libertador Simón Bolívar, 1783-1830. Bogotá: Banco de la República, Biblioteca Luis Angel Arango, 1983. 494 p.

438. Becco, Horacio Jorge. Simón Bolívar, el libertador (1783-1830), bibliografía selectiva. Washington, DC: Secretary General, Organization of American States, 1983. 61 p.

439. Brazil. Biblioteca Nacional. Simón Bolívar: informações bibliográficas. Rio de Janeiro: A Biblioteca, 1983. 66 p.

440. Castellanos, Rafael Ramón. "Los libros en el centenario del nacimiento del libertador." Academia nacional de la historia (Bogotá), Boletín, Jul-Sept 1983, 66 (263), 850-865.

441. Estévez, Irma I., and Arely Mendoza Deleon, compilers. Bibliografía de Bolívar en 250 libros. Guatemala: Editorial Universitaria de Guatemala, 1983. 69 p.

442. Flores, Ana María, and Elizabeth Delgado. "Simón Bolívar en 'Repertorio americano.'" Repertorio americano, Jul-Sept 1984, 9 (4), 24-26.

443. Sánchez, Sara M. "Simón Bolívar en la Universidad de Miami: bibliografía anotada." Los ensayistas, Mar 1984 (16-17), 7-54.

BORGES, JORGE LUIS

444. Foster, David William. Jorge Luis Borges: an annotated primary and secondary bibliography. New York: Garland, 1984. 328 p.

445. Sacerio-Garí, Enrique. "La crítica de Borges en 'El Hogar.'" Revista interamericana de bibliografía, 1983, 23 (2), 172-190.

BRANDAO, THEO

446. Sant' Ana, Moacir Medeiros de. "Bibliografia de Theo Brandão." Revista do Instituto Histórico e Geográfico de Alagoas, 1981 (37), 173-175.

BRICEÑO IRAGORRY, MARIO

447. Castellanos, Rafael Ramón. Bibliografía del doctor Mario Briceño Iragorry. Trujillo, Venezuela: Publicaciones del Ejecutivo del Estado Trujillo, 1981. 71 p.

CAILLET-BOIS, RICARDO R.

448. Barcala de Moyano, Graciela G. "Bibliografía del Doctor Ricardo R. Caillet-Bois." Revista de la Academia Nacional de la Historia (Argentina), 1979, 52, 279-315.

CARO, JOSÉ EUSEBIO

449. Aljure Chalela, Simón. "Bibliografía de José Eusebio Caro, poesía." Boletín cultural y bibliográfico, 1982, 19 (4), 116-157.

CARPENTIER, ALEJO

450. González Echevarría, Roberto, and Klaus Müller-Bergh. Alejo Carpentier: Bibliographical guide. Westport, CT: Greenwood Press, 1983. 271 p.

CAYCEDO ACOSTA, BERNARDO J.

451. "Bernardo J. Caycedo Acosta: nota bibliográfica." Boletín de historia y antigüedades, Ene-Mar 1983, 70 (740), 23-28.

CHACON, JOSÉ MARIA

452. Gutiérrez, Zenaida. Estudio bibliográfico de José María Chacón, 1913-1969. Madrid: Fundación Universitaria Española, 1982. 164 p.

CHAVEZ, ANGELINO

453. Morales, Phyllis S. Fray Angelino Chávez; a bibliography of his published writings, 1925-1978. Santa Fe, NM: Lightning Tree, 1980. 80 p.

CHOY, EMILIO

454. Rodríguez Rea, Miguel Angel. "Bibliografía de Emilio Choy." Boletín de antropología americana, Jul 1983 (7), 181-182.

COFIÑO LOPEZ, MANUEL

455. Romero, Cira. "Para una bibliografía de y sobre Manuel Cofiño." Texto crítico, May-Ag 1984, 10 (29), 120-135.

COLUMBUS, CHRISTOPHER

456. Ezquerra Abadia, Ramón. "Medio siglo de estudios colombinos." Anuario de estudios americanos, 1981 (38), 1-24.

CORTAZAR, JULIO

457. Kerr. Lucille. "Critics and Cortázar." Latin American Research Review, 1983, 18 (2), 266-275.

CRUZ SANTOS, ABEL

458. "Bibliografía del doctor Abel Cruz Santos." Boletín de historia y antigüedades, Abr-Jun 1984, 71, 342-354.

CUADRA, PABLO ANTONIO

459. Arellano, Jorge Eduardo. "Pablo Antonio Cuadra. Bibliografía fundamental." Revista del pensamiento centroamericano, Oct-Dic 1982, 38 (177), 189-200.

460. "Cronología y bibliografía fundamentales de Pablo Antonio Cuadra." Boletín nicaragüense de bibliografía y documentación, 1982, 50, 107-110.

ERRAZURIZ, CRESCENTE

461. Matte Varas, José Joaquín. "Monseñor Crescente Errázuriz, historiador en el cincuentenario de su fallecimiento." Revista chilena de historia y geografía, 1981 (149), 192-203.

EYZAGUIRRE, JAIME

462. Castellón Covarrubias, Alvaro. "Jaime Eyzaguirre: catálogo biográfico y bibliográfico." Boletín de la Academia Chilena de la Historia, 1983, 50, 59-110.

FELIPE, LEON

463. Paulino, José C. "Aportaciones para la bibliografía reciente de León Felipe." Anuario de letras, 1983, 21, 297-317.

FONSECA, CARLOS

464. "Bibliografía de y sobre Carlos Fonseca." Boletín de referencias (Nicaragua), Oct-Dic 1982, 2 (6), 45-55.

FUENTES, CARLOS

465. Reeve, Richard M. "Selected bibliography [Carlos Fuentes] 1949-1982." World literature today, Aug 1983, 57 (4), 541-546.

GABALDONI, LUIS E.

466. Lucero Nieto, Teodoro. Síntesis bio-bibliográfica del escritor Luis E. Gabaldoni. Lima: Perugraph, 1982.

GARCIA MARQUEZ, GABRIEL

467. Eyzaguirre, Luis B. "Gabriel García Márquez: contribución bibliográfica, 1955-1984." Inti, Otoño 1982-Primavera 1983 (16-17), 175-193.

GOMEZ CARRILLO, ENRIQUE

468. Castillo López, Victor. Bibliografía de Enrique Gómez Carrillo. Guatemala: Universidad de San Carlos de Guatemala, 1984. 22 p.

GOMEZ DE LA SERNA, RAMON

469. Mazzetti Cardiol, Rita. "Unpublished works of Ramón Gómez de la Serna." Anales de la literatura española contemporánea, 1982, 7 (1), 109-116.

GUILLÉN, NICOLAS

470. García Carranza, Josefina. "Síntesis bio-bibliográfica de Nicolás Guillén." Universidad de la Habana, Ene-Abr 1982 (216), 55-121.

471. Perdomo, Omar. "Nicolás Guillén en la bibliografía de Angel Augier." Santiago revista de la Universidad de Oriente, Jun 1983 (50), 199-215.

GUZMAN BRITO, ALEJANDRO

472. "Bibliografía de don Alejandro Guzmán Brito." Academia Chilena de la Historia. Boletín, 1982, 49 (93), 47-56.

KAHLO, FRIDA

473. García, Rupert. Frida Kahlo, a bibliography. Berkeley: Chicano Studies Library Publications Unit, University of California, 1983. 48 p.

LACERDA DE MOURA, MARIA

474. Leite, Miriam Lifchitz Moreira. "Uma voz feita para falar: Maria Lacerda de Moura." Boletim bibliográfico. Biblioteca Mário de Andrade, Jul-Dez 1982, 43 (3-4), 27-36.

LASCARIS, CONSTANTINO

475. Láscaris Comneno, Constantino. "Bibliografía de Constantino Láscaris." Revista de filosofía de la Universidad de Costa Rica, Ene-Dic 1981, 19 (49-50), 171-179.

LEON, CARLOS AUGUSTO

476. Bencomo de León, Guadalupe. Bibliografía de Carlos Augusto León y otras fuentes para el estudio de su obra. Caracas: Universidad Central de Venezuela, 1981. 189 p.

LEWIS, SIR ARTHUR

477. Wilkinson, Audine. "Sir Arthur Lewis: a bibliographic guide to his works to December, 1980." Social and economic studies, Dec 1980, 29 (4), 5-15.

LIMA BARRETO, AFONSO H.

478. "Lima Barreto: levantamento bibliográfico na Biblioteca Mário de Andrade." Boletim bibliográfico. Biblioteca Mário de Andrade, Jul-Set 1981, 42 (3), 99-103.

LISPECTOR, CLARICE

479. Beshers, Olga Espejo. "Clarice Lispector: a bibliography." Revista interamericana de bibliografía, 1984, 34 (3), 385-402.

480. Fitz, Earl F. "Bibliografía de y sobre Clarice Lispector." Revista iberoamericana, Ene-Mar 1984, 50 (126), 293-304.

481. Gotlib. Nádia Battella. "Clarice Lispector: a mulher e a literatura (Esboço de um itinerário crítico)." Boletim bibliográfico. Biblioteca Mário de Andrade, Jul-Dez 1982, 43 (3-4), 15-21.

LOPES CANÇADO, MAURA

482. Senra, Angela. "Os hospícios de M.L.C.--anotações." Boletim bibliográfico. Biblioteca Mário de Andrade, Jul-Dez 1982, 43 (3-4), 23-25.

MAÑACH, JORGE

483. Rovirosa, Dolores. Jorge Mañach: bibliografía. Madison: SALALM Secretariat, University of Wisconsin-Madison, c1985. 257p. (SALALM Bibliography and Reference Series, 13).

MARIATEGUI, JOSÉ CARLOS

484. Foster, David William. "A checklist of criticism on José Carlos Mariátegui." Los ensayistas; boletín informativo, Mar 1981 (10-11), 231-257.

MARQUES, RENÉ

485. Rodríguez Ramos, Esther. "Aproximación a una bibliografía: René Marques." Revista del Instituto de Cultura Puertorriqueña, Ene-Mar 1979, 22 (82), 33-47.

MARTI, JOSÉ

486. Perdomo Correa, Omar, compiler. Bibliografía martiana de Angel Augier. La Habana: Casa Natal de José Martí, 1980. 46 p.

MARTINEZ BAEZA, SERGIO

487. "Bibliografía de don Sergio Martínez Baeza." Boletín de la Academia Chilena de la Historia, 1982, 49 (93), 85-96.

MENESES, GUILLERMO

488. García Riera, Gladys. Guillermo Meneses, una bibliografía. Caracas: Centro de Investigaciones Lingüísticas y Literarias "Andrés Bello," Departamento de Castellano, Literatura y Latín, Instituto Universitario Pedagógico de Caracas, 1981. 169 p.

MERIÑO, FERNANDO ARTURO DE

489. Lluberes, Antonio. "Bibliografía sobre [Fernando Arturo de] Meriño." Estudios sociales (Dominican Republic), Dic 1983, 16 (54), 61-64.

MERINO REYES, LUIS

490. Valjalo, David. "Bibliografía de Luis Merino Reyes." Literatura chilena, creación y crítica (28), 27.

MESTRE, ANTONIO

491. González, Rosa María, compiler. Bibliografía comentada, activa y pasiva de Antonio Mestre (1834-1887). La Habana: [Centro de Estudios de Historia y Organización de la Ciencia "Carlos J. Finlay"], 1982. 49 p. (Conferencias y estudios de historia y organización de la ciencia, 30).

MILLA Y VIDAURRE, JOSÉ

492. Valenzuela de Garay, Carmen, compiler. Bibliografía de José Milla y Vidaurre, 1822-1882. Guatemala: Biblioteca "César Brañas," 1982. 27 p.

NAVARRO, DESIDERIO

493. Redonet Cook, Salvador Pedro. "Bibliografía de textos teóricos, ensayísticos y políticos sobre cultura, arte y literatura. Traducciones de Desiderio Navarro aparecidas en publicaciones nacionales." Santiago revista de la Universidad de Oriente, Sept 1983 (51), 122-130.

NEME, MARIO

494. "Bibliografía de Mário Neme." Anais do Museu Paulista, 1983, 32, 207-214.

ORTIZ, ABELARDO

495. Smith, Ronna. "Bibliografia de Ortiz." Cultura (Ecuador), May-Ag 1983, 6 (16), 197-210.

PALM, ERWIN WALTER

496. Kügelgen Kropfinger, Helga von. "Bibliografia de las publicaciones de Erwin Walter Palm." Jahrbuch für Geschichte von Staat, Wirtschaft und Gesellschaft Lateinamerikas, 1983, 20, xxxv-l.

PARRA, NICANOR

497. Fernández, Maximino. "Fichas bibliográficas sobre Nicanor Parra (II)." Revista chilena de literatura, Abr 1984, 23, 141-147.

PAZ, OCTAVIO

498. Juzyn, Olga. "Bibliografia actualizada sobre Octavio Paz." Inti, Spring 1982 (15), 98-144.

499. Verani, Hugo J. Octavio Paz: bibliografia crítica. México: Universidad Nacional Autónoma de México, 1983. 260 p.

PERON, EVA

500. Ciria, Alberto. "Flesh and fantasy: the many faces of Evita (and Juan Perón)." Latin American Research Review, 1983, 18 (2), 150-165.

PUCCIARELLI, EUGENIO

501. Parfait, Blanca H. "Bibliografia de Eugenio Pucciarelli." Cuadernos de filosofia, Ene-Dic 1983, 19 (30-31), 25-36.

PUIG, MANUEL

502. Corbatta, Jorgelina. "Bibliografia de Manuel Puig." Discurso literario, Otoño 1984, 2 (1), 245-250.

QUILES, SAMUEL

503. Adot, Juan C. Bibliografía de Ismael Quiles, S.J. Buenos Aires: Ediciones Universidad del Salvador, 1983. 81 p.

QUINTANA, MARIO

504. Faraco, Sergio, and Blasio Hickmann. "Bibliografía de Mário Quintana." Minas Gerais: suplemento literario, Mar 1982, 20 (15), 89.

QUIRARTE RUIZ, MARTIN

505. Lemoine, Ernesto. "Martín Quirarte Ruiz, 1924-1980." Estudios de historia moderna y contemporánea de México, 1983, 9, 357-365.

RAMA, ANGEL

506. Bibliografía sumaria. Angel Rama, 1926-1983. College Park: University of Maryland, Dept. of Spanish and Portuguese, 1984. 13 p.

RAMIREZ VAZQUEZ, PEDRO

507. Louie de Irizarry, Florita Z. Pedro Ramírez Vázquez, the architect. Monticello, IL: Vance Bibliographies, 1983. 4 p. (Architecture series bibliography, A-1083).

RESTREPO, JOSÉ MANUEL

508. Restrepo Manrique, Daniel. "Bibliografía del historiador don José Manuel Restrepo." Boletín de historia y antigüedades, Ene-Mar 1983, 70 (740), 255-270.

RESTREPO CANAL, CARLOS

509. "Bibliografía de Carlos Restrepo Canal." Boletín de historia y antigüedades, Ene-Mar 1984, 71 (744), 102-117.

ROCAFUERTE, VICENTE

510. Grijalva Coba, Adriana, and Samuel Guerra Bravo. "Bibliografía sobre Vicente Rocafuerte." Cultura (Ecuador), May-Ag 1983, 6 (16), 417-430.

ROJAS, GONZALO

511. Coddou, Marcelo. "Gonzalo Rojas; bibliografía." Literatura chilena, creación y crítica, Jul-Sept 1984, 8 (1), 31-32.

ROJAS, MANUEL

512. Cortés, Darío A. "Bibliografía de Manuel Rojas (Cuentos)." Literatura chilena, creación y crítica, Oct-Dec 1984, 10 (4), 30-31.

RULFO, JUAN

513. Juzyn, Olga. "Bibliografía actualizada sobre Juan Rulfo." Inti, Primavera-Otoño 1981 (13-14), 128-151.

SALOM, BARTOLOMÉ

514. Salom, Bartolomé. Archivo del general Bartolomé Salom. Caracas: Academia Nacional de la Historia, Departamento de Investigaciones Históricas, 1981. 138 p. (Biblioteca de la Academia Nacional de la Historia. Serie Archivos y Catálogos, 1). Note: "Introducción y elaboración de índice a cargo de Antonio González Antias."

SARMIENTO, DOMINGO FAUSTINO

515. Foster, David William. "A bibliography of critical monographs and articles on Domingo Faustino Sarmiento." Bulletin of bibliography, Mar 1982, 39 (1), 26-48.

SELVON, SAMUEL

516. Nasta, Susheila. "Samuel Selvon, a preliminary bibliography." Journal of Commonwealth literature, 1983, 18 (1), 131-143.

517. Nasta, Susheila. "Samuel Selvon preliminary bibliography: corrigenda." Journal of commonwealth literature, 1984, 19 (1), 153.

SOUSA DA SILVEIRA

518. Silva, Maximiliano de Carvalho e. Sousa da Silveira: o homem e a obra: sua contribução a crítica textual no Brasil. Rio de Janeiro: Presença Edições, 1984. 364 p. (Colecão linguagem, 24).

SUAREZ, FEDERICO GONZÁLEZ

519. Davidson, Russ. "Federico González: bio-bibliographical notes." Revista interamericana de bibliografía, 33, 33 (1), 13-20.

TOVAR Y TOVAR, MARTÍN

520. Aranguren, Willy. "En torno a la bibliografía de Martín Tovar y Tovar." Revista nacional de cultura, Jul-Sept 1984, 46 (254), 178-189.

TURNER, ETHEL DUFFY

521. Guía documental del archivo de Ethel Duffy Turner. [México, D.F.]: Biblioteca Nacional de Antropología e Historia, I.N.A.H., 1981. 266 p. (Serie Sección de manuscritos, 12).

VARGAS, GETULIO

522. Medeiros, Ana Ligia Silva, and Maria Celina Soares d'Araujo. Vargas e os anos cinquenta: bibliografia. Rio de Janeiro: FGV-Instituto de Documentação, Editora de Fundação Getulio Vargas, 1983. 155 p.

VASCONCELOS, JOSÉ

523. Foster, David William. "A checklist of criticism on José Vasconcelos." Los ensayistas; boletín informativo, Mar 1983, 177-212.

VIGANTI, MILCIADES ALEJO

524. Cáceres Freyre, Julián. "Bibliografía del profesor Milcíades Alejo Vignati." Boletín de la Academia Nacional de la Historia [Argentina], 1979, 52, 263-278.

VITIER, CINTIO

525. García Carranza, Araceli, and Josefina García Carranza. "Más de 40 años con la poesía: bibliografía de Cintio Vitier." Revista de la Biblioteca Nacional José Martí, May-Ag 1983, 25 (2), 69-129.

DISSERTATIONS

526. Andrade, Diva Carrero de, and Maria Angélica Rodrigues Quemel. Teses de brasileiros e sobre o Brasil defendidas na França, 1979-1980. [São Paulo]: Universidade de Sao Paulo, Faculdade de Filosofia, Letras e Ciências Humanas, 1983. 122 p. (Boletim. Biblioteca de Filosofia e Ciências Sociais. No. 2. Série especial)

527. Bandara, Samuel B. "A checklist of theses and dissertations in English on Caribbean Literature." World Literature Written in English, 1981, 20 (2), 319-334.

528. Benseler, David P. "Doctoral degrees granted in foreign languages in the United States: 1983." Modern Language Journal, autumn 1984, 68 (3), 241-257. Note: Appears annually as regular feature.

529. Buenos Aires. Universidad. Instituto Bibliotecológico. Tesis presentadas a la Universidad de Buenos Aires, 1976-1978. Buenos Aires: Universidad de Buenos Aires, Instituto Bibliotecológico, 1980. 29 leaves. (Publicación. Instituto Bibliotecológico, 58).

530. Buenos Aires. Universidad. Facultad de Derecho y Ciencias Sociales. Tesis presentadas a la Facultad de Derecho y Ciencias Sociales, 1829-1960. Suplemento, 1827-1866. Buenos Aires: Universidad de Buenos Aires, Instituto Bibliotecológico, 1982. 29 leaves.

531. Catálogo de dissertações, teses e memoriais da Universidade de São Paulo recebidos pela Biblioteca Central 1981. São Paulo: Universidade de São Paulo, Coordenadoria de Atividades Culturais, Sistema de Bibliotecas da USP, 1982. 120 p. Note: Published annually.

532. Catálogo de tesis, 1959-1981. Bahía Blanca, Argentina: Universidad Nacional del Sur, 1982. 169 p.

533. Ceará, Brasil (State). Universidade Federal. Centro de Ciencias Agrárias. Catálogo de teses do Centro de Ciencias Agrárias. Fortaleza: Universidade Federal do Ceará, 1979.

534. Chatham, James R, and Enrique Ruiz-Fornells. Dissertations in Hispanic languages and literatures: an index of dissertations completed in the United States and Canada. Lexington: University of Kentucky Press, 1970-1981. 2 vols. Note: With the collaboration of Sara Matthews Scales.

535. "Comentarios de tesis." Caribe contemporáneo, El, Ene-Abr 1981, 5, 275-280.

536. "Dissertações e tesis." Revista brasileira de estudos pedagógicos, Set-Dez 1983, 64 (148), 311-324. Note: Appears as a regular feature.

537. Duport, Claude. "Catalogue des thèses et mémoires sur l'Amérique Latine soutenus en France, 1981-1982." Cahiers des Amériques Latines, Juillet-Décembre 1982. (26), 157-206.

538. Epple, Juan Armando. "Tesis doctorales sobre literatura chilena en las universidades norteamericanas." Literatura chilena en el exilio, Ene 1980, 4 (1), 13-16.

539. González, Nelly S. Doctoral dissertations in Latin America and the Caribbean; an analysis and bibliography of dissertations accepted at American and Canadian universities, 1966-1970. Urbana, IL: Latin American Studies Association, 1980. 201 p. (Publication. Consortium of Latin American Studies Programs, 10).

540. "Grado de expertos en la enseñanza de historia de Colombia." Boletín de historia y antigüedades, Jul-Sept 1981, 68 (734), 837-842.

541. Greaves, Cecilia. Segundo catálogo de tesis sobre historia de México. México: Comité Mexicano de Ciencias Históricas, c1984. 365 p.

542. Guía Nacional de Tesis. La Paz: Ministerio de Planeamiento y Coordinación, Sistema y Fondo Nacional de Información para el Desarrollo (SYFNID), 1981-1982. 2 v. Note: v. 1 (1960-1977); v. 2 (1978-1982).

543. Híjar de Suárez, Rose. Indice de tesis: ciencias sociales 1975-1979: antropología, economía, sociología, trabajo social. Lima: Asociación Multidisciplinaria en Investigación y Docencia en Población, 1984. 294 p. (Documentación e Información sobre población. AMIDEP, 1).

544. Mantillo, Martha Eugenia, compiler. Catálogo de tesis de grado. Bogotá: Universidad de los Andes, Facultad de Economía, Centro de Estudios sobre Desarrollo Económico, [1983]. 2 vols.

545. McClendon, Carmen Chaves, and Nadine Olson. "Dissertations in the Hispanic and Luso-Brazilian languages and literatures 1983." Hispania, May 1984, 67 (2), 322-331.

546. Muñoz de Linares, Elba, and Alicia Céspedes de Reynaga. Bibliografía de tesis peruanas sobre indigenismo y ciencias sociales. Lima: Instituto Indigenista Peruano: Centro Interamericano de Administración del Trabajo, 1983. 2 vols. (Serie bibliográfica, 4).

547. Noronha, Daisy Pires. Catálogo de tesis. São Paulo: Universidade de São Paulo, Faculdade de Saúde Pública, Serviço de Biblioteca e Documentação, 1981-1982. 2 v. Note: v. 1 (1948-1971); v. 2 (1972-1981).

548. Oniki, Kazuko. "Teses e dissertaçoes de antropologia defendidas na Universidade de São Paulo, 1978-1981." Revista de antropologia, 1981, 24, 153-158.

549. Pereira, Marília Mesquita Guedes, and Norma Maria Fernandes Nogueira. Catálogo de teses defendidas na UFPb, 1970-1979. Jõao Pessoa: Universidade Federal da Paraiba, Biblioteca Central, 1980. 318 p.

550. "Positions et résumés concernant les thèses de troisième cycle soutenus en France (1979) en droit, histoire, linguistique, littérature de l'Amérique Latine." Cahiers du monde hispanique et luso-brésilien, 1980, 35, 217-308.

551. "Recent doctoral dissertations." Revista interamericana de bibliografia, 1984, 24 (3-4), 543-547. Note: This feature appears in all issues, listing U.S. and Canadian doctoral dissertations grouped by subject.

552. "Resúmenes de tesis de grado." Cuadernos de economía, Abr 1983, 20 (59), 113-118. Note: Appears as a regular feature.

553. "Resumos de dissertaçoes de mestrado, teses de doutorado ou de libre docencia defendidas em outras universidades." Revista da Pontificia Universidade Católica de São Paulo, Jan-Dez 1981. (Fasc. 100), 245-254.

554. "Resumos e/ou informes sobre dissertações de mestrado e teses de doutorado, defendidadas na Universidade em 1980 por área de conhecimiento." Revista da Pontificia Universidade Católica de São Paulo, Jan-Dez 1981. (Fasc. 100), 133-244.

555. Sánchez, María Elsa B. Tesis de técnicos paraguayos sobre temas agropecuarios y forestales (bibliografía). Asunción: Ministerio de Agricultura y Ganadería, Dirección de Investigación y Extensión Agropecuaria y Forestal, Instituto Interamericano de Ciencias Agrícolas, 1979. 21 p.

556. "Thèses soutenues sur l'Amérique Latine en 1979-1980." Cahiers des Amériques Latines, 1981. (2), 3-135.

557. "Trabajos de tesis de los graduados de la Universidad de San Carlos de Guatemala en 1978." Universidad de San Carlos, 1979, 2a. Epoca (10), 305-[381].

558. Walters, Marian C. Latin America and the Caribbean II: a

dissertation bibliography. [Ann Arbor, MI]: University Microfilms International, [198-]. 78 p.

ECONOMICS

GENERAL

559. Axline, W. Andrew. "Latin American regional integration: alternative perspectives on a changing reality." Latin American Research Review, 1981, 16 (1), 167-186.

560. Baklanoff, Eric N. "Latin American economic history: economic vs. cultural interpretations." Latin American Research Review, 1981, 16 (3), 245-249.

561. Bergquist, Charles. "What is being done? Some recent studies in the urban working class and organized labor in Latin America." Latin American Research Review, 1981, 16 (2), 203-223.

562. "Bibliografía seleccionada sobre el nuevo orden económico internacional." Revista de economía latinoamericana, Ene-Mar 1980 (59), 291-317.

563. Boisier, Sergio. "Desarrollo y planificación regional." Pensamiento iberoamericano; revista de economía política, Ene-Jun 1982 (1), 179-184.

564. Ghosh, Pradip K., editor. Developing Latin America: a modernization perspective. Westport, CT: Greenwood Press, c1984. 416 p. (International development resource book, 19).

565. Goodman, Louis Wolf. "Horizons for research on international business in developing nations." Latin American Research Review, 1980, 15 (2), 225-240.

566. Hartness-Kane, Ann. "Latin American business: library resources and services [1981]." In: Latin American economic issues: information needs and sources: papers of the twenty-sixth annual meeting of the Seminar on the Acquisition of Latin American Library Materials, Tulane University, New Orleans, La., April 1-4, 1981. Madison, WI; Los Angeles, CA: SALALM Secretariat, University of Wisconsin, Madison; UCLA Latin American Center Publications, University of California, Los Angeles, c1984, pp. 159-178.

567. Hartness-Kane, Ann. Latin America: economics and business. Austin: The University of Texas at Austin, The General Libraries, 1981 (Selected reference sources, 23).

568. Howe, Robert. "A bibliographic guide to Latin America and Caribbean government publications on foreign investments 1965-1981." Government Publications Review, Sept-Oct 1983, 10 (5), 459-477.

569. Howe, Robert. "Foreign investment in Latin America: information sources in government publications [1981]." In: Latin American economic issues: information needs and sources: papers of the twenty-sixth annual meeting of the Seminar on the Acquisition of Latin American Library Materials, Tulane University, New Orleans, La., April 1-4, 1981. Madison, WI; Los Angeles, CA: SALALM Secretariat, University of Wisconsin, Madison; UCLA Latin American Center Publications, University of California, Los Angeles, c1984, 106-120.

570. Lifschitz, Edgardo. Bibliografía analítica sobre empresas transnacionales. Analytical bibliography on transnational corporations. México: Instituto Latinoamericano de Estudios Transnacionales, c1980. 607 p. Note: Spanish and English.

571. Lundahl, Mats. "Publications of CIEPLAN [Corporación de Investigaciones Económicas para Latinoamérica]." Ibero Americana (Sweden), 1983, 13 (1), 77-79.

572. Marinho, Luiz Claudio. "Empresas transnacionales en América Latina." Pensamiento iberoamericano; revista de economía política, Jul-Dic 1982 (2), 217-226.

573. Nolff, Max. "Estrategia y experiencias del desarrollo industrial en América Latina." Pensamiento iberoamericano; revista de economía política, Jul-Dic 1982 (2), 226-235.

574. Orlandi, Alberto. "América Latina y el mercado internacional de productos básicos." Pensamiento iberoamericano; revista de economía política, Jul-Dic 1983 (4), 271-277.

575. "Publicaciones del INTAL (Instituto para la Integración de América Latina) durante 1981." Integración latinoamericana, Ag 1982, 7 (71), 78-81.

576. "Resúmenes de artículos publicados en revistas latinoamericanas." Pensamiento iberoamericano; revista de economía política, 1983 (3-4) Note: A regular feature in all issues.

577. Rieznik, Pablo Héctor, and Rodolfo Rieznik. "Capital financiero y crisis en América Latina." Pensamiento iberoamericano; revista de economía política, Ene-Jun 1983 (3), 219-226.

578. Schaffer, Ellen G., compiler. Business information sources of Latin America and the Caribbean. Washington, DC: Organization of American States, General Secretariat, Columbus

Memorial Library, 1982. 60 p. (Documentation and information series, 5).

579. Sheahan, John. "The outside and the inside: trade, finance, and domestic conflicts." Latin American Research Review, 1984, 19 (1), 173-180.

580. Sofer, Eugene F. "Recent trends in Latin American labor historiography." Latin American Research Review, 1980, 15 (1), 167-176.

581. Villareal, René. "Problemas y opciones de los países exportadores de petróleo." Pensamiento iberoamericano; revista de economía política, Ene-Jun 1982 (1), 216-220.

582. Zevallos y Muñiz, Marco Aurelio, and Augusto Pérez-Rosas Cáceres. Ciencia y tecnología para el desarrollo: una bibliografía. Lima: Universidad del Pacífico, Centro de Investigación, 1980. 270 p. (Serie cuadernos. Ensayo, 17).

ANDES REGION

583. Durand, Francisco. "La industria en el Ande: bibliografía." Revista andina, 1983, 1, 265-271.

ARGENTINA

584. Abalo, Carlos. "Enfoques sobre la crisis argentina." Pensamiento iberoamericano; revista de economía política, Jul-Dic 1983 (4), 243-251.

585. "Bibliografía económica y social de Antonio García." Trimestre económico, El, Oct-Dic 1983, 50 (200), 1869-1871.

BARBADOS

586. Williams, Maxine, and Aldeen Payne. "Select bibliography on the economy of Barbados." In: De Lisle Worrell, editor. The economy of Barbados, 1946-1980. Bridgetown: Central Bank of Barbados, 1982, 167-196.

BRAZIL

587. Ferreira, Carmosina N. Planejamento econômico e social no Brasil de 1930 à 1974: uma análise bibliográfica. Rio de Janeiro: Programa Nacional de Pesquisa Econômica, 1983. 3 vols. (Difusão e síntese. Suplemento, 1).

588. Magalhães, Alencar D'Avila. Brazilian agriculture: a manual for the foreign investor. Brasília: Ministry of Agriculture, Cordination of International Affairs, 1982. 43 p.

589. Oliveira, Franciso de. "Problemas e impasses da política económica brasileira." Pensamiento iberoamericano; revista de economía política, Jul-Dic 1982 (2), 235-239.

590. Saint, William S. "The wages of modernization: a review of the literature on temporary labor arrangements in Brazilian agriculture." Latin American Research Review, 1981, 16 (3), 91-110.

591. Sayad, Jõao. "Inflaçao brasileira." Pensamiento iberoamericano; revista de economía política, Ene-Jun 1982 (1), 220-224.

592. Souza, Paulo Renato de, and Paulo Vieira da Cunha. "Política salarial e evolução da estrutura de salário, no Brasil." Pensamiento iberoamericano; revista de economía política, Jul-Dic 1982 (2), 245-253.

593. Tausch, Arno. "German-language studies of Brazilian development." Latin American Research Review, 1983, 18 (3), 261-263.

594. Versiani, Flávio Ravelo. A literatura de economia brasileira, 1945-1975: uma bibliografia básica. [Brasília]: Fundação Universidade de Brasília, Departamento de Economia, [1981]. 34 p. (Texto para discussão, 71).

CARIBBEAN AREA

595. Towle, Edward L., and A. Robert Teytaud, compilers and annotaters. Caribbean Island resource management: an annotated bibliography of source materials focusing on the U.S. Virgin Islands' experience and its Eastern Caribbean context. Rev. ed. [St. Thomas, USVI]: Island Resources Foundation, [1982]. 40 p. (U.S. MAB miscellaneous publication, 2). Note: Prepared by the Foundation under the sponsorship of the U.S. National Commission for UNESCO, Man and the Biosphere Program.

CENTRAL AMERICA

596. Bloch, Thomas. "Central America." Government Publications Review, Jan-Feb 1983, 10 (1), 131-133.

597. "Fichas bibliográficas [acerca del tema aspectos de historia económica de Centroamérica, 1850-1950]." Revista de ciencias sociales (Costa Rica), Oct 1979 (17-18), 153-156.

598. Schaffer, Ellen G. The Central American Common Market: a selected bibliography, 1975 to the present. Washington, DC: Organization of American States, General Secretariat, Columbus Memorial Library, 1981. 10 p. (Documentation and information series, 4).

CHILE

599. Sunkel, Osvaldo, and Carmen Cariola Sutter. La historia económica de Chile: 1830 y 1930: dos ensayos y una bibliografía. Madrid: Ediciones Cultura Hispánica del Instituto de Cooperación Iberoamericana, 1982. 342 p.

COLOMBIA

600. Estrada de Asensio, Gloria; Leda Inés Arbeláez B.; and Myriam Manrique P. La información industrial en Bogotá. Bogotá: Instituto de Fomento Industrial, 1981, "varias paginaciones."

601. Hernández G., María Magdalena. Bibliografía colombiana sobre pequeña y mediana industria, 1960-1980. Bogotá: Ministerio de Educación Nacional, Fondo Colombiano de Investigaciones Científicas y Proyectos Especiales "Francisco José de Caldas," 1982 [i.e. 1983]. 90 p.

COSTA RICA

602. Edelman, Marc. "Recent literature on Costa Rica's economic crisis." Latin American Research Review, 1983, 18 (2), 166-188.

603. "Fichas bibliográficas [on Costa Rican economy]." Revista de ciencias sociales (Costa Rica), Oct 1982 (24), 81-86.

604. Jiménez, Dina. Bibliografía retrospectiva sobre política agraria en Costa Rica, 1948-1978. [San José]: Centro de Documentación, Instituto de Investigaciones Sociales, Vicerrectoría de Investigación, Universidad de Costa Rica, [1981]. 528 p.

CUBA

605. Padrón, Nicolasa, compiler. La revolución agraria en Cuba: bibliografía. [La Habana]: Departamento de Servicios Informativos, CIDA, 1982. 159 leaves.

DOMINICAN REPUBLIC

606. Banco Central de la República Dominicana. Biblioteca. Bibliografía económica dominicana 1978-1982. Santo Domingo: El Banco, 1983. 125 p. Note: Lists works in the Biblioteca "Juan Pablo Duarte" of the Banco Central.

HAITI

607. Lundahl, Mats. "Haitian undervelopment in a historical perspective." Journal of Latin American Studies, 1982, 17 (2), 465-475.

MEXICO

608. Ayala Espino, José. "Bibliografía general sobre estado y economía en México 1920-1980." A: revista de ciencias sociales y humanidades, Ene-Feb 1982, 1981 (2), 192-208.

609. Banco de México. Bibliografía económica de México 1981-1983. Banco de México, Subdirección de Investigación Económica. México, D.F.: Banco de México, 1984. 124 p.

610. Cano-Sánchez, Beatriz. "Contribución bibliográfica para la historia económica del estado de Tlaxcala: siglos XIX y XX." Ibero-amerikanisches Archiv, 1982, Neue Folge 8 (4), 403-418.

611. Carrillo Viveros, Jorge, and Alberto Hernández Hernández. La industria maquiladora en México: bibliografía, directorio e investigaciones recientes. La Jolla: Program in United States-Mexican Studies, University of California, San Diego, 1981. 130 p. (Monographs in U.S.-Mexican studies, 7).

612. Ceballos, Jorge, et al. Bibliografía general del desarrollo económico de México, 1500-1976. Florescano, Enrique, Coordinator. México: SEP, Instituto Nacional de Antropología e Historia, Departamento de Investigaciones Históricas, 1980. 3 vols. (Colección científica. Bibliografías, 76).

613. Fitzgerald, E.V.K. "Recent writings on the Mexican economy." Latin American Research Review, 1981, 16 (3), 236-244.

614. Foster, Stephenie. Economic development in the U.S.-Mexico border region: a review of the literature. Monticello, IL: Vance Bibliographies, 1981. 17 p. (Public administration series--bibliography, P-692).

615. López Rosado, Diego G. Bibliografía de historia económica y

social de México. México: Universidad Nacional Autónoma de México, 1979-1982. 13 vols. (Serie bibliografías, 8).

616. López Rosado, Diego G. Bibliografía económica de la revolución mexicana, 1910-1930. México: Universidad Nacional Autónoma de México, 1982. 362 p. (Serie bibliografías. UNAM, Instituto de Investigaciones Bibliográficas [y] Biblioteca Nacional de México, 10).

617. Lucero M., Miguel Angel. "El regimen jurídico mexicano sobre la inversión extranjera directa: una bibliografía." Comercio exterior, Feb 1983, 33 (2), 156-161.

618. Martínez Ríos, Jorge. Tenencia y explotación de la tierra en México. México: Secretaría de la Reforma Agraria, Centro de Estudios Históricos del Agrarismo en México, 1984. 184 p. (Colección fuentes para la historia del agrarismo en México).

619. Méndez N., Eloína. "Estado actual de la investigación sobre sindicatos nacionales de industria." A: revista de ciencias sociales y humanidades, Sept-Dic 1980, 1 (1), 123-152.

620. México. Secretaría de Programación y Presupuesto. Catálogo de publicaciones oficiales (diciembre 1976-junio 1979). México: Secretaría de Programación y Presupuesto, Dirección General de Documentación y Análisis, 1980. 294 p.

621. Peña, Devon Gerardo. Maquiladoras: a select annotated bibliography and critical commentary on the United States-Mexico border industry program. Austin: Center for the Study of Human Resources, University of Texas, c1981. 29, 121 p.

622. Rodríguez de Lebríja, Esperanza. Guía documental del Archivo Histórico de Hacienda. México: Archivo General de la Nación, [1981]. 2 vols.

623. Sánchez Gutiérrez, Arturo, and Luis Angel Domínguez Brito. "Bibliografía sobre el movimiento obrero en México (1940-1980)." A: revista de ciencias sociales y humanidades, Sept-Dic 1980, 1 (1), 109-122.

624. Veerkamp, Verónica. "Bibliografía sobre mercados con especial referencia a la comercialización de productos agrícolas." Nueva antropología, Jun 1982, 6 (19), 189-214.

625. Veerkamp, Verónica. "Bibliografía sobre mercados y comercio." América indígena, 1982, 42 (3), 467-504.

PARAGUAY

626. Oberbeck, Charles D. An annotated bibliography of income

distribution in Paraguay. [Washington, DC]: U.S. Agency for International Development, 1979. 22 p.

PERU

627. Durand, Francisco. "La industria en el Perú: bibliografía." Estudios andinos, 1981, 9 (17-18), 195-246.

628. González de Olarte, Efraín. "Economía campesina en el Perú." Pensamiento iberoamericano; revista de economía política, Jul-Dic 1982 (2), 212-216.

629. Pinzás García, Teobaldo. La economía peruana, 1950-1978: un ensayo bibliográfico. Lima: Instituto de Estudios Peruanos, [1981]. 156 p. (Análisis económico, 4).

TRINIDAD AND TOBAGO

630. International Institute for Educational Planning Library. Trinidad and Tobago; economics and education: a selective and annotated bibliography of documents available in the IIEP Library. Françoise Du Pouget, compiler. Paris: UNESCO, 1980. 9 p. (Bibliography. International Institute for Educational Planning, Library, 4).

VENEZUELA

631. Fundación para el Desarrollo de la Región Centro Occidental de Venezuela. Indice bibliográfico de los estudios realizados por FUDECO. Suplemento 1976-1979. Barquisimeto: Biblioteca Técnica Científica Centralizada, 1981. 258 p.

EDUCATION

GENERAL

632. Alfaro Bolaños, Flor de M., and Zaida Sánchez Moya. Bibliografía no. 1 de microfichas sobre educación en Latinoamérica. San José, C.R.: Centro multinacional de investigación educativa; Red Latinoamericana de información y documentación en educación; Centro de investigación y desarrollo educativo, 1983. 263 p.

633. "Bibliografía seleccionada: acceso a la educación superior." Docencia postsecundaria, Sept-Oct 1981, 9 (5), 133-139.

634. "Bibliografia selectiva sobre educación superior en América Latina y el Caribe." Universitas 2000, 1982, 6 (1), 151-180.

635. Bibliografia sobre educación para el trabajo. Santiago, Chile: UNESCO Oficina Regional de Educación, 1982. 14 p.

636. "Bibliografia sobre el personal docente: situación, formación, perfeccionamiento." Boletín de educación (Chile), Jul-Dic 1979, 26, 71-84.

637. Cariola, Patricio. "Bibliografia anotada de experiencias participativas en el campo de educación formal y no formal." Socialismo y participación, Jun 1981, 14, 145-157.

638. Castro de Salmerón, Alicia; Elena Saucedo Lugo; and Graciela Alvarez de Péz, compilers. Bibliografia sobre educación superior en América Latina. México: Universidad Nacional Autónoma de México, 1983. 197 p.

639. Catálogo de publicaciones didácticas latinoamericanas de formación profesional. Suplemento. Montevideo: CINTERFOR, OIT, 1981. 127 p.

640. CRESALC-UNESCO. "Bibliografia selectiva sobre educación superior en América Latina y el Caribe." Universitas 2000, 1982, 6 (3-4), 185-190. Note: "Tercera parte."

641. CRESALC-UNESCO. "Bibliografia selectiva sobre educación superior en América Latina y el Caribe." Universitas 2000, 1982, 6 (2), 201-226. Note: "Segunda parte."

642. CRESALC-UNESCO. "Bibliografia [sobre educación superior en Latinoamerica]." Universitas 2000, 1983, 7 (3-4), 137-138.

643. CRESALC-UNESCO. "Bibliografia [sobre educación superior en Latinoamerica]: IV parte." Universitas 2000, 1983, 7 (2), 155-163.

644. Dale, Doris Cruger. "Spanish-English bilingual books for children." Booklist, Sept 1981, 78 (1), 53-55.

645. Erziehung und Entwicklung in Lateinamerika: Auswahlbibliographie [Herausgeber, Institut für Iberoamerika-Kunde, Dokumentations-Leitstelle Lateinamerika]. Educación y desarrollo en América Latina: bibliografia selecta [editor, Instituto de Estudios Iberoamericanos, Centro de Documentación Latinoamericana]. Hamburg: Die Dokumentations-Leitstelle, 1980. 225 p. (Dokumentationsdienst Lateinamerika; Documentación latinoamericana, Reihe A, 3; Serie A, 3). Note: German and Spanish.

646. Galván, Max, compiler. Bibliography on bilingualism and bilingual education, 1981-1982. Trenton, NJ; New Brunswick, NJ: State Dept. of Education; Institute for Intercultural Relations and Ethnic Studies, Rutgers--The State University of New Jersey, 1982. 145 p.

647. InterAmerica Research Associates. A bibliography of bilingual-bicultural pre-school material for the Spanish-speaking child: supplement II. Washington, DC: Head Start Bureau, Administration for Children, Youth and Families, Office for Human Development Services, U.S. Department of Health and Human Services, 1981. 77 p.

648. Jungo, M.E., compiler. International bibliography for a didactics of early bilingualism in the education of underprivileged children, especially children of migrant workers. Einsiedeln, Switzerland: Bucherdienst, 1982. 140 p.

649. Lauerhass, Ludwig, and Vera Lúcia Oliveira de Araujo Haugse. Education in Latin America: a bibliography. Los Angeles, CA; Boston, MA: UCLA Latin American Center Publications, University of California, Los Angeles; G.K. Hall, [1981], c1980. 431 p. (UCLA Latin American Center Publications reference series, 9).

650. Levy, Daniel C. "Educational policy: alternative and political contexts." Latin American Research Review, 1984, 19 (3), 153-171.

651. Lulat, Y. "Comparative education bibliography." Comparative education review, Oct 1982, 26, 449-467.

652. Mackey, William F., editor. Bibliographie internationale sur le bilinguisme. International bibliography on bilingualism; with an analytic index on microfiche. 2d rev. ed. Quebec: Presses de l'Université Laval, 1982. 575 p.

653. Pérez de Zapata, Amarilis. Investigaciones latinoamericanas en educación: referencias bibliográficas de los "Resúmenes analíticos en educación" y microfichas del CIDE (Centro de Investigación y Desarrollo de la Educación) Vol. 2. Santiago, Dom. Rep.: Centro de Documentación y Investigación Educativa, Centro Nacional de REDUC: Universidad Católica Madre y Maestra, Centro de Investigaciones, 1983-.

654. "Publicaciones del proyecto 'Desarrollo y educación en América y el Caribe.'" CEPAL Review, Dec 1983 (21), 11-12.

655. Río, Martha del. "Introducción a algunas revistas de investigación educativa." Revista latinoamericana de estudios

educativos, Primavera 1981, 11 (2), 163-168. Note: Continuation of article in previous issue.

656. Río, Martha del. "Introducción a algunas revista de investigación educativa." Revista latinoamericana de estudios educativos, Invierno 1981, 11 (1), 207-211.

657. Schkolnik, Susana, et al. "Bibliografía [sobre educación superior en Latinoamerica]." Universitas 2000, 1984, 8 (1), 99-121. Note: "Séptima parte."

658. Schwartzmann, Simon. "Politics and academia in Latin American universities." Journal of Interamerican Studies and World Affairs, Aug 1983, 25 (3), 416-423.

659. Sullivan, LeRoy L. Retention of minorities in higher education: an abstracted bibliographic review (1978-1982). Little Rock: University of Arkansas at Little Rock, Office of Instructional Development, 1982. 47 p.

660. Valverde, Leonard A.; Rosa Castro Feinberg; and Esther M. Marquez, editors. Educating English-speaking Hispanics. Alexandria, VA & Washington, DC: Association for Supervision and Curriculum Development in cooperation with the National Association for Bilingual Education, c1980. 88 p.

661. Velasco Barraza, Carlos R. Bibliografía anotada sobre tecnología apropiada en educación. Carmen Del Río, reviser. Santiago, Chile: UNESCO, 1982. 77 p.

BRAZIL

662. "Fontes para uma reflexão sobre educaçao indígena." In: A questão de educação indígena. São Paulo: Brasiliense, 1981. 175-222

663. Fortes, Helvia de Luces, compiler. Bibliografia especializada em financiamento da educação. 4a ed rev e atualizada. Brasília: Fundo Nacional de Desenvolvimento da Educação. Biblioteca 'Profa. Ecilda Ramos de Souza,' 1983. 109 leaves.

664. Instituto de Estudos Avançados em Educação. Catálogo de pesquisas 1975-1983. 2a ed. Calazans, Maria Julieta Costa, Coordenadora geral de pesquisa. Rio de Janeiro: Fundação Getulio Vargas: Instituto de Estudos Avançados em Educação, 1984. 90 p. Note: Master's theses abstracts at the Instituto.

CHILE

665. Grossi, María Clara, and Ernesto Schiefelbein. Bibliografía de

la educación chilena, 1973-1980. [Santiago, Chile]: Corporación de Promoción Universitaria, [1980]. 335 p. (Serie documentos de trabajo C.P.U.)

COLOMBIA

666. Colombia. Ministerio de Educación, Dirección General de Capacitación y Perfeccionamiento Docente, Currículo y Medios Educativos. Catálogo de publicaciones 1977-1980. Bogotá: División de Documentación e Información Educativa, 1981. 26 p.

667. Müller de Ceballos, Ingrid, and Clemencia Leyva Franco. Indice acumulativo de documentos sobre educación, 1974-1980. Universidad Pedagógica Nacional. Centro de Documentación Educativa. Bogotá: El Centro, 1981. 2 vols.

COSTA RICA

668. Lafourcade V., Pedro, and Zaida Sánchez Moya. La investigación educativa en Costa Rica de 1970 a 1981. San José: Centro Multinacional de Investigación y Documentación en Educación, 1982. 21, [103] p.

669. Sánchez Moya, Zaida, and Flor de M. Alfaro Bolaños. Instrumentos utilizados en investigación educativa. San José, C.R.: Centro Multinacional de Investigación y Documentación en Educación, 1982. 66 p.

670. Solano Navarro, Yamileth, et al. Bibliografía anotada de la educación parauniversitaria en Costa Rica. San José: Centro Multinacional de Investigación Educativa, Red Latinoamericana de Información y Documentación en Educación, Centro de Investigación y Desarrollo Educativo, 1983. 236 p.

CUBA

671. Oberg, Larry R., compiler. Contemporary Cuban education: an annotated bibliography. Rev. ed. Stanford, CA: Stanford University Libraries, 1980. 40 p. Note: At head of title: Cubberley Library.

DOMINICAN REPUBLIC

672. Pérez de Zapata, Amarilis. Bibliografía de artículos de periódicos sobre educación dominicana, año 1981. Santiago de los Caballeros, Dom. Rep.: Centro de Documentación e Investigación Educativa, [1983]. 11 leaves.

673. Pérez de Zapata, Amarilis. Bibliografía de la educación dominicana antes de 1970. Santiago de los Caballeros, R.D.: Universidad Católica Madre y Maestra, Centro de Investigaciones, [1983]. 69 p.

MEXICO

674. Catálogo colectivo de material educativo de sistemas abiertos: educación media superior. México: Secretaría de Educación Pública, Consejo Coordinador de Sistemas Abiertos, 1981. 104 p.

675. Catálogo colectivo de material educativo de sistemas abiertos de educación superior. México: Secretaría de Educación Pública, Consejo Coordinador de Sistemas Abiertos de Educación Superior, 1982. 65 p.

676. Emery, Sarah Snell. Centralized education in Mexico--unification through standardization: an annotated bibliography. Monticello, IL: Vance Bibliographies, 1984. 32 p. (Public administration series--bibliography, P 1509).

677. Emery, Sarah Snell. Mexican education-generalities: an annotated bibliography. Monticello, IL: Vance Bibliographies, [1984]. 35 p. (Public administration series--bibliography, P 1485).

678. Emery, Sarah Snell. Mexico's marginal peoples--informal education projects: an annotated bibliography. Monticello, IL: Vance Bibliographies, [1984]. 30 p. (Public administration series--bibliography, P 1534).

679. Emery, Sarah Snell. The push for industrialization--Mexico's technical training and education: an annotated bibliography. Monticello, IL: Vance Bibliographies, [1984]. 40 p. (Public administration series--bibliography, P 1535).

680. "Enseñanza abierta: hemerografía." Revista mexicana de ciencias políticas, Jul-Sept 1980, Año 26, nueva época (101), 139-195.

681. Galván de Terrazas, Luz Elena. Fuentes para la historia de la educación en México. México: Centro de Investigaciones y Estudios Superiores en Antropología, 1983. 60 p.

682. Martínez Rizo, Felipe. "Calidad y distribución de la educación: estado del arte y bibliografía comentada." Revista latinoamericana de estudios educativos, 1983, 134 (4), 55-86.

683. Peña, Guillermo de la, and Luz Elena Galván de Terrazas.

Bibliografía comentada sobre la historia de la educación en México. 2a ed. [Tlalpan, D.F.]: Centro de Investigaciones Y Estudios Superiores en Antropología Social, 1980. 132 p. (Cuadernos de la Casa Chata, 12).

PARAGUAY

684. Centro Paraguayo de Documentación Social. Resúmenes analíticos en educación. Asunción: Centro Paraguayo de Estudios Sociológicos, 1981-.

685. Marecki, Sofía. Bibliografía sobre la educación en el Paraguay; período 1970-1981. Asunción: Centro Paraguayo de Estudios Sociológicos, Centro Paraguayo de Documentación, 1982. 98 p.

686. Marín de Sandoval, Concepción. Bibliografía de textos escritos por educadores paraguayos: educación primera y secundaria. Asunción: Bibliotecología, 1983. 112 p.

687. Rivarola I., Mirtha María. Bibliografía de artículos de periódicos sobre educación paraguaya. Año 1981. [Asunción]: Centro Paraguayo de Estudios Sociológicos, [1983]. 218 p.

PERU

688. Rodríguez Rea, Miguel Angel, and Gabriel Lostaunau Rubio. Bibliografía nacional de educación, 1930-1980. Lima: Instituto Nacional de Investigación y Desarrollo, 1982. 525 p.

UNITED STATES

689. Beckers, Frances López, Education and Mexican American migrant students: a topical bibliography. Rosslyn, VA: National Clearinghouse for Bilingual Education, [1982]. 45 p.

690. Cuenca, Pilar de, and Inés Alvarez Rudolph. "Library holdings of the Office of Bilingual Education, City of New York: a selected bibliography." Bilingual Review. Revista Bilingüe, May-Aug 1982, 9 (2), 127-152.

691. Outstanding dissertations in bilingual education, 1982, recognized by the National Advisory Council on Bilingual Education. Rosslyn, VA: National Clearing House for Bilingual Education, [1983?]. 125 p.

URUGUAY

692. Arrue Rius, Susana. Bibliografía sobre educación del Uruguay:

colección CIEP, 1970-1983. Montevideo: Centro de Investigación y Experimentación Pedagógica; Red Latinoamericana de Información en Educación, 1984. 29 p.

VENEZUELA

693. Morles Sánchez, Victor. Bibliografía sobre educación de postgrado en Venezuela. Caracas: Consejo Nacional de Investigaciones Científicas y Tecnológicas, Dirección de Educación y Divulgación; Universidad Central de Venezuela, Coordinación Central de Estudios para Graduados, 1981. 83 p.

FOLKLORE

694. Associação dos Bibliotecários de Minas Gerais. Grupo de Bibliotecários de Ciências Sociais e Humanidades. Bibliografia do folclore brasileiro: fontes para estudo existentes em Minas Gerais; la. parte. Belo Horizonte: O Grupo, 1983. 104 p.

695. Bibliografía del folklore de Guatemala, 1892-1980. Guatemala: Dirección General de Antropología e Historia, 1980. 174 p. (Colección antropología. Serie cultura popular. Publicación extraordinaria.)

696. Bibliografía del folklore chileno, 1782-1976. [Santiago, Chile]: Servicio de Extensión de Cultura Chilena, [between 1976 and 1980]. 35 leaves.

697. "Bibliografia do folclore brasileiro: fontes para estudo existentes em Minas Gerais." In: Simpósio de comunicações sobre pesquisas em folclore, 2. Belo Horizonte, 1980. Síntese. Belo Horizonte: Secretaria de Estado do Governo, Coordenadoria de Cultira, 1981: 95-99.

698. Cipoletti, María Susana. "Acerca de la narrativa oral del noroeste argentino." Revista andina, 1983, 1 (1), 251-263.

699. Tuleskyu, Sueli A. "Bibliografia do folclore do Paraná." Boletim da Commissão Paranaense de Folclore, Ago 1980, 4 (4), 37-41.

700. Vieira Filho, Domingos. Populário maranhense: bibliografia. [Rio de Janeiro]: Civilização Brasileira em convênio com a Secretaria de Cultura do Maranhão, 1982. 72 p.

GEOGRAPHY, CARTOGRAPHY

701. Caillavet, Chantal. "Mapas coloniales de haciendas lojanas." Cultura (Ecuador), Ene-Abr 1983, 5 (15), 513-531.

702. "Cartografia." Brazil. Biblioteca Nacional. Boletim bibliográfico, 1980, 21, 200-231. Note: Lists Brazilian maps and plans.

703. Fundação Instituto Brasileiro de Geografia e Estatística. Biblioteca Central. Mapas e outros materiais cartográficas na Biblioteca Central do IBGE. Secretaria de Planejamento da Presidência da República, Fundação Instituto Brasileiro de Geografia e Estatística, Directoria de Formação e Aperfeiçoamento de Pessoal, Biblioteca Central. Rio de Janeiro: IBGE, 1983-.

704. Gade, Daniel. "Geografía de los Andes centrales en los escritos de idioma inglés." Revista andina, 1983, 1 (1), 241-249.

705. Galloway, J.H. "Human geography in Brazil during the 1970's: debates and research." Luzo-Brazilian Review, Summer 1982, 19 (1), 1-21.

706. Guarda, Gabriel. "Los planos de la ciudad de San Marcos de Arica: siglos XVII-XVIII." Anuario de estudios americanos, 1980 (i.e. 1982), 37, 741-752. Note: 9 leaves of plates.

707. Mulcansingh, Vernon C. Titles of Caribbean studies and research papers. Department of Geography, U.W.I. Mona. [Mona, Jamaica]: The Department, [1982]. A-Y p.

708. Rey Balmaceda, Raúl. Bibliografía geográfica referida a la República Argentina. Buenos Aires: Gaea, 1983, 2 vols.

709. Rosso, Hespéria Zuma de. "Bibliografia sobre toponímia." Revista brasileira de geografia, Jul-Set 1982, 44 (3), 529-534.

710. Salmito, Adeilda Rigaud. Catálogo das cartas topográficas do nordeste. Recife: Ministerio do Interior, Superintendencia do Desenvolvimento do Nordeste, Coordenação de Informática, 1980. 196 p.

711. Sellers, John R., and Patricia Molen Van Ee, compilers. Maps and charts of North America and the West Indies, 1750-1789: a guide to the collections in the Library of Congress. Washington, DC: Library of Congress, 1980. 495 p.

712. Sternberg, Rolf. "Selected geography texts on Latin America." Latin American Research Review, 1981, 16 (3), 272-275.

HISTORY

GENERAL

713. Archer, Christon I. "The role of the military in colonial Latin America." History Teacher, May 1981, 14 (3), 413-421.

714. Arias Divito, Juan C. Expediciones científicas españolas a América en el siglo XVIII. Indice documental. Buenos Aires: Instituto Bibliográfico "Antonio Zinny," 1983. 96 p. (Colección Indices Documentales, 1).

715. Cardozo, Lubio. "Los estudios bibliográficos hispanos y europeos de la cultura humanística latinoamericana." Cuadernos hispanoamericanos, Sep 1983 (399), 116-120.

716. Díaz Acosta, América, et al. Panorama histórico-literario de nuestra América. Ciudad de La Habana: Casa de las Américas, [1982]. 2 vols. Note: t. 1 (1900-1943); t. 2 (1944-1970).

717. Larouche, Irma, et al. "Bibliografía de historia de América (I)." Revista de historia de América, Ene-Jun 1981 (91), 151-183.

718. Larouche, Irma, et al. "Bibliografía de historia de América (II)." Revista de historia de América, Jul-Dic 1981 (92), 241-271.

719. Lavrín, Asunción. "Women in Latin American History." History Teacher, May 1981, 14 (3), 387-399.

720. Lavrov, Nikolai. "Estudio de problemas de la historia y la contemporaneidad." América Latina (USSR), Sept 1983 (9), 66-73.

721. Martin, Cheryl English. "Reform, trade and insurrection in the Spanish empire." Latin American Research Review, 1984, 19 (3), 194-202.

722. Miller, Joseph C., and Larissa V. Brown. "Slavery: annual bibliographic supplement (1982) Part 1." Slavery and Abolition, Sept 1982, 3 (2), 163-208.

723. Morales Padrón, Francisco. "Guía bibliográfica general sobre historia de América." Historiografía y bibliografía americanistas, 1978, 22, 663-129. Note: Appears as a regular feature.

724. Mörner, Magnus, et al. "Comparative approaches to Latin American history." Latin American Research Review, 1982, 17 (3), 55-89.

725. Nunn, Frederick M. "Latin American military-civilian relations from independence to the present: a course conspectus." History Teacher, May 1981, 14 (3), 423-437.

726. Palmer, Colin A. "Slavery, abolition and emancipation in the New World." Latin American Research Review, 1982, 17 (3), 276-283.

727. Patterson, Orlando. "Recent studies on Caribbean slavery and the Atlantic slave trade." Latin American Research Review, 1982, 17 (3), 252-275.

728. Santos, Yolanda Lhullier dos. "A figura feminina no livro de viagem ilustrado do século XVI." Boletim bibliográfico. Biblioteca Mário de Andrade, Jul-Dez 1982, 43 (3-4), 87-91.

729. Solís, Miguel de J. Latin American independence--an historical and ideological view: a bibliography. Selected and annotated from primary sources in the Mendel Collection in the Lilly Library, Indiana University, Bloomington, Indiana. Bloomington: Latin American Studies, Indiana University, 1980. 89 p. (Latin American studies working papers, 11).

730. Werlich, David P. Research tools for Latin American historians: a select, annotated bibliography. New York: Garland Publishing Co., 1980. 269 p. (Garland reference library of social science, 60).

ANDES REGION

731. Tepaske, John J., editor. Research guide to Andean history: Bolivia, Chile, Ecuador and Peru. Durham, NC: Duke University Press, 1981, 346 p.

ARGENTINA

732. Avilés, Jorge M. "Bibliografía: las islas Malvinas y el conflicto anglo-argentino." Ideas en ciencias sociales (Belgrano, Arg.), Abr-Jun 1984, 1 (2), 113-124. Note: "Compiled from the Library of Congress and PAIS International."

733. Bohdziewicz, Jorge C. Impresos relativos a la guerra franco-argentina, 1835-1842: contribución bibliográfica y crítica. Buenos Aires, 1982. 88 p.

734. Etchepareborda, Roberto. "La bibliografía reciente sobre la cuestión Malvinas (Segunda parte)." Revista interamericana de bibliografía, 1984, 34 (2), 227-288.

735. Etchepareborda, Roberto. Historiografía militar argentina. Buenos Aires: Circulo Militar, 1984. 205 p.

736. Instituto Histórico de la Ciudad de Buenos Aires. Archivo Histórico. Indice temático general, 1880-1887: gestión Torcuato de Alvear. Estela Pagani, coordinator. Buenos Aires: Archivo Histórico, 1983. 205 p.

737. Instituto Histórico de la Ciudad de Buenos Aires. Equipo Técnico. Bibliografía básica de la historia de la ciudad de Buenos Aires. Buenos Aires: El Instituto, 1980. 23 p.

738. Libros registros cedularios del Río de la Plata, 1534-1717: catálogo. v. 1-. Buenos Aires: Instituto de Investigaciones de Historia del Derecho, 1984 (Edición de fuentes de derecho indiano, en conmemoración del V descubrimiento de América, 2).

739. Merubia, Sonia. Argentine history. Austin: Benson Latin American Collection. The General Libraries, University of Texas at Austin, 1981. 2 p. (Biblio noticias, 8).

740. Musso Ambrosi, Luis Alberto. "Anotaciones de bibliografía uruguaya sobre historia argentina en el período 1831-1852, época de Juan Manuel de Rosas." Historiografía y bibliografía americanistas, 1979, 23, 121-138.

741. Slater, William F. "Argentina: 1862--present." History Teacher, May 1981, 17 (3), 313-326.

742. Socolow, Susan M. "Recent historiography of the Río de la Plata: colonial and early national periods." Hispanic American Historical Review, Feb 1984, 64 (1), 105-120.

743. Ugalde de Chudina, María Dolores. Catálogo colectivo genealógico-heráldico de Córdoba. Córdoba: Biblioteca Mayor, 1982. 43, 18 p. Note: Copia de catálogo de obras heráldicos genealógicos en la Biblioteca Nacional de Bernardo F. Lozier Almazón.

BOLIVIA

744. Barnadas, Josep. "Panorama historiográfico de estudios recientes sobre Charcas colonial." Revista andina, Jul-Dic 1983, 1 (2), 475-543.

745. Jáuregui Cordero, Juan Heriberto. Documentación existente en el Archivo Nacional de Bolivia sobre rebeliones indígenas, 1780-1783. La Paz: Centro de Investigaciones Históricas, 1980. 38 p. (Serie índices y catálogos, 2).

746. Parejas Moreno, Alcides J. Documentos para la historia del Oriente boliviano, siglos XVI y XVII: catálogo de documentos de la sección V (Audiencia de Charcas) del Archivo General de Indias. Santa Cruz: [n.p.], 1981 [i.e. 1982]. 144 p.

747. Van den Berg, Hans. "Historiografía del oriente boliviano; logros y tareas." Shupihui, Ene-Mar 1984, 9 (29), 51-69.

BRAZIL

748. Bittencourt, Gabriel Augusto de Mello. Literatura e história, historiografia capixaba: (bibliografia de la República). Vitória-Espírito Santo: IHGES, 1984. 109 p.

749. Caldeira, Paulo da Terra, and Maria de Lourdes Borges de Carvalho. "Fontes para o estudo da Brasiliana." Revista brasileira de biblioteconomia e documentação, Jan-Jun 1982, 15 (1-2), 25-31.

750. Cervo, Amado Luis. "Fontes parlamentares brasileiras e os estudos históricos." Latin American Research Review, 1981, 16 (2), 172-181.

751. Dutra, Francis A. A guide to the history of Brazil, 1500-1822: the literature in English. Santa Barbara, CA: ABC-Clio, c1980. 625 p.

752. Leite, Miriam Moreira; María Lucía de Barros Mott; and Bertha Kauffmann Appenzeller. A mulher no Rio de Janeiro no século XIX: um índice de referencias em livros de viajantes estrangeiros. São Paulo: Fundação Carlos Chagas, 1982. 167 p.

753. Medeiros, Ana Ligia, and Monica Hirst, compilers. Bibliografia histórica: 1930-1945. Brasília: Editora Universidade de Brasília, 1982. 226 p.

754. Oliveira, Lúcia Lippi; Eduardo Rodrígues Gomes; and Maria Celina Whately. Elite intelectual e debate político nos anos 30: uma bibliografia comentada da Revoluçao de 1930. Rio de Janeiro: Fundação Getulio Vargas, em convênio com o Instituto Nacional do Livro, 1980. 355 p.

755. Peregrino, Umberto. "Autores militares em discussão." Revista do Instituto Histórico e Geográfico Brasileiro, Jan-Mar 1982 (334), 67-78.

756. Pereira, Luiz C. Bresser. "Seis interpretações sobre o Brasil." NS; North South, 1982, 7 (13), 1-34.

757. Russell-Wood, A.J.R. "An agenda and a bibliography for the

history of colonial Brazil." The Americas, 1982, 38 (3), 405-411.

758. Université de Haute Bretagne. Centre d'études portugaises, brésiliennes et de l'Afrique lusophone. Trois fonds portugais et brésiliens. Rennes: Université de Haute Bretagne, Centre d'études portugaises, brésiliennes et de l'Afrique lusophone, [1980]. 110 p.

759. Weinstein, Barbara. "Brazilian regionalism." Latin American Research Review, 1982, 17 (2), 262-276.

CARIBBEAN AREA

760. Buve, Raymond Th. J. "Bibliografía básica para la historia de las Antillas holandesas y Suriname." Historiografía y bibliografía americanistas, 1981, 25, 149-185.

761. Clarke, Colin C. "Colonialism and its social and cultural consequences in the Caribbean." Journal of Latin American Studies, Nov 1983, 18 (2), 491-503.

762. Knight, Franklin W. "The Caribbean sugar industry and slavery." Latin American Research Review, 1983, 18 (2), 219-229.

763. Miller, Joseph C. "Slavery: annual bibliographic supplement: Caribbean." Slavery and abolition, Sept 1981, 2 (2), 164-167.

CENTRAL AMERICA

764. Dunkerley, James. "Writing on revolutions." Journal of Latin American Studies, Nov 1983, 18 (2), 481-490.

765. Seckinger, Ron. "The Central American militaries: a survey of the literature." Latin American Research Review, 1981, 16 (2), 246-258.

CHILE

766. "Allende's Chile: contemporary history and the counterfactual." Journal of Latin American studies, Nov 1980, 12 (2), 445-452.

767. "Fichero bibliográfico (1981-1982)." Historia (Chile), 1983, 18, 367-436. Note: Appears as a regular feature.

768. Slater, William F. "History of Chile from the conquest to Arturo Alessandri." History Teacher, May 1981, 14 (3), 327-339.

COLOMBIA

769. Aljure Chalela, Simón. "Bibliografía relacionada con el 20 de julio de 1810." Boletín cultural y bibliográfico, 1981, 18 (1), 132-151.

CUBA

770. Pérez, Louis A., Jr. "Armed struggle and guerrilla warfare in Latin America: a bibliography of Cuban sources, 1959-1979." Revista interamericana de bibliografía, 1983, 33 (4), 507-544.

771. Pérez, Louis A. Historiography in the revolution: a bibliography of Cuban scholarship, 1959-1979. New York: Garland Publishing Co., 1982. 318 p.

ECUADOR

772. Caillavet, Chantal. "Fuentes y problemática de la historia colonial de Loja y su provincia." Cultura (Ecuador), Sep-Dic 1982, 5 (14), 409-459.

773. Caillavet, Chantal. "Relaciones coloniales inéditas de la provincia de Loja." Cultura (Ecuador), Ene-Abr 1983, 5 (15), 441-477.

774. Fauroux, Emmanuel. "Las fuentes impresas para el estudio histórico, político, económico y social de la provincia de Loja." Cultura (Ecuador), Ene-Abr 1983, 5 (15), 371-435.

775. Presidencia de Quito. La presidencia de Quito, 1822. Quito: Edit. Casa de la Cultura Ecuatoriana, 1983. 260 p.

GUATEMALA

776. Bendfeldt Rojas, Lourdes. "El Popol-Vuh: por el mundo de su bibliografía." Cultura de Guatemala, Nov-Dic 1980, 1 (3), 45-128.

777. Mulet de Cerezo, María Luisa. Bibliografía analítica de la revolución del 20 de octubre de 1944. Guatemala: Editorial Universitaria, c1980. 143 p.

HAITI

778. Geggus, David P. "Unexploited sources for the history of

the Haitian revolution." Latin American Research Review, 1983, 18 (1), 95-103.

HONDURAS

779. Argueta, Mario. Investigación y tendencias recientes de la historiografía hondureña: un ensayo bibliográfico. Tegucigalpa: UNAH, Editorial Universitaria, 1981. 28 p. (Cuadernos universitarios, 3).

780. Valle, Rafael Heliodoro. "Bibliografía histórica de Honduras." Boletín de la Academia Hondureña de la Lengua, Jun 1982, 24 (26), 205-213.

MEXICO

781. Aguirre, Carlos, et al. Fuentes para la historia de la Ciudad de México 1810-1979. México: Instituto Nacional de Antropología e Historia, [1984]. 2 vols.

782. Atondo Rodríguez, Ana María. Catálogo de documentos sobre el noroeste de México: (existentes en 7 ramos del Archivo General de la Nación, Epoca Colonial). México, DF: Archivo General de la Nación, [1980]. 2 vols. (Serie guías y catálogos, 49).

783. Barnes, Thomas Charles; Thomas H. Naylor; and Charles W. Polzer. Northern New Spain: a research guide. Tucson: University of Arizona Press, c1981. 147 p.

784. Benjamin, Thomas, and Marcial Ocasio-Meléndez. "Organizing the memory of modern Mexico: Porfirian historiography in perspective, 1880's-1890's." Hispanic American Historical Review, May 1984, 64 (2), 323-364.

785. "Catálogo del Ramo Revolución mexicana." Boletín del Archivo del Estado de México, May-Ag 1980, 5, 48-51.

786. García Moll, Roberto. Indice del archivo técnico de la Dirección de Monumentos Prehispánicos de Antropología del INAH. México: Instituto Nacional de Antropología e Historia, 1982. 304 p.

787. Glass, John B. The Boturini collection: the legal proceedings and the basic inventories, 1742-1745. Lincoln Center, MA: Conemex Associates, 1981. [73]-122 p. (Contributions to the ethnohistory of Mexico: no. 9) Note: "The Indian museum of Lorenzo Boturini," Vol. 1, Chapter 5.

788. Hanke, Lewis, et al. Guía de las fuentes en hispanoamérica para el estudio de la administración virreinal española en México y en el Perú, 1535-1700. Washington, DC: Secretaría General, Organización de los Estados Americanos, 1980. 523 p.

789. Hart, John M. "Historiographical dynamics of the Mexican Revolution." Latin American Research Review, 1984, 19 (2), 223-231.

790. Lara Tenorio, Blanca, compiler. Colección de documentos sobre Tehuacán, Pue. México: Instituto Nacional de Antropología e Historia, 1982. 167 p. (Colección científica: 133. Catálogos y bibliografías)

791. Mexico. Archivo General de la Nación. Catálogo de la Serie Armas, Fondo Presidentes Alvaro Obregon, Plutarco Elías Calles, 1920-1928. México: Archivo General de la Nación, [1980]. 153 leaves. (Serie Guías y Catálogos, 34).

792. Mexico. Archivo General de la Nación. Catálogo del Ramo Correspondencia de Virreyes, Marqués de Croix. Elena Bribiesca Sumano, et al., editors. México: Archivo General de la Nación, [1980]- (Serie guías y catálogos, 56).

793. Mexico. Archivo General de la Nación. Catálogo del Ramo de indios. Cayetano Reyes G. and Magdalena Gómez S., editors. México: Archivo General de la Nación, [1979]- (Serie guías y catálogos)

794. Mexico. Archivo General de la Nación. Catálogo del Ramo Provincias Internas, Archivo General de la Nación: índice analítico elaborado por Esperanza Rodríguez de Lebrija. México: Archivo General de la Nación, 1981. 2 v. (Serie guías y catálogos, 17).

795. Mexico. Archivo General de la Nación. Indice del Ramo alcaldes mayores. Bribiesca Sumano, María Elena, editor. México: Archivo General de la Nación, [1980]. 5 vols. in 4 (Serie guías y catálogos, 53).

796. Mexico. Archivo General de la Nación. Ramo historia. México: Archivo General de la Nación, 1981- (Serie guías y catálogos, 28). Note: Rev. y corr. por Celia Medina Mondragon.

797. Mexico. Archivo General de la Nación. Ríos y acequias, mercados, abastos y panaderías. México: Archivo General de la Nación, [1980]. 102 leaves. (Serie guías y catálogos, 54).

798. Moreno Toscano, Alejandro, and Sonia Lombardo de Ruiz.

Fuentes para la historia de la Ciudad de México, 1810-1979. México: Instituto Nacional de Antropología e Historia, [1984]. 2 vols.

799. Parcero López, María de la Luz. Historiografía mexicana, siglos XIX y XX. México: Universidad Nacional Autónoma de México, 1980.

800. Parcero López, María de la Luz. Introducción bibliográfica a la historiografía política de México, siglos XIX y XX. México: Universidad Nacional Autónoma de México, 1982. 347 p.

801. Raat, William Dirk. The Mexican revolution: an annotated guide to recent scholarship. Boston: G.K. Hall, c1982. 275 p.

802. Reyes García, Cayetano, and Hortencia Tentle J. Catálogo del Archivo de buscas. vols. 1-42. México: Archivo General de la Nación, 1981-. (Serie guías catálogos, 48).

803. Rojas R., Teresa, and Juan M. Pérez Zevallos. Indice de documentos para la historia del antiguo señorío de Xochimilco. [México]: Centro de Investigaciones y Estudios Superiores en Antropología Social, [1981]. 174 p. (Cuadernos de la Casa Chata, 43).

804. Torre Villar, Ernesto de la. Testimonios históricos mexicanos en los repositorios europeos: guía para su estudio. México: Universidad Autónoma de México, Instituto de Estudios y Documentos Históricos, 1980. 147 p. (Biblioteca del claustro. Serie guías, 1).

805. Tutino, John. "Regional diversity and national unity in the ear of Mexican independence." Latin American Research Review, 1980, 15 (1), 225-230.

806. Tutorow, Norman E., compiler and editor. The Mexican-American War: an annotated bibliography. Westport, CT: Greenwood Press, 1981. 427 p.

807. Valadés, José C. "Bibliografía: noticia para la bibliografía anarquista de México." Historia obrera, Sept 1980, 5 (20), 20-26. Note: Originally published in La Protesta, Buenos Aires.

808. Velázquez Chávez, María del Carmen. Documentos para la historia de México en colecciones austriacas. 2a ed. México: Instituto de Estudios y Documentos Históricos, 1981. 250 p. (Biblioteca del claustro. Serie guías, 2).

809. Voss, Stuart F. "The Porfiriato in time and space." Latin American Research Review, 1983, 18 (3), 246-254.

NICARAGUA

810. Booth, John A. "Celebrating the demise of Somocismo: fifty recent Spanish sources on the Nicaraguan revolution." Latin American Research Review, 1982, 17 (1), 1982.

811. Gilbert, Dennis. "Sandinistas in power." Latin American Research Review, 1984, 19 (2), 214-219.

812. Woodward, Ralph Lee, Jr. "William Walker and the history of Nicaragua in the nineteenth century." Latin American Research Review, 1980, 15 (1), 237-240.

PARAGUAY

813. Cáceres Carísimo, Cirilo. Bibliomil: ensayo de una bibliografía para militares: (los primeros 2000 títulos para servir a los SS.OO Generales y Almirantes, SS.OO Superiores y Subalternos e instituciones de las FF.AA. de la nación). Asunción: Benito Ramos Silvero Editor, 1981. 312 p.

814. Kallsen, Margarita. Referencias bibliográficas de la guerra del Chaco. Asunción: [Centro de Publicaciones de la Universidad Católica 'Nuestra Señora de la Asunción'], 1982. 68 p.

815. Whigham, Thomas Lyle, and Jerry W. Cooney. "Paraguayan history: manuscript sources in the United States." Latin American Research Review, 1983, 18 (1), 104-117.

PERU

816. Bonilla, Heraclio. "The new profile of Peruvian history." Latin American Research Review, 1981, 16 (3), 210-224.

817. Clinton, Richard Lee. "Military-led revolution in Peru: a postmortem." Latin American Research Review, 1980, 15 (1), 198-205.

818. Davies, Thomas M., Jr. "A teaching guide to the history of republican Peru, 1826-1980." History Teacher, May 1981, 14 (3), 361-386.

PUERTO RICO

819. Cibes Viadé, Alberto. Historia de Puerto Rico: guión temático y bibliografía. San Juan: Instituto de Cultura Puertorriqueña, [1980?]. 34 p. (Cuadernos del Programa Graduado de Estudios Puertorriqueños, 1).

820. Dietz, James L. "Puerto Rico's new history." Latin American Research Review, 1984, 19 (1), 210-222.

821. Scarano Fiol, Francisco, and Carmelo Rosario Natal. "Bibliografía histórica puertorriqueña de la década de los setenta (1970-1979)." Hómines (Puerto Rico), Ene-Jun 1982, 6 (2), 193-219.

822. Silvestrini Pacheco, Blanca, and María de los Angeles Castro Arroyo. "Sources for the study of Puerto Rican history: a challenge to the historian's imagination." Latin American Research Review, 1981, 16 (2), 156-171.

823. Vila Vilar, Enriqueta. "Bibliografía básica para la historia de Puerto Rico." Historiografía y bibliografía americanistas, 1979, 23, 97-116.

UNITED STATES

824. Clark, Carter Blue. "Research tools. Guide and bibliographies on New Mexico history: a selected list." Arizona and the West, 1982, 24 (2), 153-168.

825. Cruz, Alberto, and James Arthur Irby, compilers. Austin, TX: Eakin Press, 1983. 337 p.

826. Documentary relations of the southwest. [Tucson: Arizona State Museum, Documentary Relations of the Southwest Project, 198-?]. Note: Microfiches.

827. Foote, Cheryl J. "Selected sources for the Mexican period (1821-1848) in New Mexico." New Mexico Historical Review, Jan 1984, 59 (1), 81-89.

828. Oczon, Annabelle M. "Land grants in New Mexico: a selective bibliography." New Mexico Historical Review, 1982, 57 (1), 81-87.

829. Taylor, Alexander Smith. Bibliografa Californica: Supplement, or notes and materials to aid in forming a more perfect bibliography of those countries anciently called 'California'. Reprint. Sparks, NY: Falcon Hill Press, c1983. 37 p.

URUGUAY

830. Castells Montero, Carlos A. Bibliografía sobre la historia diplomática del Uruguay. Montevideo: Ministerio de Relaciones Exteriores, Dirección de Asuntos Culturales y de Información, Departamento de Relaciones Culturales, 1980. xxii leaves.

831. Musso Ambrosi, Luis Alberto. "Bibliografía básica de la historia de la república oriental del Uruguay hasta 1973 (Cuarta parte)." Historiografía y bibliografía americanistas, 1983, 27, 63-93.

832. Musso Ambrosi, Luis Alberto. "Bibliografía básica de la historia de la república oriental del Uruguay hasta 1973 (Part 2)." Historiografía y bibliografía americanistas, 1980, 24, 103-125.

833. Musso Ambrosi, Luis Alberto. "Bibliografía básica de la historia de la República Oriental del Uruguay hasta 1973 (Tercera parte)." Historiografía y bibliografía americanistas, 1982, 26, 137-171.

834. Rial, Juan, and J. Klaczko. "Historiography and historical studies in Uruguay." Latin American Research Review, 1982, 17 (3), 229-250.

835. Rodríguez de Baliero, Haydée. Selección de fuentes para el estudio del período 1750-1828: material de apoyo para la cátedra de historia del Uruguay. Montevideo: Dirección General de Extensión Universitaria, División Publicaciones y Ediciones, 1980. 118 p.

VENEZUELA

836. Fuentes para el estudio del 23 de enero de 1958. Caracas: Congreso de la República; Instituto Autónomo Biblioteca Nacional y de Servicios de Bibliotecas, 1983 (i.e. 1984). 2 vols.

837. Ramos Guédez, José Marcial. Orígenes de la emancipación venezolana; aporte bibliográfico. Caracas: Pan American Institute of Geography and History, 1982. 334 p.

WEST INDIES, FRENCH

838. Boucher, Philip. Chronique bibliographique de l'histoire des Antilles françaises, 1979-1982. [Aubenas]: [Lienhart], [1985?]. 75 p. (Notes d'histoire coloniale, 230). Note: Extrait du Bulletin de la Société d'histoire de la Guadeloupe, no. 59, ler et 2e trimestres 1984.

839. Debien, Gabriel. Chronique bibliographique de l'histoire des Antilles françaises, 1977-1979. [n.p., 1980?]. 82 p. Note: "Extrait du Bulletin de la Société d'Histoire de la Guadeloupe, 45-46, 3e-4e trimestre 1980."

INDEXES

GENERAL

840. Bibliografía latinoamericana publicada fuera de la región. 1980, no. 1-1980, no. 2. [Mexico]: Centro de Información Científica y Humanística, 1980. Note: Continued in part by: Bibliografía latinoamericana. 1, Trabajos publicados por latinoamericanos en revistas extranjeras.

841. Bibliografía latinoamericana. 1, Trabajos sobre América Latina publicados en revistas extranjeras. [Mexico]: Centro de Información Científica y Humanística, 1982-. Two issues a year. Note: Continues Bibliografía latinoamericana. Trabajos sobre América Latina publicados fuera de la región.

842. Bosque Paz, Gisela, compiler. Libros-homenaje, índice analítico. Caracas: Universidad Central de Venezuela, Facultad de Ciencias Jurídicas y Políticas, 1981. 25 p.

843. Columbus Memorial Library. Index to Latin American periodical literature, 1966-1970. Columbus Memorial Library, Organization of American States. Boston: G.K. Hall, 1980. 2 vols.

844. Felipe Herrera Library. Index of periodical articles on the economics of Latin America; Interamerican Development Bank, Felipe Herrera Library. Boston: G. K. Hall, 1983. 4 vols.

845. Indice analítico de publicaciones periódicas en ciencias penales, criminológicas y afines. 1-. Caracas: Instituto de Ciencias Penales y Criminológicas. Facultad de Ciencias Jurídicas y Políticas. Universidad de Venezuela, 1981-.

846. Indice de artículos de publicaciones periódicas en el área de ciencias sociales y humanidades. (Cumulation for 1974/1979 issued as v. 5, no. 1, 1983, in 2 pts.). Bogotá: Ministerio de Educación Nacional, Instituto Colombiano para el Fomento de la Educación Superior, División de Documentación y Fomento Bibliotecario, 1983. Note: Continues Indice Latinoamericano de ciencias sociales y humanidades.

847. Indice de diarios y semanarios de Costa Rica. 1-. San José, C.R.: Centro de Documentación y Bibliografía, Ministerio de Cultura, Juventud y Deportes; Dirección General de Bibliotecas, Jul-Ag 1981-.

848. "Indices de revistas paraguayas." Informaciones (Paraguay), Jul 1980, 8, 14-15.

849. "Indice general de revistas jurídicas de Puerto Rico." Revista

jurídica de la Universidad Interamericana de Puerto Rico, May-Ag 1982, 16 (3), 455-677. Note: Covers: Revista jurídica de la Universidad Interamericana de Puerto Rico; Revista jurídica de la Universidad de Puerto Rico; Revista de derecho puertorriqueño; Revista del Colegio de Abogados de Puerto Rico.

850. Lastarría del Alamo, Aida, and Julia Rodríguez Tamay. "Revista de las revistas." Revista andina, Ene-Jun 1983, 1 (1), 289-303. Note: A regular feature in each issue.

851. Masferrer K., Elio. Indice analítico unificado de 'América indígena,' 'Anuario indigenista,' 'Boletín indigenista' y 'Noticias indigenistas de América,' 1940-1980. México: Instituto Indigenista Interamericano, 1981. 185 p.

852. Masferrer K., Elio. Indice general de 'Boletín indigenista' y 'Noticias indigenistas de América,' 1940-1980. México: Instituto Indigenista Interamericano, 1981. 307 p. (Serie SEDIAL, 2).

853. Preliminary guide to articles in 'La Prensa' relating to Puerto Ricans in New York City between 1922 and 1929. New York: CUNY Centro de Estudios Puertorriqueños, 1981. 68 p.

854. Preliminary guide to articles in Puerto Rican newspapers relating to Puerto Rican migration between 1900-1929. New York: CUNY Centro de Estudios Puertorriqueños, 1981. 62 p.

855. "Revista de revistas iberoamericanas: a) Revistas latinoamericanas [Gives table of contents of current issues]." Pensamiento iberoamericano; revista de economía política, Ene-Jun 1983, 3, 333-354. Note: A regular feature in all issues.

856. "Revista de revistas." Ciencias administrativas, 1979 (58-60), 85-132. Note: Appears as a regular feature.

857. Salvador, Nélida, and Elena Ardissone. Bibliografía de tres revistas de vanguardia: Prisma, 1921-22; Proa, 1922-23; Proa, 1924-26. Buenos Aires: Universidad de Buenos Aires, Facultad de Filosofía y Letras, Instituto de Literatura Argentina "Ricardo Rojas," 1983 (Guías bibliográficas, 12).

858. Sánchez Moya, Zaida. Indice temático no. 1 de resúmenes analíticos en educación de Costa Rica. San José: Centro multinacional de investigación educativa--Red Latinoamericana de información y documentación en educación, 1984. 36 p. Note: Index to Boletín de Resúmenes Analíticos en Educación.

859. Valk, Barbara G., editor. Ana María Cobos, associate editor. Hispanic American Periodicals Index: HAPI. 1970-1974. Los Angeles: UCLA Latin American Center Publications, University of California, c1984. 3 v.

860. Valk, Barbara G., editor. Maj-Britt Nilsson, associate editor. Hispanic American Periodicals Index: HAPI. 1982. Los Angeles: UCLA Latin American Center Publications, University of California, 1985. Note: Began publication with the vol. for 1975 (c1977).

861. Zubatsky, David S. "An international bibliography of cumulative indices to journals publishing articles on Hispanic languages and literatures: first supplement." Hispania, Sept 1984, 67 (3), 383-393.

ACADEMIA VENEZOLANA DE LA LENGUA. BOLETIN

862. Barcelo Sifontes, Lyll. Indice de los boletines de la Academia Venezolana de la Lengua Correspondiente de la Real Española, nos. 1-150 (1934-1982). Caracas: [n.p.], 1983. 235 p.

ANTROPOLOGIA E HISTORIA DE GUATEMALA

863. Paniagua, Cándida S. de. "Indices bibliográficos de la revista Antropología e historia de Guatemala de 1949 a 1969, del vol. 1 al vol. 21 (primera época)." Antropología e historia de Guatemala, 1980, 2 (2), 261-325.

ANUARIO DE ESTUDIOS AMERICANOS

864. Henderson, Donald C. "Indice general del 'Anuario de estudios americanos' de 1964 a 1973." Anuario de estudios americanos, 1977 (i.e. 1980), 34, 819-902.

ANUARIO DE HISTORIA

865. Mucharraz de Díaz, Olga. Indice del 'Anuario de Historia,' vols. 1-10 (1961-1978). México: Universidad Nacional Autónoma de México, Facultad de Filosofía y Letras, 1981. 43 p.

ARTES DE MÉXICO

866. Barberena Blásquez, Elsa. Indice de la revista 'Artes de México,' la época, números 1-60, 1953-1965. México: Universidad Nacional Autónoma de Mexico, 1982. 301 p.

(Cuadernos de historia del arte. Instituto de Investigaciones Estéticas, 22).

BARRICADA

867. "Barricada"; índice temático y onomástico, 1980. Managua: Banco Central de Nicaragua, Biblioteca y Servicios de Información, 1981. 112 p.

868. "Barricada"; índice temático y onomástico, 1981. Managua: Banco Central de Nicaragua, 1981. 153 p.

BOLETIN DE LEGISLACION NACIONAL

869. Miranda E., Mirza. "Indice acumulativo por materia del Boletín de legislación y su continuadora, Revista de legislación y documentación en derecho y ciencias sociales, 1977-1982." Revista de legislación y documentación en derecho y ciencias sociales, Dic 1982, 4 (10), 9-24.

BOLETIN TITIKAKA

870. Rodríguez Rea, Miguel Angel. "Guía del 'Boletín Titikaka' (Puno, 1926-1930)." Hueso húmero, Jul-Oct 1981 (10), 184-204.

BULLETIN DE L'INSTITUT FRANÇAIS D'ÉTUDES ANDINES

871. "Boletín del Instituto Francés de Estudios Andinos." Bulletin de l'Institut français d'Études andines, 1980, 9 (1-2), 155-158. Note: The index covers Vols. 2-8.

CEPAL REVIEW

872. "Index of the first fifteen issues of CEPAL Review." CEPAL Review, Apr 1982 (16), 199-203.

CINE CUBANO

873. Indice de la revista 'Cine cubano,' 1960-1974. La Habana: Editorial Orbe, 1979. 181 p. Note: At head of title: Consejo Nacional de Cultura Biblioteca Nacional José Martí.

COJO ILUSTRADO

874. Milanca Guzmán, Mario. "El cojo ilustrado, 1892-1915: una investigación hemerográfica." Revista musical de Venezuela, Ene-Abr 1982, 3 (6), 73-143.

CONJUNTO

875. Layera, Ramón. "Indice bibliográfico de las obras teatrales publicadas en 'Conjunto' (1-40)." Latin American theater review, 1981, 4 (2), 57-60.

CORREO DEL DOMINGO

876. Auza, Néstor Tomás. Correo del domingo (1864-1868), (1879-1880); estudio e índice general. Buenos Aires: Instituto Histórico de la Organización Nacional, 1980. Note: Separata de la Revista Histórica, no. 5.

CUADERNOS DOMINICANOS DE CULTURA

877. "Indice general de 'Cuadernos dominicanos de cultura,' 1943-1952." Eme Eme: estudios dominicanos, Jul-Ag 1980, 9 (49), 79-103.

CUADERNOS POLITICOS

878. "Cuadernos políticos"; revista trimestral de Ediciones Era. Indice de los números 1-28 (Jul-Sept 1974--Abr-Jun 1981). México: Ediciones Era, 1981. 16 p. Note: Insert, Cuadernos políticos, no. 28.

CUADERNOS REPUBLICANOS

879. Chamorro Abadie, María Victoria. "Indice bibliográfico de la revista Cuadernos republicanos." Cuadernos republicanos, 1982 (19), 231-288.

CUBA INTERNACIONAL

880. "Indice temático: INRA (1960-1963), Cuba internacional, (1963-1979)." Cuba internacional, Ene 1980 (122), i-xxviii. Note: Index for INRA and Cuba internacional (which succeeded INRA in 1963).

DEBATE

881. "Debate; Indice 1980-1984." Debate, Mar 1984, 25, 77-86.

ESTUDIOS SOCIALES CENTROAMERICANOS

882. "[Index to vol. 4, no. 12 (Sept-Dic 1975)--Vol. 10, no. 30 (Sept-Dic 1981)]." Estudios sociales centroamericanos, Ene-Abr 1982, 11 (31), 152-172.

GACETA, LA. DIARIO OFICIAL

883. "La Gaceta. Diario oficial." Indice cronológico y temático, 1979-1980. Managua: Banco Central de Nicaragua, Biblioteca, 1981. 88 p.

GUARANIA

884. Kallsen, Margarita. Guaranía 1933-37. Asunción: [Universidad Católica "Nuestra Señora de la Asunción"], 1984. 40 p.

HISPANIA

885. Klein, Dennis A. "Decennial index for vols. 51-60 (1968-1977)." Hispania, Apr 1980, 63 (Decennial Index issue), 195-312.

HISPANIC AMERICAN HISTORICAL REVIEW

886. Ross, Stanley Robert, and Wilber A. Chaffee, editors. Guide to the "Hispanic American historical review," 1956-1975. Durham, NC: Duke University Press, 1980. 432 p. Note: 1956-1965 edited by Donald E. Worcester and Walter A. Payne.

HISTORIA

887. Ramírez Rivera, Hugo Rodolfo. "Indice general de la revista Historia (Chile), (1961-1980)." Historia (Chile), 1981, 16, 269-333.

HUESO HUMERO

888. Rodríguez Rea, Miguel Angel. "Indice de 'Hueso húmero,' vols. 1-13." Hueso húmero, Ene-Jun 1982 (12-13), 169-180.

HUMBOLDT

889. "Indice alfabético de los colaboradores y sus artículos en 'Humboldt,' números 62-77 (1977-1982)." Humboldt, 1982, 23 (77), 102-104.

ICA

890. Romero Rojas, Francisco José. "Indice sistemático de materias de la revista ICA, vol. 1-10 (1966-1974)." ICA (Colombia), 1979, 14 (Supplement).

LOGOS

891. Ruiz y Blanco, Emilio R., compiler. Indice general de "Logos" (Nos. 1-13/14, 1941-1977-78). Buenos Aires: Universidad de Buenos Aires, Facultad de Filosofía y Letras, Centro de Investigaciones Bibliotecológicas, 1983. 32 p. (Cuadernos de bibliotecología, 6).

MICROFILMING PROJECTS NEWSLETTER [SALALM]

892. Hodgman, Suzanne. Microfilming projects newsletter [SALALM]. Index, Nos. 1-20. Madison: University of Wisconsin at Madison, 1980. 38 p.

MUNDO UNIVERSITARIO

893. "Mundo universitario; revista de la Asociación Colombiana de Universidades." Mundo universitario, Abr-Jun 1981 (17), 294-300. Note: Covers no. 1-16: Oct-Dic 1972--Ene-Mar 1981.

NEW WEST INDIAN GUIDE

894. Wagenaar Hummdicks, P. "An index of articles and book reviews in the Nieuwe West Indische Gide, 1960-1981." New West Indian Guide/Nieuwe West Indische Gide, 1982, 16 (3-4), 197-244.

NEW YORK TIMES

895. Index to articles in the "New York Times" relating to Puerto Rico and Puerto Ricans between 1899 and 1930. New York: CUNY Centro de Estudios Puertorriqueños, c1981. 94 p.

NOTICIAS SOBRE EL LIBRO Y BIBLIOGRAFIA

896. "Indice temático general de la revista del CERLAL [Noticias sobre el libro y bibliografía], 1972-1980." Noticias sobre el libro y bibliografía, Dic 1980 (28), 29-33.

NUEVO MERCURIO

897. Zuleta, Ignacio M. "El Nuevo Mercurio." Revista interamericana de bibliografía, 1981, 31 (3), 385-403.

PALABRA Y EL HOMBRE

898. Arguez, Samuel. Historia, índice y prólogo de la revista "La palabra y el hombre" (1957-1970). Miami: Ediciones Universal, 1982. 99 p.

PALAU Y DULCET, ANTONIO. MANUAL DEL LIBRERO HISPANO-AMERICANO

899. Palau Claveras, Agustín. Indice alfabético de títulos-materias, correcciones, conexiones y adiciones de "Manual del librero hispanoamericano" de Antonio Palau y Dulcet. Oxford: Dolphin Book Co, 1981-.

PERU INDIGENA

900. Muñoz de Linares, Elba; Clara Cárdenas Timoteo; and Alicia Céspedes de Reynaga. Indices y resúmenes de "Perú indígena" y "Perú integral." Lima: Instituto Indigenista Peruano, Centro Interamericano de Administración del Trabajo, [1982?]. 259 p.

PLERUS

901. Indice "Plerus." Vol. 1-17 (Mayo 1967-1983). Rio Piedras: Universidad de Puerto Rico, Escuela Graduada de Planificación, [1984]. 10 p.

PONTIFICIA UNIVERSIDAD CATOLICA DEL ECUADOR. REVISTA

902. "Indice general de la Revista de la Universidad Católica del no. 1 (1972) al no. 36 (1983)." Pontificia Universidad Católica del Ecuador. Revista, Dic 1983, 11 (37), 147-158.

PROGRESO DE QUILMES

903. Ales, Oreste Carlos. Indice-resumen del periódico "Progreso de Quilmes" (4 de mayo de 1873 al 31 de mayo de 1874), "El Progreso de Quilmes" (7 de junio de 1874 al 28 de junio de 1874), "El Progreso" (3 de enero de 1875 al 29 de agosto de 1875). Buenos Aires: Platero, 1984. 197 p.

PROVINCIA DE SÃO PAULO

904. Gertz, René E. "Materias historiográficas da revista 'Provincia de São Paulo.'" Estudos iberoamericanos, Jul-Dez 1982, 9 (1-2), 221-220.

REPERTORIO AMERICANO

905. Echeverría C., Evelio. Indice general del "Repertorio americano," Vols. 1-2 (A-E). San José, C.R.: Editorial Universidad Estatal a Distancia, 1981-.

REVISTA BIMESTRE CUBANA

906. Peraza Zarausa, Norma T. "La 'Revista bimestre cubana': primera época." Revista de la Biblioteca Nacional José Martí, Sept-Dic 1981, 23 (3), 137-234. Note: [Bibliographic essay and index].

REVISTA BRASILEIRA DE ESTATISTICA

907. "'Revista brasileira de estatística' [Index to] v. 1-40 (1940-1979)." Revista brasileira de estatística, Jan-Mar 1982, 43 (169), 1-272.

REVISTA DE CIENCIA POLITICA (BRAZIL)

908. "Indice da Revista de ciência política de 1977 a 1982." Revista de ciência política (Brazil), May-Ag 1983, 26 (2), 158-167.

REVISTA DE INDIAS

909. "Indice de la 'Revista de Indias,' 1969-1980, números 115-162." Revista de Indias, Ene-Jun 1982, 42 (167-168), 247-307.

REVISTA DE LA BIBLIOTECA NACIONAL JOSÉ MARTI

910. García-Carranza, Araceli. "Indice de la Revista de la Biblioteca José Martí, 1976-1980." Revista de la Biblioteca Nacional José Martí, May-Ag 1981, 23 (2), 193-228.

REVISTA DE PLANEACION Y DESARROLLO

911. "Indice analítico enero 1969-diciembre 1979 (Indice de artículos, vol. 1, no. 1 a vol. 11, no. 3)." Revista de planeación y desarrollo, 1980, 12 (1). Note: Separata; 38 p.

REVISTA DE TEATRO

912. "Peças publicadas na Revista de teatro." Revista de teatro (Brazil), Out-Dez 1982 (444), 36. Note: Includes plays published in Nos. 396-443, Nov-Dez, 1973-Set 1982.

REVISTA DEL INSTITUTO PARAGUAYO

913. Díaz Mellán, Mafalda Victoria. "Indice de la Revista del Instituto Paraguayo, 1896-1909." Cuadernos republicanos, 1983 (21), 171-258.

914. Kallsen, Margarita. "Revista del Instituto Paraguayo" (1896-1909). Asunción: [Universidad Católica "Nuestra Señora de la Asunción"], 1984. 37 p.

REVISTA INTERAMERICANA DE BIBLIOGRAFIA

915. Revista interamericana de bibliografía. Interamerican review of bibliography. Catalog of articles, review articles and book reviews in volumes 1-34 (1951-1982) with author indexes. Washington, DC: Organization of American States, 1983. 199 p.

REVISTA NACIONAL DE LETRAS Y CIENCIAS

916. Miranda Cárabes, Celia. Indice de la "Revista nacional de letras y ciencias" (1889-1890). México: Instituto de Investigaciones Filológicas, Centro de Estudios Literarios, 1980. 158 p.

REVISTA PARAGUAYA DE SOCIOLOGIA

917. Morel Solaeche, Rubén Eugenio. Indice de la "Revista

paraguaya de sociología." Asunción: Universidad Nacional de Asunción, Escuela de Bibliotecología, 1979. 100 leaves. Note: Thesis. Universidad Nacional de Asunción.

REVISTA PUERTO RICO ILUSTRADO

918. Colon Jiménez, Elvira. Indice Bibliográfico Arte: Revista Puerto Rico Ilustrado 1910-1920. San Juan: Sociedad Amigos del Museo de la Universidad de Puerto Rico. Centro de Estudios Avanzados de Puerto Rico y El Caribe, 1983. 87 p.

REVOLUCION Y CULTURA

919. "Indice de 'Revolución y cultura' del número 45 al 74." Revolución y cultura, Dic 1978 (76), 76-84.

SALALM NEWSLETTER

920. Valk, Barbara G. "SALALM Newsletter" cumulative index; volumes VI-X; subject and author lists. Madison: SALALM Secretariat, Memorial Library, University of Wisconsin, 1983. 29 p.

SIGNO

921. "Signo: cuadernos bolivianos de cultura." Guía bibliográfica de "Signo." Indice del número 1-10. La Paz: Don Bosco. 48 p.

SUPLEMENTO ANTROPOLOGICO DEL ATENEO PARAGUAYO

922. Mora Gutiérrez, Dominga Venancia. "Indice de la revista Suplemento antropológico del Ateneo paraguayo, vol. 1, no. 1, 1965-vol. 14, no. 2, 1979." Cuadernos republicanos, 1982 (20), 231-274.

TEOLOGIA Y VIDA

923. Barrios Valdés, Marciano. Teología y vida. Indice general de los vols. 1-20, 1960-1979. Santiago: Universidad Católica de Chile. Facultad de Teología, 1981. 72 p.

TRES AMÉRICAS

924. "[Las tres Américas, N.Y.] Indice de contenido de cada

número de la revista; índice alfabético de autores; indice de reseñas bibliográficas." In: Orihuela, Augusto Germán. "Las Tres Américas" y el modernismo. Caracas: Centro de Estudios Rómulo Gallegos. Consejo Nacional de la Cultura, 1983, 89-229.

ZONA FRANCA

925. "Zona franca. 2a. época 1977-1982. Indice de autores de los números 1 al 28." Zona franca, Nov 1982-Feb 1983, 2a. época, 5, 55-67.

INTERNATIONAL RELATIONS

926. Araya Incera, Manuel E. Materiales para la historia de las relaciones internacionales de Costa Rica: bibliografía, fuentes impresas. San Pedro, Costa Rica: Centro de Investigaciones Históricas, Universidad de Costa Rica, 1980. 91 p.

927. Bibliografía de artículos sobre las relaciones internacionales de América Latina y el Caribe: 1975-1982. Washington: Secretaría General de al Organización de los Estados Americanos, 1982. 56 p.

928. Bustamente, Jorge A., and Francisco Malagamba A. México-Estados Unidos: bibliografía general sobre estudios fronterizos. México: El Colegio de México, 1980. 251 p.

929. Campillo Celado, Rosa C. Indice anotado de la colección de tratados de la República Dominicana. Santo Domingo: CENAPEC, 1984. 188 p.

930. Castells Montero, Carlos A. Bibliografía sobre la historia diplomática del Uruguay. Montevideo: Ministerio de Relaciones Exteriores, Dirección de Asuntos Culturales y de Información, Departamento de Relaciones Culturales, 1980. 22 leaves.

931. Fernández-Kelly, María Patricia. "The U.S.-Mexico border: recent publications and the state of current research." Latin American Research Review, 1981, 16 (3), 250-267.

932. Fernández P, María Angélica, and María del Valle Stark O. "Instrumentos internacionales, Ministerio de Relaciones Exteriores de la República de Chile, Junio 1979-Marzo 1981." Revista de legislación y documentación en derecho y ciencias sociales, Ene-Mar 1981, 3 (1), 11-25.

933. Finan, John J., and John Child. Latin America, international relations: a guide to information sources. Detroit: Gale Research Co., c1981. 236 p. (International relations information guide series, 11).

934. Fischer de Figueroa, Marie Claire, compiler. Relaciones México-Estados Unidos: Bibliografía anual. México: Colegio de Mexico, 1982-.

935. Grindle, Merilee. "Armed intervention and U.S.-Latin American relations." Latin American Research Review, 1981, 16 (1), 207-217.

936. Hernández Ruigómez, Manuel. "El diferendo anglo-argentino en el Atlántico sur: un acicate para la producción bibliográfica." Revista de Indias, Ene-Jun 1984, 44 (173), 293-307.

937. Kaufman, Debra. Mexico-United States relations, a bibliography. Los Angeles: Chicano Studies Research Center Publications Unit, University of California at Los Angeles, c1982.

938. Lima, María Regina Soares de, and Gerson Moura. "Brasil-Argentina: fontes bibliográficas." Revista interamericana de bibliografía, 1982, 32 (3-4), 295-321.

939. Lowenthal, Abraham F. "Research in Latin America and the Caribbean on international relations and foreign policy: some impressions." Latin American Research Review, 1983, 18 (1), 95-103.

940. Mercader Martínez, Yolanda, and Pablo Valentino Ramírez, compilers. Testimonios de las relaciones México-norteamericanas desde fines del siglo XVIII a la primera mitad del siglo XIX. [México]: Biblioteca Nacional de Antropología e Historia, [1982]. 428 p.

941. Muñoz, Heraldo. "Beyond the Malvinas crisis: Perspectives on Inter-American relations." Latin American Research Review, 1984, 19 (1), 158-172.

942. Nodal, Roberto. The Cuban presence in Africa: a bibliography. [Milwaukee]: University of Wisconsin-Milwaukee, [1980]. 16 leaves. (Afro-American studies report, 12).

943. Portales, Carlos. Bibliografía sobre relaciones internacionales y política exterior de Chile, 1964-1980. Santiago de Chile: Facultad Latinoamericana de Ciencias Sociales, [1981]. 19 p. (Documento de trabajo; Programa de FLACSO--Santiago de Chile, 108).

944. Ramírez R, Rubén. "Hemerografía básica sobre política exterior

de México actual." Relaciones internacionales, Abr-Jun 1984, 11 (32), 111-118.

945. Rauls, Martina. Die Beziehungen des Karibischen Raumes zu Afrika. Las relaciones entre el area del Caribe y Africa. Relations between the Caribbean area and Africa. Hamburg: Institut für Iberoamerika-Kunde, Dokumentations-Leitstelle Lateinamerika, 1980. 24 leaves. Note: Citations in English, French, Portuguese and Spanish.

946. Sloan, John W. "Challenges to U.S. influence in Latin America." Latin American Research Review, 1984, 19 (1), 223-234.

LANGUAGE AND LITERATURE

GENERAL

947. Alarcón, Norma, and Sylvia Kossmar. Bibliography of Hispanic women writers. Bloomington, IN: Chicano-Riqueño Studies, 1980. 86 p. (Chicano-Riqueño studies bibliography series, 1).

948. Almeida, Horácio de. Catálogo de dicionários portugueses e brasileiros. Rio de Janeiro: Companhia Brasileira de Artes Gráficas, 1983. 132 p.

949. Ariza Viguera, Manuel. Intento de bibliografía de la onomástica hispánica. Cáceres: Universidad de Extremadura, 1981. 116 p. (Anejos del anuario de estudios filológicos, 4).

950. Averbuck, Lígia. "A Mulher e o texto da intimidade." Boletim bibliográfico. Biblioteca Mário de Andrade, Jul-Dez 1982, 43 (3-4), 49-55.

951. Baird, Keith E. A critical annotated bibliography of African linguistic continuities in the Spanish-speaking Americas. Cincinnati: Union for Experimenting Colleges and Universities, 1982. 130 p. Note: Thesis (Ph.D.).

952. Barrios Pintos, Anibal. Contribución a la bibliografía de vocabularios técnicos. Montevideo: Academia Nacional de Letras, 1981. 24, 5 p.

953. Becco, Horácio Jorge. Diccionario de literatura hispanoamericana. Buenos Aires: Huemul, 1984. 313 p.

954. Benson, John. "García Márquez en 'Alternativa' 1978-1980: una bibliografía comentada." Chasqui, Feb-May 1981, 10 (2-3), 41-46.

955. Bernal García, Cristina; David Arriaga Weiss; and Ernestina Zenzes Eisenbach. "Literatura y sociedad (hemerografía)." Revista mexicana de ciencias políticas y sociales, Oct-Dic 1980, 26 (102), 191-212.

956. "Bibliografía [on linguistics]." Nueva revista de filología hispánica, 1980, 19 (2), 596-702.

957. Bibliografia 1973-1980: 1) Literatura de autoria indígena; 2) Linguística e antropologia; 3) Linguística aplicada; 4) Material arquivado no Museu do Rio de Janeiro e na Fundação Nacional do Indio. Brasília: Summer Institute of Linguistics, 1981. 84 p.

958. Bleznick, Donald W. A sourcebook for Hispanic literature and language: a selected annotated guide to Spanish, Spanish-American and Chicano bibliography, literature, linguistics, journals and other source materials. 2d ed. Metuchen, NJ: Scarecrow Press, 1983. 303 p.

959. Brazil. Biblioteca Nacional. Goethe 1749-1842: catálogo da exposição organizado pela Seção de Promoções Culturais. Rio de Janeiro: A Biblioteca, 1982. 81 p.

960. Burton, Julianne. The new Latin American cinema: an annotated bibliography of sources in English, Spanish and Portuguese, 1960-1980. New York: Smyrna Press, 1983. 80 p.

961. Carpenter, Charles A. "Latin American theater criticism, 1966-1974: some addenda to Lyday and Woodyard." Revista interamericana de bibliografía, 1080, 30 (3), 246-253.

962. Carpenter, Charles A. "Modern drama studies: an annual bibliography." Modern drama, Jun 1980, 23 (2), 121-199. Note: Contains a section on Latin American drama.

963. Castro-Klarén, Sara, and Héctor Campos. "Traducciones, tirajes, ventas y estrellas: el 'boom.'" Ideologies and Literature, Sept-Oct 1983, 4 (2d cycle) (17), 319-338.

964. Corvalán, Graciela N.V. Latin American women writers in English translation: a bibliography. Los Angeles: Latin American Studies Center, California State University, c1980. 109 p. (Latin America bibliography series, 9).

965. Dale, Doris Cruger. "Spanish-English bilingual books for children: the expanding frontier." Top of the News, Summer 1981, 37 (4), 333-343.

966. Davis, Jack Emory. The Spanish of Argentina and Uruguay: an annotated bibliography for 1940-1978. New York: Mouton, 1982. 360 p. (Janua linguarum. Series minor, 105).

967. Díaz, Marco. "La referencia a la obra arquitectónica en la prosa y la poesía de la Nueva España, siglo XVII." Anuario de estudios americanos, 1981 (i.e., 1983), 38, 417-440.

968. Elkin, Judith Laikin. Multi-racial books for the classroom: a select list of children's books. 3d rev. ed. [Birmingham, England]: Library Association, Youth Libraries Group, 1980. 134 p. (YLG pamphlet, 22).

969. Espinosa Elerick, María Luz. Annotated bibliography of technical and specialized dictionaries in Spanish-Spanish and Spanish ... with commentary. Bibliografía anotada y comentada de diccionarios técnicos y especializados en español-español y español.... Troy, NY: Whitston Pub. Co., 1982. 100 p.

970. Ferrer Andrade, Guadalupe, and Ernestina Zenzes Eisenbach. "Literatura y comunicación (hemerografía)." Revista mexicana de ciencias políticas y sociales, Abr-Jun 1980, 26 (100), 157-172.

971. Foster, David William. "Bibliografía del indigenismo hispanoamericano." Revista iberoamericana, Abr-Jun 1984, 50 (127), 587-620.

972. Foster, David William. "Bibliografía literaria hispanoamericana, 1980-1981." Revista iberoamericana, Ene-Mar 1983, 49 (122), 235-241.

973. Hoffman, Herbert H. Latin American play index. Metuchen, NJ: Scarecrow Press, 1983-84. 2 vols.

974. Jackson, Richard L. The Afro-Spanish American author: an annotated bibliography of criticism. New York: Garland Pub. Co., 1980. 129 p. (Garland reference library of the humanities, 194).

975. Kensinger, Kenneth M. "Recent publications in Panoan linguistics." International journal of American linguistics, Jan 1981, 47 (1), 68-74.

976. Larsen, Jurgen Ingemann. Bibliografi over latinamerikansk skønlitteratur paa dansk samt over danske bidras til den latinamerikansek litteraturs historie. Kobenhavn: J. Ingemann Larsen, 1982. 122 p.

977. Laurenti, Joseph L. Bibliografía de la literatura picaresca. Suplemento. A bibliography of picaresque literature. Supplement. New York: AMS Press, 1981. 163 p.

978. Lindstrom, Naomi. "Feminist criticism of Latin American

literature: bibliographic notes." Latin American Research Review, 1980, 15 (1), 151-159.

979. "Literatura infanto-juvenil." Oficina de livros, Jan-Dez 1980, 315-324.

980. Losada, Alejandro. "Bibliografía para una periodización de la literatura en la sociedad de América Latina, 1800-1980." Revista de crítica literaria latinoamericana, 1983, 9 (17), 31-37.

981. Lozano, Eduardo. "Recent books on Indian literatures: bibliography." Latin American Indian Literatures, Fall 1983, 7 (2), 182-193.

982. Mayman, Valerie. Hispanic literature: a guide to reference sources. Montreal: McGill University, McLennan Library, 1982. 19 p.

983. McMurray, George R. "Recent criticism of Spanish American fiction." Latin American Research Review, 1984, 19 (3), 184-193.

984. Meehan, Thomas C. "Bibliografía de y sobre la literatura fantástica." Revista iberoamericana, Ene-Jun 1980, 46 (110-111), 243-256.

985. Montes Huidobro, Matías. "Nueva generación." Chasqui, Nov 1979, 9 (1), 39-74.

986. Nuessel, Frank H., Jr. "A supplementary enumerative bibliography of generative-based grammatical analyses of Spanish, 1979-1981: phonology and morphology, syntax and semantics." Lenguaje y ciencias, Jun, Dic 1981, 21 (2, 4), 41-54, 101-111.

987. Nuessel, Frank H., Jr. "A supplementary enumerative bibliography of generative-based grammatical analyses of Spanish, 1981-1983: phonology and morphology, syntax and semantics." Lenguage y ciencias, Sept 1983, 23 (3), 131-145.

988. Osorio Tejeda, Nelson. "Contribución a una bibliografía sobre el vanguardismo hispanoamericano." Revista de crítica literaria hispanoamericana, 1982, 18 (15), 141-150.

989. Quilis, Antonio. Bibliografía de fonética y fonología españolas. Madrid: Consejo Superior de Investigaciones Científicas, Instituto "Miguel de Cervantes," 1984. 481 p. (Collectanea phonetica, 9).

990. Rela, Walter. Spanish-American literature: a selected bibliography, 1970-1980. East Lansing, MI: Michigan State University, 1982, 231 p.

991. Resnick, Margery, and Isabelle De Courtivron. Women writers in translation: an annotated bibliography, 1945-1981. New York: Garland Pub., 1984. 272 p. (Garland reference library of the humanities, 228). Note: Contains section on Latin American authors.

992. Rocard, Marcienne. "La littérature hispano-américaine et son image." Caravelle, 1982 (39), 125-129.

993. Rodríguez Castelo, Hernán. Grandes libros para todos: 700 obras de narrativa para lectura de niños y jóvenes, guía por edades, con una sección dedicada a la literatura boliviana. La Paz: Editorial Khana Cruz, 1980. 152 p.

994. Román Lagunas, Jorge. "La literatura hispanoamericana en 'Cahiers du monde hispanique et luso-brésilien (Caravelle),' 1963-1979." Cahiers du monde hispanique et luso-brésilien, 1980 (35), 59-88.

995. Román-Lagunas, Jorge. "La literatura hispanoamericana en 'La nouvelle revue française.'" Revista chilena de literatura, Abr 1982 (19), 115-121.

996. Roy, Joaquín. "Latin American poetry and various critical tendencies." Latin American Research Review, 1983, 18 (3), 243-245.

997. Sáez-Godoy, Leopoldo. "Las computadoras en el estudio del español; bibliografía." Thesaurus, May-Ag 1983, 38 (2), 340-375.

998. Schon, Isabel. Books in Spanish for children and young adults--series II: an annotated guide. Metuchen, NJ: Scarecrow Press, c1983. 162p.

999. Schon, Isabel. A Hispanic heritage: a guide to juvenile books about Hispanic people and cultures. Metuchen, NJ: Scarecrow Press, 1980. 168 p.

1000. Schon, Isabel. A Hispanic heritage, series II: a guide to juvenile books about Hispanic people and cultures. Metuchen, NJ: Scarecrow Press, 1985. 153 p.

1001. Schon, Isabel. "Recent outstanding books for young readers from Spanish-speaking countries." Reading Teacher, Nov 1982, 36 (2), 206-209.

1002. Schon, Isabel. "Trends in literature in Spanish for children and adolescents: an annotated bibliography." Hispania, Sept 1984, 67 (3), 422-426.

1003. Schon, Isabel, and Patricia Kennedy. "Noteworthy books in Spanish for children and young adults from Spanish-speaking countries." Reading Teacher, Nov 1983, 37 (2), 138-142.

1004. "Selección bibliográfica de humoristas latinoamericanos." Comunicación (Caracas), Jun 1982 (38), 95-98.

1005. Sheetz de Eherd, Pamela, compiler. Bibliografía del Instituto Lingüístico de Verano de Centroamérica 1952-1982. Guatemala: El Instituto, 1983. 118 p.

1006. Simón Díaz, José. Bibliografía de la literatura hispánica. 3a. ed. corr. y actualizada. Madrid: Consejo Superior de Investigaciones Científicas, Instituto "Miguel de Cervantes" de Filología Hispánica, 1983-.

1007. Simón Palmer, María del Carmen. "Información bibliográfica." Revista de literatura, Ene 1982, 44 (87), 171-305.

1008. Simón Palmer, María del Carmen. "Información bibliográfica." Revista de literatura, Jun 1982, 44 (88), 217-230.

1009. "Spanish language books for young adults and children." Booklist, Sept 1, Oct 1 1981, 78 (1, 3), 38-40. 190-191.

1010. Stuart, George E. "Some recent books and Maya hieroglyphic writing." Latin American Research Review, 1982, 17 (1), 255-262.

1011. "Survey of Latin American children's literature [Bibliographic essays on the literature of 13 countries]." Phaedrus; an international annual of children's literature, 1984, 10, 11-74.

1012. Valis, Noel. "Directory of publication sources in the fields of Hispanic language and literature." Hispania, May 1981, 64 (2), 226-257.

1013. Ventur, Pierre. "Mayan texts." Latin American Indian literatures, Spring 1981, 5 (1), 16-18.

1014. West, Dennis Deforest. "Latin American film studies: some recent anthologies." Latin American Research Review, 1983, 18 (1), 179-188.

1015. Wood, Richard E. "Current sociolinguistics in Latin America." Latin American Research Review, 1981, 16 (1), 240-251.

1016. Zeitz, Eileen, and Richard A. Seybolt. "Hacia una bibliografía sobre el realismo mágico." Hispanic journal, 1981, 3 (1), 159-167.

ARGENTINA

1017. Cattarossi Arana, Nelly. Literatura de Mendoza: historia documentada desde sus orígenes a la actualidad, 1829-1980. Mendoza, Argentina: Inca Editorial, 1982. 2 vols.

1018. Costilla, María Isabel. Relevamiento de bibliografía literaria de Tucumán. Tucumán, Argentina: Dirección General de Cultura, Departamento de Literatura, [1981]. 55 p.

1019. Foster, David William. Argentine literature: a research guide. 2d rev. and expanded ed. New York: Garland Publishing Co., 1982, 778 p.

1020. Lewald, H. Ernest. "Two generations of River Plate women writers." Latin American Research Review, 1980, 15 (1), 231-236.

1021. Masiello, Francine R. "Contemporary Argentine fiction: liberal (pre-)texts in a reign of terror." Latin American Research Review, 1981, 16 (1), 218-224.

1022. Pio del Corro, Gaspar, et al. Villa Dolores. Córdoba: Instituto de Literature Argentina e Iberoamericana, Facultad de Filosofía y Humanidades, Universidad Nacional de Córdoba, 1981. 90 p. (Bibliografía crítica de la literatura de Córdoba, 2).

BRAZIL

1023. Bagby, Albert Ian, Jr. "Machado de Assis traduzido." Veritas, Mar 1980, 25 (97), 89-102.

1024. Berrini, Beatriz. "Presença feminina em Eça de Queiroz." Boletim bibliográfico. Biblioteca Mário de Andrade, Jul-Dez 1982, 43 (3-4), 81-86.

1025. Bibliografia da dramaturgia brasileira. São Paulo: Escola de Comunicações e Artes de Universidade de São Paulo: Associaçao Museu Lasar Segall, 1981-1983. 2 vols.

1026. Chamberlain, Bobby J. "A consumer guide to developing a Brazilian literature reference library." Hispania, May 1981, 64 (2), 260-264.

1027. Coelho, Nelly Novaes. "A Presença da nova mulher na ficção brasileira atual (1981-1982)." Boletim bibliográfico. Biblioteca Mário de Andrade, Jul-Dez 1982, 43 (3-4), 57-68.

1028. Dietrich, Wolf. Bibliografia da língua portuguesa do Brasil.

Tübingen: Gunter Narr Verlag, 1980. 292 p. (Tübinger Beiträge zur Linguistik, 120).

1029. Gerber, Raquel. O cinema brasileiro e o processo político e cultural (de 1950 a 1978): bibliografia e filmografia crítica e selectiva. Rio de Janeiro: Departamento de Assuntos Culturais, Empresa Brasileira de Filmes, 1982. 290 p.

1030. Luyten, Joseph Maria. Bibliografia especializada sobre literatura popular em verso. São Paulo: Escola de comunicações e Artes, Universidade de São Paulo, 1981. 104 p.

1031. Oliveira, Joanyr de. Brasilia na poesia brasileira. Rio de Janeiro: Brasília: Livraria Editora Catedra; Instituto Nacional do Livro, Fundação Nacional Pro Memoria, 1982. 163 p.

1032. Paes, José Paulo, and Massaud Moisés. Pequeno dicionário de literatura brasileira. 2a ed. rev e ampliada. São Paulo: Editora Cultrix, 1980. 462 p.

1033. Pinto, Regina Pahin. "A Imagem da mulher através dos livros didáticos." Boletim bibliográfico. Biblioteca Mário de Andrade, Jul-Dez 1982, 43 (3-4), 125-131.

1034. Rodríguez, Rita de Cassia. Jornalismo científico: bibliografia. São Paulo: Universidade de São Paulo, Escola de Comunicações e Artes, Biblioteca, 1982. 49 leaves.

1035. Silveira Santos, Daury Da. Bibliografia toponímica de linguística nacionais. Recife: [Editora Universitaria da Univ. Fed. de Pernambuco], 1983. 59 p.

1036. Simoes, Neusa Quirino. "Dedicatórias a Mário de Andrade." Boletim bibliográfico. Biblioteca Mário de Andrade, Out-Dez 1981, 42 (4), 15-59.

1037. Stern, Irwin. "Brazilian literature." Review, Jan-Apr 1981 (28), 69-72.

CARIBBEAN AREA

1038. Bandara, Samuel B. "A bibliography of theses and dissertations written in English on Caribbean novels." Commonwealth Novel in English, Jul 1983, 2 (2), 50-93.

1039. Finch, Mark S. "A selective bibliography on Caribbean literature." Revista-Review interamericana, Summer 1981, 11 (2), 283-300.

1040. Marting, Diane. Hispanic women writers of the Caribbean. New Brunswick, NJ: D. Marting, 1980. 17 p.

CHILE

1041. Castillo, Homero. "La literatura chilena en los Estados Unidos de América (Suplemento)." Revista chilena de literatura, Nov 1981 (18), 159-177.

1042. Castillo, Homero. "La literatura chilena en los Estados Unidos de América, II." Revista chilena de literatura, Abr 1982 (19), 75-94.

1043. Castillo, Homero. "La literatura chilena en los Estados Unidos de América, III." Revista chilena de literatura, Nov 1982 (20), 133-145.

1044. "Cronología del cine chileno en el exilio 1973-1983." Literatura chilena, creación y crítica, Ene-Mar 1984, 8 (1), 15-21.

1045. Fleak, Kenneth. "The Chilean generation of 1950: an introduction and a bibliography to its original works." Chasqui, Feb-May 1981, 10 (2-3), 26-36.

1046. Rafide, Matías. Diccionario de autores de la region del Maule: bio-bibliográfico y crítico. Talca, Chile: Delta, 1984. 572 p.

1047. Román-Lagunas, Jorge. "La novela chilena: estado de las investigaciones y fuentes generales de la información." Revista chilena de literatura, Nov 1984 (24), 103-118.

1048. Rubio de Lertora, Patricio. "La Nación 1970-1973: bibliografía de literatura chilena." Literatura chilena; creación y crítica, Jul-Sept 1983 (25), 29-36.

1049. Szmulewicz, Efraín. Diccionario de la literatura chilena. 2a ed corr y aum. Santiago de Chile: Editorial Andrés Bello, [1984]. 484 p.

COLOMBIA

1050. Cobo Borda, J.G. "La nueva poesía colombiana: una década, 1979-1980." Boletín cultural y bibliográfico, 1979, 16 (9-10), 75-80.

1051. Pluto, Joseph A. "Contribución a una bibliografía anotada de los estudios sobre el español de Colombia." Thesaurus, May-Ag 1980, 35 (2), 288-358.

1052. Universidad de Antioquía. Departamento de Bibliotecas, Medellín. Bibliografía especializada: literatura colombiana. [Medellín]: Centro de Documentación, [1981]. 216 p. (Serie: Actualización profesional, 57).

CUBA

1053. Espinosa Domínguez, Carlos. "Las ediciones cubanas de teatro." Conjunto, Ene-Mar 1982 (51), 118-119.

1054. Figueras, Myriam, compiler. Catálogo de la colección de la literatura cubana en la Biblioteca Colón. Washington, DC: Biblioteca Colón, Organización de los Estados Americanos, 1984. 114 p. (Documentation and information series, 9).

1055. Foster, David William. Cuban literature: a research guide. New York: Garland Pub., 1985. 522 p. (Garland reference library of the humanities, 511).

1056. García, Enildo Alberto. Cuba en la obra de Plácido (1809-1844): análisis y bibliografía comentada. New York: New York University, 1982. 426 p. Note: Ph.D. dissertation.

1057. García-Carranza, Araceli. "Bibliografía de [Los pasos perdidos] 1953-1983." Revista de la Biblioteca Nacional José Martí, Ene-Abr 1983, 25 (1), 133-156.

1058. García González, José, and María E. Díaz Gámez. "Bibliografía sobre el español de Cuba, 1978-1982." Islas, Ene-Abr 1984 (77), 175-181.

1059. Graupera Arango, Elena. Bibliografía sobre teatro cubano: libros y folletos. La Habana: Biblioteca Nacional José Martí, Departamento de Información y Documentación de la Cultura, 1981. 27 leaves.

1060. Gutiérrez de la Solana, Alberto. Investigación y crítica literaria y lingüística cubana. New York: Senda Nueva de Ediciones, c1978. 246 p. (Senda bibliográfica, 1).

1061. Larraga, Ricardo. "Mariano Brull y la poesía pura en Cuba: bibliografía y evolución." New York: New York University, 1981. Note: Dissertation (Ph.D.).

1062. López Iñiguez, Iraida. "Bibliografía comentada de estudios lingüísticos publicados en Cuba, 1959-1980." Cuban Studies, Winter 1983, 13 (1), 41-68.

1063. Smith, Paul Christopher. "Theater and political criteria in Cuba: Casa de las Américas Awards, 1960-1983." Cuban Studies, Winter 1984, 14 (1), 43-47.

DOMINICAN REPUBLIC

1064. Olivera, Otto. Bibliografía de la literatura dominicana (1960-

1982). Lincoln, NE: Society of Spanish and Spanish-American Studies, c1984. 86 p.

ECUADOR

1065. Luzuriaga, Gerardo. "Bibliografía del teatro ecuatoriano." Cultura (Ecuador), May-Ag 1982, 5 (13), 227-232.

1066. Luzuriaga, Gerardo. Bibliografía del teatro ecuatoriano, 1900-1982. Quito: Editorial Casa de la Cultura Ecuatoriana, 1984. 132 p.

1067. Sacoto, Antonio. "La novela ecuatoriana a partir de 1975." Cultura (Ecuador), Ene-Abr 1981, 3 (9), 317-331.

1068. Salomon, Frank. "El quichua de los Andes ecuatoriales: algunos aportes recientes." Revista andina, Jul-Dic 1983, 1 (2), 393-405.

GUATEMALA

1069. Albizúrez Palma, Francisco. Grandes momentos de la literatura guatemalteca. Indice bio-bibliográfico de la literatura guatemalteca. Guatemala: Editorial "José de Pinedo Ibarra," 1983. 125 p.

1070. Menton, Seymour. "Los señores presidentes y los guerrilleros: the new and the old Guatemalan novel: 1976-1982." Latin American Research Review, 1984, 19 (2), 93-117.

HAITI

1071. Hoffman, Léon-François. "Pour une bibliographie des études littéraires haitiennes." Conjonction, Jan 1983 (152), 43-57.

JAMAICA

1072. Brathwaite, Edward Kamau. Jamaica poetry: a checklist: books, pamphlets, broadsheets: 1686-1978. Kingston: Jamaica Library Service, 1979. 36 p.

MEXICO

1073. Foster, David William. Mexican literature: a bibliography of secondary sources. Metuchen, NJ: Scarecrow Press, 1981. 386 p.

1074. León-Portilla, Ascensión H. de. "Publicaciones sobre lengua literatura nahuas." Estudios de cultura nahuatl, 1982, 15 291-296.

1075. Manrique Casteñeda, Leonardo. "Fray Andrés de Olmos: notas críticas sobre su obra lingüística." Estudios de cultura nahuatl, 1982, 15, 27-35.

1076. Parodi, Claudia. La investigación lingüística en México, 1970-1980. México: Universidad Nacional Autónoma de México, 1981. 205 p. (Cuadernos del Instituto de Investigaciones Filológicas, UNAM).

MEXICO (MEXICAN AMERICAN)

1077. Anzaldúa, Mike. Mexican American literature: a preliminary bibliography of literary criticism. Austin, TX: Institute of Latin American Studies, c1980. 29 p. (Latin American curriculum units for junior and community colleges, 3).

1078. Arora, Shirley L. "A critical bibliography of Mexican-American proverbs." Aztlán, Spring-Fall 1982, 13 (1-2), 71-80.

1079. Eger, Ernestina. A bibliography of criticism of contemporary Chicano literature. Berkeley: Chicano Studies Library Publications, University of California, 1982, c1980. 295 p. (Chicano Studies Library Publications Series, 5).

1080. León-Portilla, Ascención H. de. "Algunas publicaciones recientes sobre lengua y literatura nahuas." Estudios de cultura nahuatl, 1980 (14), 419-432.

1081. León-Portilla, Ascención H. de. "Publicaciones sobre lengua y literatura nahuas." Estudios de cultura nahuatl, 1983 (16), 349-373.

1082. Martínez, Julio A., and Francisco A. Lomeli, editors. Chicano literature: a reference guide. Westport, CT: Greenwood Press,c1984. 512 p.

1083. Ordoñez, Elizabeth J. "Chicana literature and related sources: a selected and annotated bibliography." Bilingual review. Revista bilingüe, May-Ag 1980, 8 (2), 143-164.

1084. Rivero, Eliana. "Literatura chicana: introducción y contexto." Areito, 1981, 7 (25), 38-40.

1085. Trujillo, Roberto G., et al. "A comprehensive bibliography (1970-1979)." In: Luis Leal et al. A decade of Chicano literature (1970-1979): critical essays and bibliography. Santa Barbara, CA: La Causa, 1982, 107-128.

1086. Trujillo, Roberto G., and Andrés Rodríguez, compilers. A current bibliography of Chicano literature: creative and critical writings through 1984. Stanford, CA: Stanford University Libraries, Collection Development Program, Chicano Collection, 1984. 75 leaves. (Working bibliography series: Stanford University Libraries, Collection Development Program, Chicano Collections, 2).

1087. Trujillo, Roberto G., compiler. Literatura Chicana: a comprehensive bibliography (1980-1984). Stanford, CA: Stanford University Libraries, Collection Development Program, Chicano Collections, 1984. 21 leaves. (Working bibliography series: Stanford University Libraries, Collection Development Program, Chicano Collections, 1).

1088. Velasco, Ana María. Literatura chicana en el exilio; índice general 1977-1980. Los Angeles: Ed. de la Frontera, 1981.

1089. Zimmerman, Enid. "An annotated bibliography of Chicano literature: novels, short fiction, poetry and drama, 1970-1980." Bilingual review. Revista bilingüe, Sept-Dec 1982, 9 (3), 227-251.

NICARAGUA

1090. Arellano, Jorge Eduardo. "Diccionario de las letras nicaragüenses. Primera entrega: escritores de la época colonial y el siglo XIX." Cuadernos de bibliografía nicaragüense, Ene-Dic 1982 (3-4), 1-144.

1091. Arellano, Jorge Eduardo. El español en Nicaragua: bibliografía fundamental y analítica (1837-1980). 3a ed. Managua: Departamento de Español, UNAN, 1980. 64 leaves.

PARAGUAY

1092. Obras de autores nacionales: bibliografía. Asunción: Ministerio de Educación y Culto, 1980. 18 p.

PERU

1093. Arriola Grande, Maurilio. Diccionario literario del Perú. 2a ed corr y aum. Lima: Editorial Universo, [1983]. 2 vols.

1094. Ballón, Enrique. "La semiótica en el Perú." Apuntes, 1981, 6 (11), 39-59.

1095. Cabel, Jesús. Bibliografía de la poesía peruana, 65-79. Lima: Amaru Editores, 1980. 142 p.

1096. Chavarría Mendoza, María C. Bibliografía pano-tacana. [Perú]: Universidad Nacional Mayor de San Marcos Centro de Investigación de Lingüística Aplicada, 1983. 166 p. (Documento de trabajo, 47).

1097. Corbera Mori, Angel. Bibliografía de la familia lingüística jíbaro. San Marcos, Peru: Universidad Nacional Mayor de San Marcos, Centro de Investigación de Lingüística Aplicada, 1984. 98 p.

1098. Foster, David William. Peruvian literature: a bibliography of secondary sources. Westport, CT: Greenwood Press, 1981. 324 p.

1099. Jordan, Anne H. Contemporary Peruvian literature. Austin: Benson Latin American Collection, University of Texas at Austin, 1983. 2 p. (Biblio noticias, 20).

1100. Natella, Arthur A., Jr. "Bibliography of Peruvian theatre: 1946-1970." Hispanic journal, 1981, 2 (2), 141-147.

1101. Rodríguez Rea, Miguel Angel. "Bibliografías: poesía peruana del siglo XX, 1921-1930." Hueso húmero, Ene-Mar 1981, 8, 132-149.

1102. Rodríguez Rea, Miguel Angel. "Bibliografías: poesía peruana del siglo XX, 1931-1935." Hueso húmero, Abr-Jun 1981, 9, 148-158.

1103. Rodríguez Rea, Miguel Angel. "Poesía peruana del siglo XX (1936-1940)." Hueso húmero, 1982, 14, 186-203.

PUERTO RICO

1104. Foster, David W. Puerto Rican literature: a bibliography of secondary sources. Westport, CT: Greenwood Press, 1982. 232 p.

1105. Rivera de Alvarez, Josefina. "Genesis y desarrollo de la dramaturgia puertorriqueña hasta los umbrales de la generación del treinta." Revista del Instituto de Cultura Puertorriqueña, Jul-Dic 1977, 20 (76-77), 19-30.

TRINIDAD AND TOBAGO

1106. González, Ansón. "Bibliography of creative writing [Trinidad and Tobago], 1962-1977." New voices, Apr 1978, 6 (11), 22-43.

URUGUAY

1107. Puentes de Oyenard, Sylvia. Indice bibliográfico de literatura infantil de autores uruguayos. Montevideo: Club de Leones Barrio Sur y Palermo, 1980. 24 p.

VENEZUELA

1108. Hernández, Luis Guillermo. Bibliografía de la poesía femenina zuliana. Maracaibo, 1980. 30 leaves.

1109. López de Valdivieso, Miriam. Indice general de los discursos de incorporación a la Academia Venezolana de la Lengua. Caracas: Centenario de la Academia Venezolana Correspondiente de la Real Española, 1983. 96 p.

1110. Lovera de Sola, Roberto J. Bibliografía de la crítica literaria venezolana, 1847-1977. Caracas: Instituto Autónomo Biblioteca Nacional y de Servicios de bibliotecas, 1982. 489 p.

1111. Nazoa, Aquiles. "Selección bibliográfica de humoristas venezolanos de este siglo." Comunicación (Caracas), Jun 1982 (38), 94-95.

1112. Pedrique, Vilma; Amarilis Ruiz; and Ana Cecilia Rojas. "Guía filmográfica venezolana (1975-1979)." Comunicación (Caracas), May 1980, 27, 66-71.

1113. Querales, Juandemaro. Estudio bibliográfico de la poesía larense. Caracas: Academia Nacional de la Historia, 1981. 94 p.

1114. Rivas, Rafael Angel, et al. Bibliografía sobre las lenguas indígenas de Venezuela. Caracas: Instituto Autónomo Biblioteca Nacional y de Servicios de Bibliotecas, Instituto Universitario Pedagógico de Caracas, 1983. 162 p.

1115. Rojas Uzcátegui, José de la Cruz, and Lubio Cardozo. Bibliografía del teatro venezolano. Mérida, Venezuela: Universidad de los Andes, Facultad de Humanidades y Educación, Instituto de Investigaciones Literarias "Gonzalo Picón Febres," 1980. 199 p.

VIRGIN ISLANDS

1116. Sabino, Robin, compiler. A selected bibliography of materials on language varieties spoken in the Virgin Islands. [Charlotte Amalie, St. Thomas]: Bureau of Libraries, Museums and Archaeological Services, Dept. of Conservation and Cultural Affairs, Govt. of the Virgin Islands, 1980. 8 p. (Occasional paper, 6).

WEST INDIES

1117. Allis, Jeannette B. West Indian literature: an index to criticism, 1930-1975. Boston: G.K. Hall, c1981. 353 p.

1118. "Bibliography: West Indian exiles' bibliography of West Indian literature." Trinidad and Tobago review, 1977, 2, 4-6.

1119. Carnegie, Jenipher R. Critics on West Indian literature: a selected bibliography. Barbados: Research and Publications Committee, University of the West Indies, 1979. 74 p.

1120. McWatt, Mark. "The West Indies." Journal of Commonwealth literature, Feb 1982, 16 (2), 132-140. Note: In "Annual bibliography of Commonwealth literature for 1980."

1121. Singh, Sydney. "Bibliography of critical writing on the West Indian novel." World literature written in English, Spring 1983, 22 (1), 107-142.

1122. West Indian books for children. Kingston, Jamaica: Jamaica Library Service, 1983. 8 p.

LAW

1123. Arteaga Sáenz, Juan José; Silvia Reyes; and Sergio Silva. Constitución de 1830: bibliografía. Montevideo: Instituto de Filosofía, Ciencias y Letras, Departamento de Investigación y Estudios Superiores de Historia Americana, 1981. 82 p.

1124. Bernal, Marie-Louise H.; Rubens Medina; and Ivan Sipkov, compilers. Bibliografía de obras sobre el derecho de los Estados Unidos de América en lenguas extranjeras: entrega hispánica; División de Derecho Europeo y División de Derecho Hispánico, Biblioteca de Derecho. Washington, DC: Library of Congress, 1984. 38 p.

1125. Bibliografía sobre derecho de menores, legislación relativa a familia y a menores, codificación en materia de menores y familia, y tribunales de menores y de familia. Montevideo:

Organización de los Estados Americanos, Instituto Interamericano del Niño, 1980. 95 p.

1126. Centro de Estudios Puertorriqueños, New York. Preliminary guide to resolutions relating to Puerto Rico presented before the Annual Conventions of the American Federation of Labor, and articles, editorials and labor reports on Puerto Rico in the 'American Federationist,' 1902-1930. New York: Research Foundation of the City University of New York, 1981. 20 p.

1127. Cornejo, Atilio. Bibliografía jurídica de salteños: ensayos. Salta, Argentina: Ediciones Limache, [1983]. 233 p.

1128. Hernández de Caldas, Angela, and Gloria Chapetón de Ortiz. Legislación forestal colombiana 1919-1980 [Bibliografía]. Bogotá: Corporación Nacional de Investigación y Fomento Forestal, 1981. 20 p.

1129. Hurtado Mánguez, Eugenio. Bibliografía general. México: Instituto de Investigaciones Jurídicas, Universidas Nacional Autónoma de México, 1981. 37 p. (Serie A--Fuentes. Instituto de Investigaciones de Jurídicas. Textos y estudios legislativos, 50).

1130. Jara, Alvaro, and Sonia Pinto, compilers. Fuentes para la historia del trabajo en el Reino de Chile: legislación, 1546-1810. Santiago: Editorial Andrés Bello, [1982-1983]. 2 v.

1131. Moss, Sylvia Grace, compiler. Environmental legislation of the Commonwealth Caribbean. The Garrison, Barbados: Caribbean Conservation Association, 1982. 155 leaves. Note: Compiled in collaboration with the Caribbean Conservation Association.

1132. Newton, Velma, and Sylvia Moss. Law in Caribbean society: an annotated guide to University of the West Indies Law in Society Dissertations, 1973-1977. [Bridgetown? Barbados]: Research and Publications Fund Committee, University of the West Indies, 1980. 151 p.

.133. Olmo, Rosa del. "Indice bibliográfico de criminología latinoamericana." Anuario del Instituto de Ciencias Penales y Criminológicas (Caracas), 1976-77, 125-189.

1134. Rivera de Bayrón, Vilma. La bibliotecología jurídica: estudio de sus fuentes bibliográficas de investigación. Rio Piedras, P.R.: Escuela Graduada de Bibliotecología, Universidad de Puerto Rico, 1981. 33 p.

1135. Rodríguez, Selma C. "Selective bibliography on legal aspects of the petroleum industry in the I.D.B. regional member countries." International journal of legal information, Aug 1982, 10, 158-168.

1136. Snyder, Frederick E., compiler. Latin American society and legal culture: a bibliography. Westport, CT: Greenwood Press, c1985. (Bibliographies and indexes in law and political science, 5).

1137. Verner, Joel G. "The independence of Supreme Courts in Latin America: a review of the literature." Journal of Latin American Studies, Nov 1984, 16 (2), 463-506.

1138. Villasmil de Losada, Helen. "Sección de bibliografía." Boletín del Instituto de Derecho Privado, Universidad Central de Venezuela, Jun 1980. (23-24), 85-93.

LIBRARIES AND ARCHIVES

GENERAL

1139. Nauman, Ann Keith. A handbook of Latin American and Caribbean national archives. Guía de los archivos nacionales de América Latina y el Caribe. Detroit: Blaine Ethridge Books, c1983. 127 p. Note: English and Spanish.

ARGENTINA

1140. Biblioteca de Martín Ferreyra. Sección Historia, Genealogía y Heráldica. Catálogo. Sección historia, genealogía y heráldica. Córdoba, Arg.: Biblioteca de Martín Ferreyra, 1982. 253 p.

1141. Biblioteca Dr. Juan José Nissen. Catálogo de materiales especiales de la Biblioteca Dr. Juan José Nissen. San Juan, Arg.: Universidad Nacional de San Juan, Facultad de Filosofía, Humanidades y Artes, Biblioteca Dr. Juan José Nissen, 1982. 37 p.

1142. Buenos Aires. Universidad. Biblioteca. Argentine bibliography: a union catalog of Argentine holdings in the libraries of the University of Buenos Aires. Bibliografía argentina: catálogo de materiales argentinos en las bibliotecas de la Universidad de Buenos Aires. Boston: G.K. Hall, 1980. 7 vols.

1143. Buenos Aires, Universidad. Catálogo de la biblioteca: Obras 3. Buenos Aires: Universidad de Buenos Aires, 1980. 178 p. Note: Suplemento 3.

1144. Córdoba. Universidad Nacional. Biblioteca Mayor. Catálogo de la donación Jorge Hieronymus. Funes, Antonieta del Valle. Córdoba, Argentina: Biblioteca Mayor, 1980. 30 leaves, [6] leaves of plates.

1145. Córdoba. Universidad Nacional. Biblioteca Mayor. Catálogo de la donación Velez Sarsfield. Córdoba, Argentina: Biblioteca Mayor, 1980. 152 leaves. (Publicaciones de la Biblioteca Mayor, 13).

1146. Instituto Argentino del Petroleo. Comisión de Biblioteca. Catálogo de hemeroteca. María Adela d'Auro and María Eugenia Stratta, compilers. [Buenos Aires]: El Instituto, 1983.

BAHAMAS

1147. Boultbee, Paul G., compiler. Bahamian reference collection: bibliography. 2d ed. Nassau, Bahamas: College of the Bahamas, Library, [1981]. 57 p.

BOLIVIA

1148. Lewinski, Liliana. "Archivos históricos de Oruro." Latin American Research Review, 1980, 15 (3), 195-198.

1149. Lorini, Irma. Catálogo de folletería minera del Repositorio Nacional. La Paz: Instituto Boliviano de Cultura, Departamento de Historia, 1979. [62] p.

BRAZIL

1150. Aragão Dias Freire, Maria Ines, compiler. Catálogo da coleção Clidenor Coelho Galvão. Escola Superior de Mossoró, Biblioteca Orlando Teixeira. Mossoró, Brasil: A Biblioteca, 1982. 53 p.

1151. Arquivo Histórico do Rio Grande so Sul. Falas e relatórios dos presidentes da Província do Rio Grande do Sul. Estado do Rio Grande do Sul, Secretaria de Cultura, Desporto e Turismo, Arquivo Histórico do Rio Grande do Sul. [Porto Alegre]: O Arquivo, [1983-?].

1152. Associação Catariense de Bibliotecarios. Grupo de Bibliotecarios em Informação e Documentação em Processos Técnicos. Catálogo de obras catarienenses nas bibliotecas de Florianopolis. Florianopolis: A Associação: Fundação Catarinense de Cultura, 198-.

1153. Biblioteca Pública do Paraná. Divisão de Documentação Paranaense. Catalogo bibliográfico. Curitiba, Brazil: Secretaria da Cultura e do Esporte, 1980. 537 p.

1154. Brazil. Ministério das Relações Exteriores. Arquivo Histórico. Catálogo do arquivo particular do visconde do Rio Branco. Ferreira, Nadir Duarte, editor. Brasília: Editora Universidade de Brasília, c1981. 201p. (Coleção temas brasileiros, 9).

1155. Ferreira, Sonia Campos. "Avaliaçao de Coleção bibliográfica da Biblioteca Central da Universidade Federal do Rio Grande do Norte." Revista de Biblioteconomia de Brasília, Jan-Jun 1980, 8 (1), 44-51.

1156. Guia de obras de referencia em tecnologia das bibliotecas de Curitiba. Curitiba: Associação Bibliotecaria do Parana, Grupo de Trabalho em Informação e Documentação Tecnologia, 1979. 65 p.

1157. Leonel, Maria Célia de Moras, and Sandra Guardini Teixeira Vasconcelos. "Arquivo Guimarães Rosa." Revista do Instituto de Estudos Brasileiros, 1982. (24), 178-180.

1158. "Registro bibliográfico." Boletim bibliográfico. Biblioteca Mário de Andrade, Jan-Jun 1980, 41 (1-2), 145-157. Note: Atualização do acervo da Biblioteca Mário de Andrade.

1159. Rondinelli, Roseli Curi, and Alice Ferry de Moraes. Arquivo de Rui Barbosa repertório da série corrêspondencia geral. Rio de Janeiro: Fundação Casa de Rui Barbosa. Centro de Documentação Arquivo Histórico, 1983. 91 p.

1160. Vasque, Josetine. Catálogo dos 854 títulos da batalha da cultura, Prefeitura Municipal de Mossoró, 1948-1973, Escola Superior de Agricultura de Mossoró, 1974-1983, Fundação Guimarães Duque, 1978-1983; boletim bibliográfico, 153 números, Coleção mossoroense, série A, 25 volumes, série B, 414 plaquetas, série C, 262 livros; incluídos índices de autores e de assuntos. [Mossoró, Brazil]: Escola Superior de Agricultura de Mossoró: Fundação Guimarães Duque, 1983. 123 p. (Coleção mossorense, 259).

CHILE

1161. Barrios Valdés, Marciano. "Bibliografía sumaria del profesor Dr. Julio Jiménez Berguecio, S.J." Anales de la Facultad de Teología. Pontificia Universidad Católica de Chile, Santiago de Chile, 1982, 23, 15-22.

1162. "Documentos de don Hugo Rodolfo Ramírez Rivera (con explicación y notas del mismo)." Academia Chilena de la Historia. Boletín, 1981, 92, 309-330.

1163. "Documentos del archivo de don Sergio Fernández Larraín (con explicaciones y notas del mismo)." Academia Chilena de la Historia. Boletín, 1981, 92, 285-307.

1164. Eyzaguirre E., Juan. "Guía de los archivos de Chile." Boletín interamericano de archivos, 1978, 5, 161-188.

1165. Eyzaguirre [E.], Juan, et al. Guía de los Archivos Históricos de Santiago. Santiago de Chile: Instituto Panamericano de Geografía e Historia, Sección Chilena, 1982. 100 p.

1166. Falch Frey, Jorge. "Archivo de los antiguos libros parroquiales de la Iglesia chilena." Revista católica (Chile), 1981, 81 (1050), 51-52.

1167. González Echenique, Javier. Documentos de la misión de don Mariano Egaña en Londres (1824-29). Santiago: Ministerio de Relaciones Exteriores de Chile, 1984. 655 p.

1168. "Indice de documentos del Archivo del Convento de Santo Domingo de Santiago de Chile: censos y capellanias, siglos XVI a XX." Historia (Chile), 1983, 18, 235-344.

1169. Provincia Franciscana de Chile. Descripción del Archivo del Convento Máximo de Santiago. Santiago de Chile, 1980. 12 p. (Cuadernos del Archivo de la Provincia Franciscana de Chile, 1).

1170. Provincia Franciscana de Chile. Indice del Archivo del Colegio San Ildefonso de Chillán, 1651-1799. Santiago de Chile: [n.p.], 1980. 57 p. (Cuadernos del Archivo de la Provincia Franciscana de Chile, 5, 8).

1171. Provincia Franciscana de Chile. Indices del Archivo del Convento de San Francisco de Santiago de Chile. Santiago de Chile: [n.p.], 1980. 231 p. (Cuadernos del Archivo de la Provincia Franciscana de Chile, 2, 7, 9-14).

1172. Von dem Bussche, Gastón. "Gabriela Mistral y su herencia literaria. Indice de la colección de microfilmes de Gabriela Mistral (Serie I-IV, poesía, prosa, correspondencia etc.)." Academia (Chile), 1983, 5-6, 135-174.

COLOMBIA

1173. Alvarez, Victor, and Beatriz Patiño. Inventario de fuentes documentales en Antioquía: 42 municipios, 347 archivos. Medellín: Fundación Antioqueña para los Estudios Sociales, 1981. 316 p.

1174. "Archives in Pamplona, norte de Santander, Colombia." The Americas, Oct 1980, 37 (2), 223-225.

1175. Banco de la República, Bogotá. Hemeroteca Luis López de Mesa: catálogo general. Vol. 1. Bogotá: Talleres Gráficos del Banco de la República, [1980?]. 199 p.

1176. Colombia. Ministerio de Relaciones Exteriores. Biblioteca. Catálogo de la Biblioteca 'Marco Fidel Suárez.' [Bogotá]: [Multilith Minrelaciones Exteriores], 1981. 207 p.

1177. Fundación Mariano Ospina Pérez. Servicio de Documentación e Información. Fondo bibliográfico Armando Samper Gnecco. María Ramirez de Díaz, and María del Pilar Ortiz de López, compilers. Bogotá: El Servicio, 1980. 313 p.

CUBA

1178. Echevarría, Israel, et al. "Bibliografía de la Biblioteca Nacional José Martí (1901-1981)." Revista de la Biblioteca Nacional José Martí, May-Ag 1981, Año 72 (tercera época), 23 (2), 105-192.

1179. Echevarría, Israel, et al. "Catálogo de libros del siglo XVI existentes en la Biblioteca Nacional José Martí." Revista de la Biblioteca Nacional José Martí, May-Ag 1981, Año 72 (tercera época), 23 (2), 29-56.

1180. Pérez, Louis A., Jr. "Record collections at the Cuban National Archives: a descriptive survey." Latin American Research Review, 1984, 19 (1), 142-156.

ECUADOR

1181. Archivo Nacional de Historia (Ecuador). Guía del Archivo Nacional de Historia. Quito: Edit. Casa de la Cultura Ecuatoriana, 1981. 219 p.

1182. Caillavet, Chantal. "Les archives équatoriennes." Cahiers du monde hispanique et luso-brésilien, 1980, 34, 171-175.

1183. "Los índices del fondo Jacinto Jijón y Caamaño, Archivo Histórico del Banco Central del Ecuador. Cuarta colección, Vols. 1-10 (1822-34)." Cultura (Ecuador), May-Ag 1982, 5 (13), 303-360.

1184. "Los índices del fondo Jacinto Jijón y Caamaño. Archivo Histórico del Banco Central del Ecuador. Cuarta colección. Vols. 11-17 (1835-49)." Cultura (Ecuador), Sept-Dic 1982, 5 (14), 409-459.

1185. Luna Tamayo, Milton, and Patricio Ordoñez Chiriboga. Fondo Jijón y Caamaño: Banco Central del Ecuador. Archivo Histórico. [Quito]: Centro de Investigación y Cultura, Banco Central del Ecuador, 1983-. (Catálogos del Archivo Histórico, 2-).

1186. Villacis V., Eduardo. "Los índices del Archivo Jacinto Jijón y Caamaño." Cultura (Ecuador), May-Ag 1980, 3 (7), 286-346. Note: Continues indexing of this archive that began in v. 2, no. 5 (Sept-Dic 1979).

1187. Villacis V., Eduardo. "Los índices del Archivo Histórico del Banco Central; Fondo Jijón y Caamaño. Tercera colección. Vols. 1-10 (1805-1835)." Cultura (Ecuador), Sept-Dic 1980, 3 (8), 284-345.

1188. Villacis V., Eduardo. "Los índices del Archivo Histórico del Banco Central; Fondo Jijón y Caamaño. Tercera colección. Vols. 11-15 (1836-58)." Cultura (Ecuador), May-Ag 1981, 4 (10), 315-361.

1189. Villacis V., Eduardo. "Los índices del Archivo Jacinto Jijón y Caamaño. Tercera colección. Vols. 16-19 (1859-74)." Cultura (Ecuador), Sept-Dic 1981, 4 (11), 463-512.

ENGLAND

1190. Price, Robin. An annotated catalogue of medical Americana in the library of the Wellcome Institute for the History of Medicine. London: Wellcome Institute for the History of Medicine, 1983. 319 p. (Publications of the Wellcome Institute for the History of Medicine. Catalogue series America, 1).

FRANCE

1191. France. Archives Nationales. Guide des sources de l'histoire de l'Amérique Latine et des Antilles dans les archives françaises. Paris: Archives Nationales, 1984. 711 p.

1192. Jackson, William Vernon. Resources for Brazilian studies at the Bibliothèque Nationale. Austin, TX: [n.p.], 1980. 57 p.

1193. Université de Paris IV: Paris-Sorbonne. Institut d'Études Hispaniques. Bibliothèque. Catalogue du fonds ancien de la bibliothèque de l'Institut d'Études Hispaniques de Paris. Jean-Michel Guittard, compiler. Paris: Klincksieck, 1982. 172 p.

GUATEMALA

1194. Feldman, Lawrence H. Colonial manuscripts of Chiquimula, El Progreso and Zacapa Departments. [n.p., 1982]. 597 p.

1195. Feldman, Lawrence H., and Teresa Mayaweski. "Indice de planos de tierras y pueblos del oriente de Guatemala, existentes en el Archivo General de Centroamérica (siglos XVIII y XIX)." Antropología e historia de Guatemala, 1981, 2 (3), 197-228.

1196. Jackson, William Vernon. "Situación archivística actual en Guatemala." Universidad de San Carlos, 1979, 2a época, 10, 25-101.

1197. Lutz, Cristóbal H., and Stephen Webre. "El Archivo General de Centroamérica, Ciudad de Guatemala." Mesoamérica, 1980, 1 (1), 274-285.

1198. Tobar Cruz, Pedro. "Indice de los documentos que se encuentran en la biblioteca del IDAEH (1870-1885)." Antropología e historia de Guatemala, 1981, 2 (3), 229-238.

MARTINIQUE

1199. Martinique. Archives. Guide des Archives de la Martinique. Chauleau, Liliane. Fort-de-France: Archives départementales, 1978. 68 p.

MEXICO

1200. Aguilar Zarandona, Irene; Marcela Pellón Caballero; and Alejandro Vigil Batista. Indice del archivo parroquial de Zacualpan de Amilpas. México: Universidad Iberoamericana, Departamento de Historia, 1978. 110 p. (Cuadernos de trabajo, 1).

1201. Alanís Boyso, José Luis. "Los archivos históricos municipales de los Reyes La Paz, Chicoloapan, Chimalhuacán, Ixtapaluca, Atenco, Tezoyuca, Acolman, Nopaltepec, Axapusco, Temascalapa, Apaxco, Ayapango, Atlautla, Ecatzingo, Huixquilucan, Tlazala, Jilotepec, Metepec, Tenancingo y Tejupilco." Boletín del Archivo General del Estado de México, Ene-Abr 1981, 7, 32-48.

1202. Alanís Boyso, José Luis. "Los archivos históricos municipales de Santa Cruz Atizapan, Temascalcingo, Villa Victoria, Tacámac, Polotitlán, Zinacantepec, San Martín de la Pirámides, San Mateo Atenco, Xonacatlán, Otzolotepec, Jalatlaco, Joquicingo, Texcaltitlán, Almoloya de Alquisiras, Coatepec Harinas y Tonatico." Boletín del Archivo General del Estado de México, May-Ag 1980, 5, 35-47.

1203. Alanís Boyso, José Luis. "Los archivos históricos municipales de Sultepec, Lerma, Aculco, Villa de Allende, Temascaltepec, Donato Guerra, Amanalco de Becerra, Jiquipilco, Texcalyacac, Temoaya, Zumpahuacan y Villa Guerrero." Boletín del Archivo General del Estado de México, Sept-Dic 1980, 6, 49-59.

1204. Arnold, Linda. Directorio de burócratas en la ciudad de México, 1761-1832. México: Archivo General de la Nación, [1980]. 301, [6] p. (Serie guías y catálogos, 52).

1205. Bazant, Jan. "Los archivos de notarías de Zacatecas." Historia mexicana, Jul-Sept 1980, 30:1 (117), 134-136.

1206. Beltrán González, Ignacio, and Pedro Rodríguez Chávez. Catálogo de folletos existentes en la Biblioteca 'Manuel Orozco y Berra.' México: Departamento de Investigaciones Históricas, INAH, 1979. 111 p.

1207. Biblioteca Nacional de Antropología e Historia. Archivo Histórico. Documentos sobre Mesoamérica en el Archivo Histórico de la Biblioteca Nacional de Antropología e Historia. María de los Angeles Ojeda Díaz, editor. México: La Biblioteca, [1979]. 92 p.

1208. Bribiesca Sumano, María Elena. Guía del Ramo títulos y despachos de guerra: copias. México: Archivo General de la Nación, 1980. 88 leaves. (Serie guías y catálogos, 9).

1209. Catálogo de documentos sobre el Instituto Literario del Estado. Toluca, México: Universidad Autónoma del Estado de México, c1980. 98 p.

1210. García Moll, Roberto. Indice del archivo técnico de la Dirección de Monumentos Prehispánicos del INAH. México: Instituto Nacional de Antropología e Historia, 1982. 304 p.

1211. Garibay Alvarez, Jorge. Archivo parroquial sagrario León, Guanajuato. México: Archivo General de la Nación, 1981. 11 p.

1212. Garibay Alvarez, Jorge. Inventario del archivo parroquial de Ixtacamaxitlán, Puebla. México: Archivo General de la Nación, 1981. 17 p.

1213. Garritz Ruiz, Amaya. Guía del Archivo Amado Aguirre. México: Universidad Autónoma de México, Instituto de Investigaciones Históricas, 1982. 291 p.

1214. González Cícero, Stella María. Archivo histórico del teatro Esperanza Iris. México: Archivo General de la Nación, c1981. 17 p.

1215. González Cícero, Stella María. Archivo Municipal de Xocchel, Yucatán. México: Archivo General de la Nación, 1981. 11 p.

1216. González Cícero, Stella María. Inventario del Archivo Municipal de Ahuacatlán, Nayarit. México: Archivo General de la Nación, 1981. 8 p.

1217. González Cícero, Stella María. Inventario del Archivo Municipal de Rosamorada, Nayarit. México: Archivo General de la Nación, 1981. 13 p.

1218. González Cícero, Stella María. Inventario del Archivo Municipal de Ruiz, Nayarit. México: Archivo General de la Nación, 1981. 11 p.

1219. González Cícero, Stella María. Inventario del Archivo Municipal de Santa María del Oro. México: Archivo General de la Nación, 1981. 20 p.

1220. González Cícero, Stella María. Inventario del Archivo Municipal de Santiago Ixcuintla, Nayarit. México: Archivo General de la Nación, 1981. 19 p.

1221. La France, David G. "The Madero collection in Mexico's Archivo General de la Nación." Revista interamericana de bibliografía, 1983, 33 (2), 191-197.

1222. Lechuga Barrios, Carmen. "Sección catálogos: (El Archivo General del Estado de México)." Boletín del Archivo General del Estado de México, Ene-Abr 1981, 7, 52-54.

1223. Luna, Laurentino, et al. Archivo de Genovevo de la O. México: Archivo General de la Nación, [1980]. 8, 149 leaves. (Serie guías y catálogos, 36).

1224. Luna Marez, Patricia. Guía de documentos de los Ramos de mercados y traslados de tierras en el Archivo General de la Nación. México: Biblioteca Nacional de Antropología e Historia, I.N.A.H., 1980. 87 p. (Cuadernos de la biblioteca. Serie bibliografía, 12).

1225. Luna Marez, Patricia. Guía del Ramo de aguardiente de caña en el Archivo General de la Nación. [México]: Biblioteca Nacional de Antropología e Historia, I.N.A.H., 1980. 137 p. (Serie bibliografía. Biblioteca Nacional e Antropología e Historia, 8).

1226. Luna Marez, Patricia. Guía del Ramo de almacenes Reales en el Archivo General de la nación. [México]: Biblioteca Nacional de Antropología e Historia, 1980. 83 p. (Serie bibliografía: Biblioteca Nacional de Antropología e Historia, 6).

1227. Mexico. Archivo General de la Nación. Archivo de Alfredo Robles Domínguez. México: Archivo General de la Nación, [1981]. 5 vols. (Serie guías y catálogos, 45).

1228. Mexico. Archivo General de la Nación. Archivo de guerra. Martínez Bribiesca, Gilberto, compiler. México: Archivo General de la Nación, 1982. 2 vols.

1229. Mexico. Archivo General de la Nación. Catálogo de documentos sobre el noroeste [existentes en siete ramos del Archivo General de la Nación]. Ana María Atondo Rodríguez, compiler. México: Archivo General de la Nación, [1980]. 2 vols. (Serie guías y catálogos, 49).

1230. Mexico. Archivo General de la Nación. Catálogo de ilustraciones. México: Centro de Información Gráfica del Archivo General de la Nación, 1979. 2 vols.

1231. Mexico. Archivo General de la Nación. Catálogo de los Ramos Oficio de Soria y Oficio de Hurtado. María Elena Bribiesca, editor. México: Archivo General de la Nación, [1980]. 84 leaves.

1232. Mexico. Archivo General de la Nación. Catálogo del Ramo escribanos. Abel González Flores et al., editors. México: Archivo General de la Nación, 1980. 168 leaves. (Serie guías y catálogos, 55).

1233. Mexico. Archivo General de la Nación. Fondo Presidente Abelardo L. Rodríguez: índice de serie confederaciones, uniones y organizaciones. Angeles Suárez et al., compilers. México: Archivo General de la Nación, [1980]. 4, 199, 23 leaves. (Serie guías y catálogos, 50).

1234. Mexico. Archivo General de la Nación. Guía del archivo histórico de la Compañia de Minas de Real del Monte y Pachuca; Instituto Nacional de Antropología e Historia, Dirección de Estudios Históricos [y] Archivo General de la Nación. México: Dirección de Difusión y Publicaciones del Archivo General de la Nación, [1981]. 173 leaves. (Serie guías y catálogos, 62).

1235. Mexico. Archivo General de la Nación. Guía general de los fondos que contiene el Archivo General de la Nación. México: Dirección de Difusión y Publicaciones del Archivo General de la Nación, 1981. 194 p.

1236. Mexico. Archivo General de la Nación. Ramo historia. Celia Medina Mondragón, editor. México: Archivo General de la Nación, 1981. 4 vols. (Serie guías y catálogos, 28).

1237. Museo Nacional de Historia (Mexico). Josefina González de Arellano, editor. Archivo "Espinosa de los Monteros." Vol. 1-5, 7-. México: Instituto Nacional de Antropología e Historia, 1982-. Note: Catalog of documents compiled by S. Espinosa de los Monteros in the Museo Nacional de Historia.

1238. Pérez Herrero, Pedro. Ramo consulados. México: Archivo General de la Nación, 1982-. (Serie guías y catálogos, 69).

1239. Potash, Robert A.; Jan Bazant; and Josefina Z. Vázquez. Guide to the notarial records of the Archivo General de Notarías, Mexico City, for the year 1829. Amherst, MA: [University Computing Center], 1982. 301 leaves.

1240. Potash, Robert A.; Jan Bazant; and Josefina Z. Vázquez. Guide to the notarial records of the Archivo General de Notarías, Mexico City, for the year 1847. Guía de los protocolos notariales del Archivo General de Notarías, México, D.F., año 1847. Amherst, MA: University Computing Center, 1983. 237 leaves.

1241. Potash, Robert A.; Jan Bazant; and Josefina Z. Vázquez. Guide to the notarial records of the Archivo General de Notarías, Mexico City, for the year 1875. Guía de los protocolos notariales del Archivo General de Notarías, México, D.F., año 1875. Amherst, MA: University Computing Center, 1984. 2 vols.

1242. Robinson, David James. Research inventory of the Mexican collection of colonial parish registers. Salt Lake City: University of Utah Press, 1980. 288 p. (Finding aids to the microfilmed manuscript collection of the Genealogical Society of Utah, 6).

1243. Rodríguez de Lebrija, Esperanza. Guía documental del Archivo Histórico de Hacienda. México: Archivo General de la Nación, [1981]. 2 vols. (Serie guías y catálogos, 61).

1244. Universidad Iberoamericana. Centro de Información Académica. Catálogo de documentos--carta de la Colección Porfirio Díaz. [México]: Universidad Iberoamericana, Centro de Información Académica, Departamento de Historia, 1982-. (Catálogos de fondos documentales de la UIA. Serie CPD, Documentos-Carta)

1245. Valentino Ramírez, Pablo. General Jesús González Ortega, colección bibliográfica. México: Biblioteca Nacional de Antropología e Historia, INAH, 1981. 510 p.

NICARAGUA

1246. "Archivo Carlos Fonesca." Boletín de referencias (Nicaragua), Oct-Dic 1982, 2 (6), 57-89.

PANAMA

1247. Panama. Archivo Nacional. Indice de los tomos I y II de reales cédulas correspondientes a la Audiencia de Panamá, procedentes del Archivo de Indias de Sevilla, expedidas de 1573 a 1627. Mercedes Figueroa, editor. Panamá: Archivos Nacionales de Panamá, [1982]. [2] 68 leaves.

PARAGUAY

1248. Biblioteca Presidente Carlos A. López. Catálogo de obras paraguayas existentes en la Biblioteca del CRESR. Ramona Sosa de Macial, editor. San Lorenzo, Paraguay: Ministerio de Educación y Culto, Centro Regional de Educación Saturio Rios, Biblioteca Presidente Carlos A. López, 1982. 82 p.

PERU

1249. "Catálogo general del Archivo del Monasterio de Santa Catalina del Cusco, Perú." Revista andina, Ene-Jun 1983, 1 (1), 127-133.

1250. Málaga Medina, Alejandro. Archivos arquipenses. Arequipa, Perú: Ed. Publiunsa, 1980. 101 p.

1251. Málaga Medina, Alejandro. "Organización del Archivo Municipal de Arequipa." Boletín interamericano de archivos, 1978-79. (6-7), 211-221.

1252. Perú. Biblioteca Nacional, Lima. Catálogo de autores de la Colección Peruana, Biblioteca Nacional del Perú. Boston: G.K. Hall, 1979. 6 vols.

1253. Perú. Dirección de Archivo Colonial. Inventario, Serie Real Aduana. Archivo General de la Nación, Dirección General de

Archivo Histórico, Dirección de Archivo Colonial. Lima: Archivo General de la Nación, Dirección General de Archivo Histórico, Dirección de Archivo Colonial. v. 1-, 1984-.

SPAIN

1254. Archivo General de Indias. Catálogo de las consultas del Consejo de Indias. v. 1-. Antonia Heredia Herrera, Javier Rubiales Torrejón, and María Dolores Vargas Zúñiga, editors. Sevilla: Diputación Provincial, 1983-. (V Centenario del descubrimiento de América, 1-).

1255. Contreras, Remedios. Fondos americanistas de la Colección Salazar y Castro: catálogo. Madrid: Real Academia de la Historia, 1979. 259 p.

1256. Cuesta Domingo, Mariano, and Nieves Sáenz Gracia. "Fondos de la Biblioteca del Ultramar en el Museo de América de Madrid." Historiografía y Bibliografía Americanistas, 1980, 24, 127-187.

1257. López Díaz, María T., and A. Dominguez Camacho. Catálogo de documentos farmacéuticos del Archivo General de Indias. Sevilla: [n.p.], 1983.

1258. Rodríguez Vicente, Encarnación. Catálogo de la Colección Caballero de Rodas. Madrid: Real Academia de la Historia, 1981. 279 p.

UNITED STATES

1259. Arrigunaga Coello, Maritza. Catálogo de las fotocopias de los documentos y periódicos yucatecos en la biblioteca de la Universidad de Texas en Arlington. Arlington, TX: Center for Mesoamerican Studies, University of Texas at Arlington Library, 1983.

1260. Central America Resource Center (Minneapolis). Library. The Central America Resource Center Library catalogue. Minneapolis: The Center, 1984. 37 p.

1261. Church of Jesus Christ of Latter-Day Saints. Genealogical Department. Bibliographic guide to the Guatemalan collection. Shirley A. Weathers et al., compilers. Salt Lake City: University of Utah Press, 1981. 533 p. (Finding aids to the microfilmed manuscript collection of the Genealogical Society of Utah, 7).

1262. Columbus Memorial Library. Catálogo de la colección de la literatura chilena en la Biblioteca Colón. Thomas L. Welch, compiler. Washington, DC: Columbus Memorial Library, 1983. 154 p.

1263. Cotera, Martha. Mexican American archives at the Benson Collection: a supplement for educators. [Austin]: University of Texas at Austin, The General Libraries, 1981. 94 p.

1264. Flores, María G., compiler. Mexican American archives at the Benson Collection: a guide for users. Laura Gutiérrez-Witt, editor. Austin: University of Texas at Austin, General Libraries, 1981. 74 leaves.

1265. Gibbs, Donald. Mexican archives: new journals and guides. Austin: Benson Latin American Collection, The General Libraries, University of Texas at Austin, 1982. 2 p. (Biblio noticias, 15).

1266. Glass, John B. The Boturini collection: documents No. 1743 (1) through 1743 (2-6). Lincoln Center, MA: Conemex Associates, 1981. 178 p. (Contributions to the Ethnohistory of Mexico, 10). Note: "The Indian museum of Lorenzo Boturini." Vol. 2, part 3.

1267. Hartness-Kane, Ann. Revolution and counterrevolution in Guatemala 1944-1963: an annotated bibliography of materials in the Benson Latin American Collection. Austin: University of Texas, General Libraries, 1984.

1268. Henderson, Donald C., and Grace R. Pérez, compilers and translators. Literature and politics in Latin America: an annotated calendar of the Luis Alberto Sánchez correspondence, 1919-1980. University Park: Pennsylvania State University, 1982. 498 p.

1269. Pérez, Lisandro. "The holdings of the Library of Congress on the population of Cuba." Cuban studies, Winter 1983, 13 (1), 69-76.

1270. Phillips, Glenn O. "The Caribbean collection at the Moorland-Spingarn Research Center, Howard University." Latin American Research Review, 1980, 15 (2), 162-178.

1271. Poyo, Gerald E., and Jane Garner. Inventory of the records of the Cuban Consulate, Key West, Florida, 1886-1961, on microfilm. [Austin]: University of Texas at Austin, The General Libraries, 1983. 48 p.

1272. San Diego State University. Library. Department of Special Collections. The Henry Raup Wagner collection in the Department of Special Collections of the San Diego State University Library. Stephen A. Colston, compiler. San Diego, CA: The Library, 1982. 30 p.

1273. Sandos, James. "Latin American holdings of the U.S. Military History Institute." Revista interamericana de bibliografía, 1983, 23 (1), 21-27.

1274. Sonntag, Iliana L.; Shelley F. Phipps; and Ross W. McLachlan, compilers. Guide to Chicano resources in the University of Arizona Library. 2d rev. corr. and enl. ed. Tucson, AZ: [n.p.], 1980. 186 p.

1275. Tyler, Daniel. "The Carrizal archives: a source for the Mexican period." New Mexico Historial Review, Jul 1982, 57 (257-267).

1276. Wilson, Lofton, editor; Lisa Browar, Anna Fernicola, and Miryam A. Ospina, compilers. Guide to Latin American pamphlets from the Yale University Library: selections from 1600-1900. New York: Clearwater Pub. Co., c1985. 7v.

1277. Yale University. Library. Historical Manuscripts and Archives. Subject guide to the Latin American pamphlet collection: Mexican pamphlets. Lisa Browar, Ann Fernicola, and Miryam Ospina, compilers. New Haven, CT: [Yale University Library], 1983. 2 vols.

WEST INDIES

1278. Institute of Jamaica, Kingston. West India Reference Library. The catalogue of the West India Reference Library. Millwood, NY: Kraus International Publications, [1980]. 6 vols.

LIBRARY SCIENCE

1279. Catálogo de dissertações e teses em ciencias da informação e biblioteconomia. Brasília: Instituto Brasileiro de Informação em Ciencia e Tecnologia, 1982. 92 p.

1280. Dorn, Georgette Magassy. "Of libraries and bibliographies." Latin American Research Review, 1981, 16 (3), 268-271.

1281. Freudenthal, Juan R., and Héctor Gómez Fuentes. "Information and documentation in Chile: progress report; bibliography 1974-1978." Journal of the American Society for Information Science, Nov 1980, 31 (445-448).

1282. Gómez de Matos, Patricia, and Ana María Morais da Cruz. Ciencia da informação; catálogo coletivo do Piaui. Teresina, Brasil: ABEPI, 1981. 53 leaves.

1283. Martínez, Manuela O. Bibliografía selectiva anotada de diversos aspectos de la bibliotecología jurídica, 1976-1981. San Juan, PR: Sociedad de Bibliotecarios de Puerto Rico, 1981. 18, [5] leaves. (Cuaderno bibliográfico, 3).

1284. Moriya de Freundorfer, Yoshiko, and Rosa Amarilla de Ferreira de Costa. Clasificación de temas relacionados al Paraguay. Asunción: Universidad Nacional de Asunción, Escuela de Bibliotecología, 1981. 63 leaves.

1285. Nocetti, Milton A. Bibliografía brasileira sobre automação de serviços bibliotecarios: 1968-1981. Brasília: Empresa Brasileira de Pesquisa Agropecuaria, Departamento de Informação e Documentação, 1982. 75 p.

1286. Stenzel, Norma, and Gloria Isabel Sattamini Ferreira. "Revisão seletiva da literatura sobre metodologia em biblioteconomia comparada." Revista de biblioteconomia de Brasília, Jan-Jun 1980, 8 (1), 60-64.

MANUSCRIPTS AND RARE BOOKS

1287. Andrade, Ana Isabel de Souza Leão; Carmen Lúcia de Souza Leao; and Tereza Cristina de Souza Dantas. Catálogo de correspondência de Joaquim Nabuco. Vols. 1-2 (1865-1889). Recife, Brazil: Ministerio da Educação e Cultura, Instituto Joaquim Nabuco de Pesquisas Sociais, 1978-80.

1288. Argüelles Espinosa, Luis Angel. "Catálogo de manuscritos sobre México en la Biblioteca Nacional de Cuba." Revista de la Biblioteca Nacional José Martí, Sept-Dic 1982, 24 (3), 181-202.

1289. Barnes, Catherine A., and David M. Szewczyk, editors. The Viceroyalty of New Spain and early independent Mexico: a guide to original manuscripts in the collections of the Rosenbach Museum and Library. Philadelphia: Rosenbach Museum and Library, 1980. 139 p.

1290. Borba de Moraes, Rubens Borba de. Bibliographia brasiliana: rare books about Brazil published from 1504 to 1900 and works by Brazilian authors of the colonial period. Rev. and enl. ed. Los Angeles; Rio de Janeiro: UCLA Latin American Center

Publications; Livraria Kosmos, 1983. 2 vols. (UCLA Latin American Center publications reference series, 10).

1291. Brazil. Ministério da Justiça. Biblioteca. Obras raras na Biblioteca do Ministério da Justiça. Neuma Pinheiro Salomão Gonçalves and Maria Cristina Pedrinha de Lima, editors. Brasília: A Biblioteca, 1981. 147 p.

1292. Brazil. Ministerio da Fazenda. Biblioteca. Obras raras existentes na BMF-RJ. Rio de Janeiro: Centro de Serv. Graf. do IBGE, 1984. 125 p. Note: "Elaboradas pelas bibliotecárias: Isaura Lima Maciel Soares, Regina Maria Silva Carríco, Vera Lucia Guilhon Costa."

1293. "Catálogo de manuscritos sobre o Rio de Janeiro existentes na Biblioteca Nacional." Brazil. Biblioteca Nacional. Anais, 1982, 102, 5-220.

1294. "Catálogo de manuscritos sobre o Rio Grande do Sul existentes na Biblioteca Nacional." Brazil. Biblioteca Nacional. Anais, 1979, 99, 3-142.

1295. Contreras, Remedios. Catálogo de la colección Manuscritos sobre América de la Real Academia de la Historia. Badajoz: Real Academia de la Historia, Institución 'Pedro Valencia,' 1978. 101 p.

1296. Glass, John B. The Boturini collection and the Mexican National Museum and General Archive, 1821-1826. Lincoln Center, MA: Conemex Associates, 1977. 25 p. (Contributions to the ethnohistory of Mexico, 5). Note: "The Indian museum of Lorenzo Boturini," Vol. 1, Chapter 12.

1297. Reyes García, Cayetano, et al. Documentos mexicanos. [México]: Archivo General de la Nación, 1982. 2 vols. (Serie guías y catálogos, 72).

1298. Rocha Nogueira, Arlinda; Heloisa Liberalli Bellotto; and Lucy Maffei Hunter. Inventário analítico dos manuscritos da Coleção Lamego. São Paulo: Instituto de Estudos Brasileiros da Universidade de São Paulo, 1983. 2 vols.

1299. Rosenberg Library. Manuscript sources in the Rosenberg Library: a selective guide. Jane A. Kenamore and Michael E. Wilson, editors. College Station: Published for the Rosenberg Library by the Texas A&M University Press, c1983. 174 p.

1300. A supplementary guide to selected Latin American manuscripts in the Lilly Library of Indiana University. Bloomington: Latin American Studies Program, Indiana University, 1980. 24 leaves. (Latin American studies working papers, 10). Note: Original guide published in 1974.

1301. Szewczyk, David M., compiler. A guide to the manuscript books of Fernando Pinzón, 1776 and 1778. Philadelphia: Rosenbach Museum and Library, 1981. 36 leaves.

1302. Universidad de Oriente (Santiago de Cuba). Catálogo de libros raros. Ricardo García, Ismaela, compiler. [Santiago de Cuba?]: Dirección de Información Científico Técnica, Universidad de Oriente, 1981. 130 p.

MASS MEDIA

1303. "Dossier bibliográfico: periodismo y nuevas tecnologías." Comunicación, Sept-Oct 1981. (33-34), 64-67.

1304. "Fichas bibliográficas [on the Costa Rican press]." Revista de ciencias sociales (Costa Rica), Oct 1983. (26), 87-99.

1305. García Saucedo, Jaime. "Investigación descriptiva documental de los trabajos de grado de la Facultad de Ciencias de la Comunicación Social en el área de la radiodifusión." Lotería, Nov-Dic 1984. (344-345), 53-59.

1306. Heeter, Carrie. Mass communication and Hispanic Americans: a bibliography. East Lansing, MI: Department of Communication, Michigan State University, 1980. 17 p. (CASA report, 2).

1307. John F. Kennedy Library, Guyana. Communications media: press, radio, journals: bibliography. Georgetown: The Library, 1981. 15 leaves.

1308. Lent, John A. Caribbean mass communications: a comprehensive bibliography. [Waltham, MA]: Crossroads Press, c[1981]. 152 p.

1309. "Para una evalucación del impacto de las nuevas tecnologías de comunicación en Venezuela." Comunicación, Sept-Oct 1981. (33-34), 79-83.

1310. Sonntag, Iliana L. "International communications and political parties: a review of recent literature." Latin American Research Review, 1984, 19(2), 182-192.

1311. Teja Angeles, Ileana de la. "Hemerografía chicana sobre medios de comunicación masiva." Revista mexicana de ciencias políticas y sociales, Abr-Sept 1981, 27, Nueva época (104-105), 257-266.

MICROFORMS

1312. Brazil. Biblioteca Nacional. Periódicos brasileiros en microformas: catálogo colectivo. Rio de Janeiro: A Biblioteca, 1981. 296 p. (Coleção Rodolfo Garcia, 18; Serie B-Catálogos e bibliografias).

1313. Caballero, César; Susana Delgado; and Bud Newman, compilers. Mexico and the Southwest: microfilm holdings of historical documents and rare books at the University of Texas at El Paso Library. El Paso: University of Texas at El Paso Libraries, Special Collections Dept., 1984. 33 p.

1314. Garner, Jane, compiler. Archives and manuscripts on microfilm in the Nettie Lee Benson Latin American Collection: a checklist. [Austin]: University of Texas at Austin, The General Libraries, 1980. 48 leaves. (Contributions to librarianship, 3).

1315. Hodgman, Suzanne. "Bibliography of microform projects 1981 [1981]." In: Latin American economic issues: information needs and sources: papers of the twenty-sixth annual meeting of the Seminar on the Acquisition of Latin American Library Materials, Tulane University, New Orleans, La., April 1-4, 1981. Madison: SALALM Secretariat, University of Wisconsin-Madison; Los Angeles: UCLA Latin American Center Publications, University of California, Los Angeles, c1984: 345-351.

1316. Hodgman, Suzanne. "Bibliography of microform projects 1982 [1982]." In: Public policy issues and Latin American library resources: papers of the twenty-seventh annual meeting of the Seminar on the Acquisition of Latin American Library Materials, Washington, D.C., March 2-5, 1982. Madison: SALALM Secretariat, University of Wisconsin-Madison; Los Angeles; UCLA Latin American Center Publications, University of California, Los Angeles, c1984: 209-217.

1317. Hodgman, Suzanne, and Anne Vandenburgh, compilers. Ibero-American studies: microforms in the University of Wisconsin, Madison Libraries. [Madison]: University of Wisconsin--Madison Libraries, 1982. 124 p. (Occasional papers of the University of Wisconsin--Madison Libraries, 4).

1318. Malish, Basil Microfilming Projects Newsletter. No. 25, 1983. Submitted for SALALM XXVIII San José, Costa Rica, June 30-July 4, 1983. Compiled at the Library of Congress, Washington, DC, 1983. 31 p.

1319. Malish, Basil. Microfilming Projects Newsletter. No. 26, 1984. Submitted for SALALM XXIX, Chapel Hill, N.C., June 2-7, 1984. Compiled at the Library of Congress, Washington, DC, 1984. 71 p.

1320. "Microfilming Projects Newsletter 1979. Committee on Acquisitions, SALALM." In: Windward, leeward and main: Caribbean studies and library resources: University of California, Los Angeles, California, June 17-22, 1979 (Seminar on the Acquisition of Latin American Library Materials: 24). Madison, WI: SALALM Secretariat, 1980: 111-121.

1321. "Microfilming Projects Newsletter. Index, Numbers 1-20. Prepared by Committee on Acqusitions, SALALM." In: Library resources on Latin America: new perspectives for the 1980's; University of New Mexico, Albuquerque, N.M., June 1-5, 1980 (Seminar on the Acquisition of Latin American Library Materials; 25). Madison: University of Wisconsin-Madison, SALALM Secretariat, 1981: 61-121.

1322. Spain. Centro Nacional de Microfilm. Publicaciones en microfilm/microficha. Madrid: Instituto Bibliográfico Hispánico, 1980. 25 p.

MINORITY GROUPS

1323. An annotated bibliography of materials on the Puerto Rican and Mexican cultures. Albany, NY: State Education Dept., Bureau of Bilingual Education, 1982. 115 p.

1324. Berry-Cabán, Cristóbal, et al. Hispanics in Wisconsin: a bibliography of resource materials. Hispanos en Wisconsin: una bibliografía de materiales de recurso. Madison: State Historical Society of Wisconsin, 1981. 258 p.

1325. Casas, Jesús Manuel. "The Mexican American in higher education: an example of subtle stereotyping." Personnel and Guidance Journal, Mar 1981, 59 (7), 473-476.

1326. Chavaría, Elvira. Mexican American studies. Austin: University of Texas, The General Libraries, 1981. 15 p. (Selected reference sources, 17).

1327. Chavaría, Elvira, editor. Chicano film guide. 2d ed. Austin: Mexican American Library Project, Benson Latin American Collection, General Libraries, University of Texas at Austin, 1983.

1328. Chicano periodical index: a cumulative index to selected Chicano periodicals between 1967 and 1978. Produced by the Committee for the Development of Subject Access to Chicano Literatures. Boston: G.K. Hall, 1981. 972 p.

1329. Chicano periodical index: a cumulative index to selected periodicals, 1979-1981, with selected serials indexed retrospectively. Compiled by the Chicano Periodical Indexing Project. Francisco García-Ayvens and Richard Chabrán, editors. Boston: G.K. Hall, 1983, 648 p.

1330. Derpich Gallo, Wilma. "Estudios históricos sobre los chinos en el Perú." Apuntes, 1983. (13), 97-101.

1331. Díaz, Marta, editor. Data clearinghouse: a project of the National Chicano Research Network. 2d ed. Ann Arbor, MI: The Network, c1982. 60 p.

1332. Donahue, Mary Kaye. Studies on the Mexican American voter as a political force: a bibliographic essay. Monticello, IL: Vance Bibliographies, [1984]. 19 p. (Public administration series--bibliography, P-1360).

1333. Elkin, Judith Laikin. Latin American Jewish studies. Cincinnati: American Jewish Archives, c1980. 53 p.

1334. Elkin, Judith Laikin, editor. Resources for Latin American Jewish studies; proceedings of the first research conference of the Latin American Jewish Studies Association, held on the Cincinnati campus of Hebrew Union College--Jewish Institute of Religion on October 30-November 1, 1982. Ann Arbor, MI: Latin American Jewish Studies Association, c1984. 60 p. (Publication [Latin American Jewish Studies Association], 1).

1335. García-Ayvens, Francisco, and Richard F. Chabrán, editors. Biblio-politica: Chicano perspectives on library service in the United States. Berkeley: Chicano Studies Library Publications Unit, University of California, 1984. 284 p. (Chicano studies library publications series, 10).

1336. García-Ayvens, Francisco; Darien Fisher; and Hilda Villarreal, compilers. Quien sabe?: a preliminary list of Chicano reference materials. Los Angeles: Bibliographic Research and Collection Development Unit, Chicano Studies Research Center, UCLA, 1981. 116 p. (Bibliographic and reference series, Chicano Studies Research Center, 11).

1337. Gray, Silvia Sims. A source book in child welfare: serving Chicano families and children. Ann Arbor: National Child Welfare Training Center, School of Social Work, University of Michigan, 1983. 136 p.

1338. Kim, Vivian C. List of publications on American Indians, Alaskan Natives, Asian-Pacific Americans, Blacks and Hispanics resulting from ADAMHA-supported research on minorities 1972-1981. Rockville, MD: U.S. Dept. of Health and Human Services, Public Health Service, Alcohol, Drug Abuse and Mental Health Administration, 1984. 95 p.

1339. Hennessy, Alistair. "The rise of the Hispanics: Chicanos." Journal of Latin American studies, May 1984, 16 (1), 171-194.

1340. Leon (Swadesh) Quintana, Frances, and Gilbert Benito Córdova. "The Chicano heritage." American anthropologist, Mar 1980, 82 (1), 100-107.

1341. Lotchin, Roger W., and David Weber. "The new Chicano Urban history: two perspectives." History Teacher, 1983, 16 (2), 219-247.

1342. MacCorkle, Lyn, compiler. Cubans in the United States: a bibliography for research in the social and behavioral sciences, 1960-1983. Westport, CT: Greenwood Press, c1984. 227 p. (Bibliographies and indexes in sociology, 1).

1343. McKinnon, Linda T. Mexican American education fact sheets and mini reviews. Las Cruces, NM: ERIC Clearinghouse on Rural Education and Small Schools, 1980. 18 p.

1344. Meier, Matt S., compiler. Bibliography of Mexican American history. Westport, CT: Greenwood Press, c1984. 500 p.

1345. Robinson, Barbara J., and Joy Cordell Robinson. The Mexican American: a critical guide to research aids. Greenwich, CT: JAI Press, c1980. 287 p. (Foundations in library and information science, 1).

1346. Rodríguez, Humberto. "Los inmigrantes chinos en el Perú." Apuntes, 1984. (14), 137-164.

1347. Rodríguez Pastor, Humberto. Chinos culíes. Bibliografía y fuentes, documentos y ensayos. Lima: Instituto de Apoyo Agrario, Instituto de Historia Rural Andina, 1984. 212 p. (Serie historia, 2).

1348. Roscoe, Lori A, et al. Interpersonal communication and Hispanic Americans: an annotated bibliography. [East Lansing]: Dept. of Communication, Michigan State University, [1981]. 94 leaves.

1349. Santos, María, and Toby Montes. A bibliography for counselors working with Chicano students. Oakland, CA: The National Hispanic Center and University, [1981 or 1982]. 20 leaves.

1350. Stark, Greg; Kathryn Guthrie; and Cheryl Selinsky. Annotated bibliography of recent research on Chicanos and Latinos in Minnesota. Minneapolis: Center for Urban and Regional Affairs, 1980. 56 p.

1351. Tatum, Charles. "An overview of Chicano library materials: abstract and bibliography." In: Library resources on Latin America: new perspectives for the 1980's: University of New Mexico, Albuquerque, N.M., June 1-5, 1980 (Seminar on the Acquisition of Latin American Library Materials; 25). Madison: University of Wisconsin-Madison, SALALM Secretariat, 1981: 293-299.

1352. Tigner, James L. "Japanese settlement in eastern Bolivia and Brazil." Journal of Interamerican Studies and World Affairs, Nov 1982, 24 (4), 496-517.

1353. Valdés, Dennis Nodin. Materials on the history of Latinos in Michigan and the Midwest: an annotated bibliography. Detroit: Wayne State University, College of Education, c1982. 34 p.

1354. Vásquez, James A. Factors that affect learning among minority youth: a partial bibliography. Los Angeles: Evaluation, Dissemination and Assessment Center, California State University, Los Angeles, 1981. 277 p.

1355. Wagoner, Shirley A. "Mexican-Americans in children's literature since 1970." Reading teacher, Dec 1982, 36 (3), 274-279.

1356. Weiss, David; Ileana de la Teja Angeles; and Luis Saînz Chávez. "Estados Unidos: cinco realidades contemporáneas; hemerografía." Revista mexicana de ciencias políticas y sociales, Abr-Sept 1981, 27, nueva época (104-105), 239-255.

1357. Woods, Richard D. "Mexican American reference books, 1979-1980." In: Library resources on Latin America: new perspectives for the 1980's; University of New Mexico, Albuquerque, N.M., June 1-5, 1980 (Seminar on the Acquisition of Latin American Library Materials; 25). Madison: University of Wisconsin-Madison, SALALM Secretariat, 1981: 313-316.

MUSIC

1358. African-Caribbean Institute of Jamaica. Music in the Caribbean, excluding Jamaica: a bibliography. Kingston, Jamaica: ACIJ, 1983. 9 p.

1359. Arellano, Jorge Eduardo. "Breve bibliografía de la música nicaragüense." Boletín nicaragüense de bibliografía y documentación, 1982. (49), 1-7.

1360. "Bolivian nineteenth-century developments." Inter-American Music Review, Spr-Sum 1983, 5 (2), 119-123.

1361. Bustillos Vallejo, Freddy. Bibliografía boliviana de etnomusicología. La Paz: Instituto Nacional de Antropología, Departamento de Etnomusicología y Folklore, 1982. 21 p.

1362. "Caribbean music history. A selective annotated bibliography with musical supplement." Inter-American music review, 1981, 4(1), 1-112.

1363. Cobo, Eugenio. "Bibliografía flamenca." Cuadernos hispanoamericanos, Aug 1984. (410), 184-188.

1364. De Lerma, Dominique-René. Bibliography of Black music. Westport, CT: Greenwood Press, 1981-1984. 4 vols.

1365. Doyle, John Godfrey. Louis Moreau Gottschalk, 1829-1869: a bibliographical study and catalog of works. Detroit: Published for the College Music Society by Information Coordinators, 1982, c1983. 386 p.

1366. Eisenhood, Elizabeth D. Brazilian materials in the archive of folk song. Washington, DC: Library of Congress, 1980. 3 p.

1367. Estupiñan, Argentina Ch. de. "La música popular frente a la mujer." Cultura (Ecuador), Sept-Dic 1981, 4 (11), 357-369.

1368. "Haydn anniversary literature in Spanish." Inter-American music review, 1982, 4 (2), 77-78.

1369. Lapique Becali, Zoila. Música colonial cubana en las publicaciones periódicas (1812-1902). Vol. 1. La Habana: Editorial Letras Cubanas, 1979-.

1370. "Latin America in 'Ilustración musical hispano-americana.'" Inter-American music review, 1981, 3 (2), 151-158.

1371. Lotis, Howard. Latin American music materials available at the University of Pittsburgh and at Carnegie Library of Pittsburgh. Pittsburgh: University of Pittsburgh, Center for Latin American Studies (distributor), 1981. 145 p.

1372. Peñín, José. "Los estudios musicológicos en Venezuela." Revista musical de Venezuela, Sept-Dic 1980, 1 (2), 75-87.

1373. Thompson, Annie Figueroa. Puerto Rican newspapers and journals of the Spanish colonial period as source materials for musicological research; an analysis of their musical content. 501 p. Note: Dissertation. Ph.D. University of Florida State, 1980.

1374. White, Garth. The development of Jamaican popular music with special reference to the music of Bob Marley: a bibliography. Kingston: African-Caribbean Institute of Jamaica, 1983. 49 p.

PERIODICALS

GENERAL

1375. Boland, Roy, and Alun Kenwood, compilers. A select bibliography of serials relating to Hispanic language, literature, and civilization held by libraries in Australia and New Zealand. [Auckland, N.Z.]: Auckland University Library, 1984. 64 p.

1376. Centro Internacional de Agricultura Tropical. Unidad de Servicios de Documentación. Catálogo de publicaciones periódicas: Unidad de Servicios de Documentación del CIAT. Cali, Colombia: El Centro, 1980. 129 p.

1377. Covington, Paula Anne. Indexed journals; a selection of Latin American serials. Submitted for SALALM XXVI, Tulane University, April 1-4, 1981. Madison: SALALM Secretariat, Memorial Library, University of Wisconsin, 1981. 21 p.

1378. Covington, Paula Hattox. Indexed journals: a guide to Latin American serials. Madison, WI: SALALM Secretariat, 1983. 458 p. (SALALM Bibliography series, 8).

1379. Guevara de Bejarano, Martha, and Francisco A. Salazar Alonso. Catálogo de publicaciones periódicas BAC (Biblioteca Agropecuaria de Colombia). 3d ed. Bogotá: Instituto Colombiano Agropecuario, Subgerencia de Desarrollo Rural, División de Comunicación, Biblioteca Agropecuaria de Colombia, 1981. 424 p.

1380. Revistas. An annotated bibliography of Spanish-language periodicals for public libraries. Compiled by Bibliotecas para la Gente, Periodical Committee. Berkeley: Chicano Studies Library Publications Unit, University of California, 1983. 31 leaves. (Chicano Studies Library Publications Series, 9).

1381. Ruiz-Fornells, Enrique. "Bibliografía de revistas y

publicaciones hispánicas en los Estados Unidos: 1979." Cuadernos hispanoamericanos, Oct-Dic 1981. (376-378), 953-969.

1382. Sonntag, Iliana L. "Sampling of new periodicals." SALALM Newsletter, Dec 1980, 8 (2), 4-6.

1383. Sonntag, Iliana L. "Selected and annotated list of Chicano periodicals." SALALM Newsletter, Jun 1980, 7 (4), 6-8.

1384. University of California, Berkeley. Library. Hispanic periodical publications received currently by the University of California libraries at Berkeley. Berkeley: University of California, 1983. 4 vols.

1385. Williams, Gayle. "New periodicals: new titles; title changes; ceased titles." SALALM Newsletter, Mar 1984, 11 (3), 11-12.

1386. Williams, Gayle. "New titles; title changes." SALALM Newsletter, Dec 1984, 12 (2), 11-12.

ARGENTINA

1387. Ardissone, Elena. Bibliografía de índices de publicaciones periódicas argentinas. Buenos Aires: Universidad de Buenos Aires, Instituto Bibliotecológico, 1984, 52 p. (Publicación, 64).

1388. Carrera de Mangiola, Silvia, compiler. Catálogo hemerográfico: Estado Mayor Conjunto; Biblioteca y Centro de Documentación. [Argentina]: La Biblioteca, 1983. 49 p. Note: Anexo al catálogo hemerográfico 1983.

BOLIVIA

1389. Catálogo colectivo de publicaciones periódicas [existentes en las unidades de información de Bolivia]. La Paz: Ministerio de Planeamiento y Coordinación, Sistema y Fondo Nacional de Información para el Desarrollo, 1981. 322 p.

BRAZIL

1390. Arujo, Marta Maria Alencar. Catalogo coletivo de periodicos EMBRAPA. Rio de Janeiro: Empresa Brasileira de Pesquisa Agropecuaria, 1982. 435 p.

1391. Biblioteca Pública do Estado (Santa Catarina, Brazil). Catálogo de jornais catarinenses, 1850-1980. Florianápolis:

Secretaria de Cultura, Esporte e Turismo, Fundação Catarinense de Cultura, 1980. 120 p.

1392. Fernandes, Antônia Régia Mendonça, and Hilda de Sena Corrêa Wiederhecker. Catálogo coletivo dos periódicos brasileiros relacionados com educação. Brasília: Conselho de Reitores das Universidades Brasileiras, 1982. 483 p.

1393. Fundaçao Instituto Brasileiro de Geografia e Estatística. Catálogo de publicações periódicas do IBGE. Rio de Janeiro: Instituto Brasileiro de Geografia e Estatística, 1982. 99 p.

1394. Periódicos brasileiros em microformas: catálogo coletivo. Rio de Janeiro: Biblioteca Nacional, 1981. 296 p.

1395. Universidade Federal de Goiás. Biblioteca Central. Seção de Periódicos. Catálogo de periódicos. Goiânia: A Seção, 1980. 217, [50] leaves.

CARIBBEAN AREA

1396. Annotated bibliography of the present available Caribbean periodicals in the Public Library of Curação, Netherlands Antilles. Curação: The Library, 1981. 12 leaves.

CHILE

1397. Massone, Juan Antonio. "Indice de diez revistas literarias fugaces." Revista chilena de literatura, Abr 1983. (21), 123-135.

COLOMBIA

1398. Alvarez, Jesús, and María Teresa Uribe de H. Indice de prensa colombiana, 1840-1890: periódicos existentes en la Biblioteca Central. Medellín: Sección de Documentación, Departamento de Bibliotecas, Universidad de Antioquia, 1984. 240 p, [6] leaves of plates.

1399. Zapata Cuéncar, Heriberto. Antioquia, periódicos de provincia. Medellín, Colombia: Editorial Lealon, 1981. 135 p.

COSTA RICA

1400. Costa Rica. Oficina de Planificacón Nacional y Política Económica. Centro de Documentación. Catálogo de publicaciones periódicas existentes en el CEDOP. San José: CEDOP, [1980]. 155 leaves.

1401. Inter-American Center for Documentation and Agriculture Information. Biblioteca y Terminal de Servicios. Catálogo colectivo de publicaciones periódicas de las bibliotecas del CIDIA. Turrialba, Costa Rica: Centro Interamericano de Documentación e Información Agrícola, Biblioteca y Terminal de Servicios, 1981. 520 p. (Documentación e información agrícola, 96).

1402. López M. de Badilla, María del Rocío. Catálogo colectivo de publicaciones existentes en Costa Rica. San José: Consejo Nacional de Investigaciones Científicas y Tecnológicas, 1982. 750 p.

CUBA

1403. Lozano, Eduardo. Cuban periodicals in the University of Pittsburgh libraries. 3d ed. Pittsburgh: University of Pittsburgh Libraries, 1981. 87 p.

1404. Revistas y periódicas cubanos. Cuban reviews and newspapers. La Habana: Ediciones Cubanas, c1980. 86 p.

1405. Tamayo Rodríguez, Carlos. "Notas para el estudio de las publicaciones periódicas en Santiago de Cuba (1900-1930)." Santiago revista de la Universidad de Oriente, Mar 1983, 49, 125-159.

1406. Valdés, Nelson P. "A bibliography of Cuban periodicals related to women." Cuban studies, Jul 1982, 12 (2), 73-80.

DOMINICAN REPUBLIC

1407. Centro de Informacion Científica y Tecnológica, compiler. Catálogo colectivo de publicaciones periódicas de la República Dominicana. [Santo Domingo]: INDOTEC, CENICIT, [1981]. 252 p.

1408. Martínez Paulino, Marcos Antonio. Publicaciones periódicas dominicanas desde la colonia. 2a corr y aum ed. San Pedro de Macoris: Universidad Central del Este, 1984. 287 p. (UCE Publicaciones v. 54. Serie bibliográfica, 1).

1409. "Un siglo de cultura dominicana; tabla cronológica." Eme Eme; estudios dominicanos, Ene-Feb 1981, 9 (52), 85-116.

GUYANA

1410. Union list of scientific and technical periodicals held in libraries in Guyana. Edited for the Guyana Library Association

Bibliographic Subcommittee. Lutishoor Salisbury, editor. Georgetown: The Association, 1982. 128 p.

MEXICO

1411. Catálogo general de publicaciones periódicas mexicanas, 1983-1984. México: Distribuidora internacional de revistas, S.A. (DIRSA), 1984. 86 p. Note: Publicación anual. Primera edición 1983-84.

1412. "Comunicación alternativa: cuatro revistas feministas, parte I." Fem, Ag-Sept 1983, 8 (29), 61-62.

1413. "Comunicación alternativa: cuatro revistas feministas, parte II." Fem, Oct-Nov 1983, 8 (30), 63-64.

1414. Coronado Rodríguez, José. Catálogo colectivo de publicaciones periódicas y seriadas de la bibliotecas del CIANO (Centro de Investigaciones Agrícolas del Noroeste). Ciudad Obregon, México: Secretaría de Agricultura y Recursos Hidraúlicos, Instituto Nacional de Investigaciones Agrícolas del Noroeste, 1980. 91 p. (Publicación especial CIANO, 34).

1415. Khorramzadeh, Heshmatallah, compiler. Directorio de publicaciones periódicas mexicanas, 1981. Guanajuato: Departamento de Investigaciones Bibliotecológicas, Dirección General de Bibliotecas, Universidad de Guanajuato, c1982. 200 p.

1416. Mace, Carroll Edward. "Libraries of Mérida, Yucatán and a checklist of nineteenth-century serials in the 'Hemeroteca José María Pino Suárez.'" The Americas, Oct 1981, 38 (2), 249-267.

1417. McGowan, Gerald L. Lista de fichas hemerográficas. México: Dirección de Difusión y Publicaciones, Archivo General de la Nación, 1981. 150 p. (Serie guías y catálogos, 63).

1418. Montejano y Aguiñaga, Rafael. Nueva hemerografía potosina, 1828-1978. México: Universidad Nacional Autónoma de México, 1982. 373 p. (Serie Hemerografías: Biblioteca de historia potosina. Serie documentos, 6).

1419. Universidad Nacional Autónoma de México. Instituto de Investigaciones Sociales. Lista de revistas de la Biblioteca del Instituto de Investigaciones Sociales. México: UNAM, Instituto de Investigaciones Sociales, 1981. 64 p.

NICARAGUA

1420. Nicaragua. Centro de Investigaciones y Estudios de la Reforma Agraria. Biblioteca. Catálogo de publicaciones periódicas, Biblioteca CIERA. Managua: Biblioteca CIERA, 1982. 18 p.

PERU

1421. Catálogo colectivo de publicaciones periódicas. Lima: Centro Nacional de Información y Documentación Científica y Tecnológica, Consejo Nacional de Ciencia y Tecnología, 1983. 499 p.

URUGUAY

1422. Catálogo colectivo de publicaciones periódicas existentes en las bibliotecas universitarias del Uruguay: actualización 1969-1975. Universidad de la República, Escuela Universitaria de Bibliotecología y Ciencias Afines Ing. Federico E. Capurro. v. 1-3. Montevideo: La Escuela, 1977-. Note: v. 1-3 (A-N).

VENEZUELA

1423. Fernández, David W. "Los periódicos de Guarenas." Boletín de la Academia Nacional de la Historia (Venezuela), Abr-Jun 1983, 66 (262), 419-435.

1424. Nieschulz de Stockhausen, Elke. "Periodismo y política en Venezuela: cincuenta años de historia." Montalbán, 1980, 10, 715-911.

1425. Paz, Miguel Angel. Periódicos y revistas del estado Falcón. [n.p.]: [Asamblea Legislativa del Estado Falcón, Comisión de Cultura], [1982 or 1983]. 200 p.

1426. Universidad de Oriente (Cumaná, Venezuela). Dirección de Bibliotecas. Catálogo colectivo de publicaciones en serie del sistema bibliotecario de la UDO hasta 1979. Cumaná: UDODB, 1982. 250 leaves. (Publicación UDODB, 5).

VIRGIN ISLANDS

1427. Gregg, Kathleen, editor. Virgin Island newspapers, 1770-1983. Charlotte Amalie, St. Thomas, USVI: Dept. of Conservation & Cultural Affairs, Bureau of Libraries, Museums & Archaeological Services, 1984.

PHILOSOPHY

1428. Albán, María Elena. "Bibliografía de filosofía ecuatoriana." Revista de historia de las ideas, 1983. (4, 2a época), 263-275.

1429. Astorquiza Pizarro, Fernando. Bio-bibliografía de la filosofía en Chile desde el siglo XVI hasta 1980. Santiago, Chile; Barcelona: Empresa Industrial Gráfica, 1982. 295 p.

1430. Becco, Horacio Jorge. Contribución para una bibliografía de las ideas latinoamericanas. Paris: UNESCO, 1981. 230 P.

1431. "Catálogo de libros de filosofía en el Ecuador y de otros que interesan para el estudio de dicha ciencia." Cultura (Ecuador), May-Ag 1979, 2 (4), 389-415.

1432. Díaz Díaz, Gonzalo, and Ceferino Santos Escudero. Bibliografía filosófica hispánica (1901-1970). Madrid: Consejo Superior de Investigaciones Científicas, Instituto de Filosofía "Luis Vives," Departamento de Filosofía Española, 1982. 1371 p.

1433. Lertora Mendoza, Celia Ana, and Matilde Isabel García Losada. Bibliografía filosófica argentina (1900-1975). Buenos Aires: Fundación para la Educación, la Ciencia y la Cultura, 1983. 359 p.

1434. Martí, Oscar R. "Bibliography [on Gabino Barreda]." Aztlán, Fall 1983, 14 (2), 405-417.

1435. Moreno, M.A. "Fichero de revistas latinoamericanas: fichero de teología, fichero de filosofía." Stromata, Jul-Dic 1981, 37 (3-4), 339-382.

1436. Paím, Antonio. "Bibliografia filosófica brasileira 1982." Revista brasileira de filosofia, Abr-Jun 1983, 33 (130), 209-215. Note: Appears annually as a regular feature.

POLITICAL SCIENCE

GENERAL

1437. Bibliografía geopolítica, 1879-1980. [Montevideo, Uruguay]: Asociación Sudamericana de Estudios Geopolíticos e Internacionales, [1980]. 31 p. (Geosur, 12).

1438. Bibliografia sobre política. Buenos Aires: Moreno, 1983, c1983. 27 p.

1439. "Conflicto político e información en Latinoamérica y el Caribe." Comunicación (Caracas), Dic 1979-Ene 1980. (25-26), 118-131.

1440. Franco, Rolando. "Estados burocráticos-autoritarios y democracia." Pensamiento iberoamericano; revista de economía política, Ene-Jun 1982. (1), 185-192.

1441. Latin American politics: a historical bibliography. Santa Barbara, CA: ABC-Clio Information Services, 1984. 290 p.

1442. Portantiero, Juan Carlos. "Discusiones en torno a democracia y socialismo." Pensamiento iberoamericano; revista de economía política, Jul-Dic 1982. (2), 240-245.

1443. Stemplowski, Ryszard. "Latin America, the United States and diplomacy; new books, old problems." Latin American Research Review, 1980, 14 (1), 206-210.

1444. Vanden, Harry E. Latin American marxism: a bibliography. New York: Garland, 1985. 300 p.

ARGENTINA

1445. Bilsky, Edgardo. Contribution à l'histoire du mouvement ouvrier et social argentin: bibliographie et sources documentaires de la région parisienne. Nanterre; Toulouse: Bibliothèque de documentation internationale contemporaine; GRECO 25, Université de Toulouse-LeMirail, 1983. 229 p.

1446. Ferrari, Gustavo. "La política exterior argentina a través de la bibliografía general." Revista interamericana de bibliografía, 1980, 30 (2), 133-147.

BRAZIL

1447. Bibliografia sobre a campanha civilista. Rio de Janeiro: Fundação Casa de Rui Barbosa, 1981, 117 p. (Bibliografias, 1).

1448. Chilcote, Ronald H. Brazil and its radical left: an annotated bibliography on the communist movement and the rise of Marxism, 1922-1972. Millwood, NY: Kraus International Publications, c1980. 455 p.

1449. Mendes, Evelyse Maria Freire. Bibliografia do pensamento político republicano (1870-1970). Vol. 1. Brasília: Editôra Universidade de Brasília, 1981. 210 p.

CENTRAL AMERICA

1450. Ruhl, J. Mark. "Understanding Central American politics." Latin American Research Review, 1984, 19 (2), 143-152.

1451. Torre-Rivas, Edelberto. "Sobre la crisis en Centroamérica." Pensamiento iberoamericano; revista de economía política, Jul-Dic 1982. (2), 253-260.

CHILE

1452. Nef, Jorge. "The revolution that never was: perspectives on democracy, socialism and reaction in Chile." Latin American Research Review, 1983, 18 (1), 228-245.

COSTA RICA

1453. Gudmundson, Lowell. "Costa Rica and the 1948 Revolution: rethinking the social democratic paradigm." Latin American Research Review, 1984, 19 (1), 235-242.

CUBA

1454. LeoGrande, William M. "Two decades of socialism in Cuba." Latin American Research Review, 1981, 16 (1), 187-206.

1455. Pérez López, Jorge F. "Two decades of Cuban socialism: the economic context." Latin American Research Review, 1983, 18 (3), 227-242.

1456.-1457. Pérez Stable, Marifeli. "Towards a Marxist school of Cuban studies." Latin American Research Review, 1980, 15 (2), 248-256.

ECUADOR

1458. Fitch, J. Samuel. "Class structure, populism and the armed forces in contemporary Ecuador." Latin American Research Review, 1984, 19 (1), 270-274.

EL SALVADOR

1459. Tosstorff, Reiner. "Neuerscheinungen zum Bürgerkrieg in El Salvador." Iberoamericana, 1982, 6 (16-17), 81-85.

HONDURAS

1460. Oqueli, Ramón. "Bibliografía sociopolítica de Honduras." Boletín de la Academia Hondureña de la Lengua, Ene 1979, 22, 237-321.

1461. Oqueli, Ramón. Bibliografía sociopolítica de Honduras. Tegucigalpa: Editorial Universitaria, 1981. 106 p. (Colección cuadernos universitarios, 15).

MEXICO

1462. Grindle, Merilee. "Black gold in Mexico and in U.S.-Mexican relations." Latin American Research Review, 1983, 18 (2), 230-239.

1463. Köppen, Elke. "Bibliografía electoral." Nueva antropología, Oct 1984, 7 (25), 183-197.

PERU

1464. Becker, David G. "Recent political development in Peru: dependency or postdependency?" Latin American Research Review, 1984, 19 (2), 225-242.

1465. Portocarrero, Felipe, and Pedro Jibaja. "Estado, régimen político y democracia en el Perú." Pensamiento iberoamericano; revista de economía política, Jul-Dic 1983. (4), 277-281.

PUERTO RICO

1466. Miranda, Altagracia. El status político de Puerto Rico, 1952-1983: bibliografía de libros y artículos de revistas que se encuentran en la Biblioteca de Derecho de la Universidad de Puerto Rico. [San Juan?]: Biblioteca de Derecho, Universidad de Puerto Rico, 1984. 15 p.

UNITED STATES

1467. Nazario, Olga. "Las elecciones presidenciales norteamericanas de 1980: imagen brasileña de 'Veja.'" Los ensayistas: boletín informativo, Mar 1982. (12-13), 215-218.

VENEZUELA

1468. Alexander, Robert J. "Democracy in Venezuela." Latin American Research Review, 1980, 15 (2), 241-247.

PUBLISHERS

1469. Academia Nacional de la Historia, Caracas. Departamento de Publicaciones. Catálogo. 3 agosto 1958-3 agosto 1983. Caracas: La Academia, 1983, 524 p.

1470. "Algunas publicaciones de la CEPAL. Some CEPAL publications." CEPAL review, 1983, 19-21. Note: Appears as a regular feature.

1471. Bruna V., Alicia. Publicaciones del INIA sobre hortalizas 1964-1980. Santiago de Chile: Instituto de Investigaciones Agropecuarias, Estación Experimental La Platina, 1980. 20 p.

1472. Centro de Investigaciones y Estudios Superiores en Antropología Social. Catálogo de publicaciones 1983. México: El Centro, 1983, 32 p.

1473. Centro de Publicaciones de Organismos Internacionales. Publicaciones editadas en español, 1980-1981. México: El Centro, 1981. 3 vols.

1474. Centro Latinoamericano de Demografía. Catálogo de publicaciones, 1980-1981. Santiago de Chile, 1980. 66 p.

1475. Fundación Mariano Ospina Pérez, Bogotá. Catálogo de publicaciones. [Bogotá]: [Edit. Dintel], [1981]. 12 p.

1476. García Blasquez, Raúl, and César Ramón Cordova. Bibliografía de los estudios y publicaciones del Instituto Indigenista Peruano, 1961-1969. Lima: Instituto Indigenista Peruano, 1982. 126 p. (Serie bibliográfica, 1).

1477. Instituto de Desenvolvimento de Pernambuco. Catálogo de publicações do CONDEPE, 1952-1982. Secretaria de Planejamento, Instituto de Desenvolvimento de Pernambuco-CONDEPE. Recife, Brasil: CONDEPE, 1982. 65 leaves.

1478. Leal, Maria Antonieta Oliveira de Barros. Catálogo de publicações da SUDENE 1970-1980. Recife: Ministério do Interior, Superintendência do Desenvolvimento do Nordeste, Coordenação de Informática, 1983. 132 p.

1479. México. Secretaría de Programación y Presupuesto. Coordinación General de Estadística, Geografía e Informática. Catálogo de publicaciones de la Coordinación General de los Servicios Nacionales de Estadística, Geografía e Informática. 3a ed. México: La Secretaría, 1982. 396 p.

1480. Mexico. Secretaría de Educación Pública. Indice de publicaciones hasta 1982. México: SEP, 1982. 100 leaves.

1481. "Obras publicadas por el Banco de la República, 1923-1982." Boletín cultural y bibliográfico, 1983, 20 (1), 195-216.

1482. Organization of American States. Catalog of publications. Catálogo de publicaciones. Washington, DC: [OAS], 1980. 44 p.

1483. Programa Regional del Empleo para América Latina y el Caribe. Lista de publicaciones PREALC. Santiago de Chile: PREALC, 1982. 22 p.

1484. "Publications of the OAS and its specialized organizations." Revista interamericana de bibliografía, 1981, 31 (1), 130.

1485. Sabelli de Louzao, Martha. Catálogo de publicaciones, CIESU, 1975-1981. Montevideo: Biblioteca CIESU, Centro de Informaciones Y Estudios del Uruguay, 1982. 33 p. (Serie bibliográfica, 4).

1486. Zapata, Megala de. Catálogo de publicaciones, 1964-1981: Corporación de los Andes. Mérida, Venezuela: Corporación de los Andes, [1981]. 118 leaves.

RELIGION

1487. Alves, Ephraim Ferreira. "Teologia da libertação: pequena bibliografia." Vozes (Brazil), Maio 1982, 76 (4), 64-66.

1488. Bamat, Thomas. "The Catholic church and Latin American politics." Latin American Research Review, 1983, 18 (3), 219-226.

1489. Bibliografia sobre religiosidade popular. São Paulo: Edições

Paulinas, 1981. 101 p. (Coleção estudos da Conferência Nacional dos Bispos do Brasil, 27).

1490. Bisio, Carlos A. Contribución bibliográfica para el estudio de las Iglesias Cristianas Evangélicas en Argentina. Buenos Aires: Instituto Bibliográfico "Antonio Zinny," 1982. 120 p.

1491. Callender, Jean A. The church in the Caribbean: a select bibliography. Cave Hill, Barbados: Main Library, University of the West Indies, 1981. 24 p.

1492. Canedo, Lino Gómez. Archivos franciscanos de México. 2a ed. México: Universidad Nacional Autónoma de México, Instituto de Estudios y Documentos Históricos, 1982, c1981. 208 p. (Serie guías, 3).

1493. Dahlin, Terry, and Reed Nelson. "Caribbean religion: a survey and bibliography." In: Windward, leeward and main: Caribbean studies and library resources: University of California, Los Angeles, California, June 17-22, 1979 (Seminar on the Acquisition of Latin American Library Materials: 24). Madison, WI: SALALM Secretariat, 1980: 339-352.

1494. González Martínez, José Luis, and Teresa María van Ronzelen. Religiosidad popular en el Perú: bibliografía, antropología, historia, sociología y pastoral. Lima: Centro de Estudios y Publicaciones (CEP), 1983. 375 p.

1495. Kennedy Troya, Alexandra. Catálogo del Archivo General de la Orden Franciscana del Ecuador. Quito: Banco Central del Ecuador, Instituto Nacional de Patrimonio Cultural, c1980. 330 p. (Colección archivos y bibliotecas, 1).

1496. Mansutti Rodríguez, Alejandro. Catálogo del Ramo Bulas y Santa Cruzada. México: Archivo General de la Nación, [1979]. 55 leaves. (Serie guías y catálogos, 41).

1497. Meireles, Mário M. "Catálogo dos bispos e arcebispos de São Luis do Maranhão." Revista do Instituto Histórico e Geográfico Brasileiro, Out-Dez 1982. (337), 67-78.

1498. Mexico. Archivo General de la Nación. Catálogo del Ramo de congregaciones. México: Archivo General de la Nación, 1980. 63 leaves. (Serie guías y catálogos, 43). Note: Elaborado por Delia Pezzat Arzave.

1499. Mexico. Archivo General de la Nación. Catálogo del Ramo misiones. México: Archivo General de la Nación, 1981. 198 leaves. (Serie guías y catálogos, 16). Note: Elaborado por Enrique González Ponce.

1500. Mexico. Archivo General de la Nación. Obras pías, derechos parroquiales, cultos religiosos e iglesias. México: Dirección de Difusión y Publicaciones del Archivo General de la Nación, [1980]. 41 leaves. (Serie guías y catálogos, 57).

1501. Miceli, Sergio. Fontes para o estudo da elite eclesiástica brasileira. São Paulo: Instituto de Estudos Econômicos, Sociais e Políticos de São Paulo, 1983. 29 leaves. (Textos/ IDESP, 3).

1502. Millones, Luis. "Las religiones nativas del Perú: recuento y evaluación de su estudio." Bulletin de l'Institut Français d'Etudes Andines, 1979, 8 (1), 35-48.

1503. Paolucci, Gabriella. Bibliografia su religioni e società nel Centro America (1976-1981). Pisa: Giardini, [1982]. 121 p.

1504. Reich, Peter L. "Algunos archivos para el estudio de la historia eclesiástica mexicana en el siglo XX." Historia mexicana, Jul-Sept 1980, 30:1(117), 126-133.

1505. Storni, Hugo. Catálogo de los Jesuitas de la provincia del Paraguay (Cuenca del Plata), 1585-1768. Roma: Institutum Historicum S.I., 1980. 350 p. (Subsidia ad historiam S.I., 9).

SOCIAL SCIENCES

GENERAL

1506. Anrup, Roland. "Feminist research in Latin America." Ibero-Americana, 1984, 13 (2), 77-83.

1507. Arnold, Bill R., and Susan B. Hancock. The Hispanic handicapped: a bibliographic listing of relevant attitudinal research. [Austin, TX, 1982]. 21 p. Note: Distributed at the joint Texas Rehabilitation Association--Southwest Region, National Rehabilitation Association annual conference.

1508. Arretx, Carmen; Rolando Mellafe; and Jorge L. Somoza. Demografía histórica en América Latina: fuentes y métodos. San José, C.R.: Centro Latinoamericano de Demografía, c1983. 265 p. (Serie E. Centro Latinoamericano de Demografía, 1002).

1509. Arriaga Weiss, David, and Guadalupe Ferrer Andrade. "Grupos étnicos y cuestion racional (hemerografía)." Revista mexicana de ciencias políticas y sociales, Ene-Mar 1981, 27 (103), 223-260.

1510. Asdrúbal Silva, Hernán, et al. Bibliografía sobre el impacto del proceso inmigratorio masivo en el Cono Sur de América: Argentina, Brasil, Chile, Uruguay. México: Instituto Panamericano de Geografía e Historia, 1984. 207 p. (Serie inmigración, 1).

1511. Bailey, Juan P., and Freya Headlam, compilers. Intercontinental migration to Latin America: a select bibliography. London: Institute of Latin American Studies, University of London, 1980. 62 p.

1512. Becerra, Rosina M. and David Shaw. The Hispanic elderly: a research reference guide. Lanham, MD: University Press of America, 1984, c1983. 144 p.

1513. Bloch, Thomas. "Some recent Latin American documents." Government publications review, 1980, 7A (4), 337-340.

1514. Brem, Walter B., Jr. "Energy resources of Latin America [1981]." In: Latin American economic issues: papers of the twenty-sixth annual meeting of the Seminar on the Acquisition of Latin American Library Materials, Tulane University, New Orleans, La. April 1-4, 1981. Madison: SALALM Secretariat, University of Wisconsin-Madison; Los Angeles: UCLA Latin American Center Publications, University of California, Los Angeles, c1984: 121-128.

1515. Canak, William L. "Structural transformation in rural social relations." Latin American Research Review, 1982, 17 (1), 223-234.

1516.-1517. Collado Ardón, Rolando; Galia Castro Campillo; and Elías Cáceres Castro. Salud mental y enfermedad mental en América Latina: bibliografía sociológica. México: Universidad Nacional Autónoma de México, 1982. 101 p.

1518. Computer-readable data for use in Latin American studies research. [Princeton, NJ: Princeton University Computer Center, 1981]. [87] p.

1519. Corvalán-Vásquez, Oscar. Youth employment and training in developing countries: an annotated bibliography. Geneva: International Labour Office, 1984. 172 p.

1520. Dahlin, Therrin C.; Gary P. Gillum; and Mark L. Grover. The Catholic left in Latin America: a comprehensive bibliography. Boston: G.K. Hall, c1981. 410 p.

1521. De Irizarry, Florita Z. Louie. U.S. women of Spanish origin in the employment sector: a selected bibliography. Monticello, IL: Vance Bibliographies, 1982. 12 p.

1522. Delgado, Melvin. "Hispanic cultural values: implications for groups." Small group behavior, Feb 1981, 12 (1), 69-80.

1523. Delorme, Robert. Latin America, 1979-1983: a social science bibliography. Santa Barbara, CA: ABC-Clio Information Services, c1984. 225 p.

1524. Documentos producidos por el Fondo Simón Bolívar. San José, C.R.: IICA, Centro Interamericano de Documentación e Información Agrícola, 1980. 24 leaves. (Documentación e información agrícola, 84).

1525. Drake, Paul W. "Population in South America." Latin American Research Review, 1982, 17 (1), 190-199.

1526. Drogadicción, conducta desviada, agresión y violencia. Lista de libros en venta en español y portugués. Mexicali, México: Asociación Latinoamericana de Ecodesarrollo, 1981. 72 p.

1527. Feijoó, María del Carmen. La mujer, el desarrollo y las tendencias de población en América Latina: bibliografía comentada. Buenos Aires: Centro de Estudios de Estado y Sociedad, 1980. 59 p. (Estudios CEDES, v. 3, no. 1).

1528. Flores Colombino, Andrés. Catálogo latinoamericano de publicaciones sexológicas. Vol. 1. [Montevideo]: Federación Latinoamericana de Sociedades de Sexología y Educación Sexual, [1982-].

1529. Fundación Ecuatoriana de Estudios Sociales. Pensamiento humanista y comunitario; bibliografía básica. Quito: La Paz, 1979. 24 p.

1530. González, Nelly S. "A meta-bibliography of publications on land tenure, agrarian reform and rural migration [1981]." In: Latin American economic issues: information needs and sources: papers of the twenty-sixth annual meeting of the Seminar on the Acquisition of Latin American Library Materials, Tulane University, New Orleans, La., April 1-4, 1981. Madison: SALALM Secretariat, University of Wisconsin-Madison; Los Angeles: UCLA Latin American Center Publications, University of California, Los Angeles, c1984: 78-105.

1531. Goyer, Doreen S., and Elaine Domschke. The handbook of national population censuses: Latin America and the Caribbean, North America and Oceania. Westport, CT: Greenwood Press, 1983. 711 p.

1532. Graciarena, Jorge. "Crisis y cambio histórico." Pensamiento iberoamericano; revista de economía política, Ene-Jun 1983. (3), 192-195.

1533. Greenfield, Richard. "The human rights literature of Latin America." Human rights quarterly, May 1982, 4 (2), 275-298.

1534. "Guía bibliográfica: conflicto político e información en Latinoamericana y el Caribe." Comunicación (Venezuela), Ene 1980. (25-26), 118-131.

1535. Guide to Latin American and West Indian census material: a bibliography and union list. No. 2: Chile. Compiled by Carole Travis. London: SCONUL Advisory Committee on Latin American Materials, 1982. 32 p.

1536. Haines, David W. and Augustine Ha T. Vinh. Refugee settlement in the United States: an annotated bibliography on the adjustment of Cuban, Soviet and the Southeast Asian refugees. Washington, DC: Office of Refugee Resettlement, Department of Health and Human Services, 1981. 104 p.

1537. Human rights in Latin America, 1954-1980: a selective annotated bibliography compiled and edited by the Hispanic Division. Washington, DC: Library of Congress, 1983. 257 p. Note: Compiled in cooperation with the Latin American Studies Association.

1538. Inter-American Center for Documentation and Agriculture Information. Bibliografía, participación de la mujer en el desarrollo rural de América Latina y el Caribe, enero 1980. San José, C.R.: OEA, Instituto Interamericano de Ciencias Agrícolas, Centro Interamericano de Documentación e Información Agrícola, [1980]. 103 [5] p. (Serie documentación e información agrícola, 78).

1539. Jaramillo, Phillip. Hispanic health services research: a preliminary bibliography. [Hyattsville, MD]: U.S. Dept. of Health and Human Services, Public Health Service, Office of Health Research, Statistics and Technology, National Center for Health Services Research, 1981. 15 p. (NCHSER research report series, 81-3300).

1540. Kenton, Charlotte. Health needs and services for Hispanic Americans. Bethesda, MD: U.S. Department of Health and Human Services, Public Health Service, National Institute of Health, 1982. 7 p. Note: Covers January 1980-July 1982: 96 citations.

1541. Lavrin, Asunción. "Recent studies on women in Latin America." Latin American Research Review, 1984, 19 (1), 181-189.

1542. Levine, Daniel H. "Religion, society and politics; states of the art." Latin American Research Review, 1981, 16 (3), 185-209.

1543. Levine, Robert M. Race and ethnic relations in Latin America and the Caribbean: an historical dictionary and bibliography. Metuchen, NJ: Scarecrow Press, 1980. 252 p.

1544. Luján Muñoz, Jorge. "Literatura notarial en España e Hispanoamérica, 1500-1820." Anuario de estudios americanos, 1981, 38, 101-116.

1545. Marichal, Carlos, and Guy Pierre. "Bibliografía selectiva sobre la teoría y la historia de los ciclos y las crisis del capitalismo." Iztapalapa; revista de ciencias sociales y humanidades, Ene-Jun 1982, 3 (6), 162-171.

1546. Mesa-Lago, Carmelo. "Seguridad social en América Latina: avances, problemas y reformas." Pensamiento iberoamericano; revista de economía política, Jul-Dic 1983, (4), 266-271.

1547. Metress, Eileen S. and Seamus Metress. The Euro-American elderly: an ethnic bibliography. Monticello, IL: Vance Bibliographies, [1983]. 18 p.

1548. Mosquera, Martha. "Perfil Universitario: Fundación Bariloche." Universitas 2000, 1982, 6 (2), 185-192.

1549. Nocetti, Milton A, and Cecília Moreira. Bibliografia sobre disseminação seletiva da informação: fontes para pesquisa e estudo, 1961 a 1979. Brasília: Empresa Brasileira de Pesquisa Agropecuária, Departmaneto de Informação, 1980. 71 p.

1550. Papkov, Oleg. "Balance de la labor científica de investigación del Instituto de América Latina en 1981-1982." América Latina (USSR), Sept 1983. (9), 74-76.

1551. Planindex: resúmenes de documentos sobre planificación. Santiago de Chile: Naciones Unidas, CEPAL/CLADES/ILPES, 1980-. Note: Semiannual.

1552. Portes, Alejandro. "Migration, poverty and the city in Latin America." Latin American Research Review, 1981, 16 (3), 225-235.

1553. Reyna, José Luis, and Ignacio Marván Laborde. "Tendencias recientes del movimiento sindical en tres países de América Latina: los casos de Argentina, Brasil y México." Pensamiento iberoamericano; revista de economía política, Ene-Jun 1983. (3), 213-218.

1554. Scheidesser, Elisabeth. Población y desarrollo: la evolución demográfica y el desarrollo económico y social de América Latina; bibliografía seleccionada, 1960-1974. Geneva, Switzerland: Instituto Internacional de Estudios Laborales, [1980?]. 111 p.

1555. Schmidt, Steffen W. "Women, politics and development." Latin American Research Review, 1983, 18 (1), 210-227.

1556. Schultz, Rosario A., compiler. Resource materials available in Spanish concerning exceptional children. Arlington Heights, IL: Illinois Resource Center for Exceptional Bilingual Children, 1982. 131 p.

1557. Smith, John David. Black slavery in the Americas: an interdisciplinary bibliography, 1865-1980. Westport, CT: Greenwood Press, c1982. 2 vols.

1558. Terrazos Contreras, Máximo. Guía bibliográfica de ciencias sociales. [Lima: Sección Publicación y Difusión de la Universidad Nacional "Federico Villareal"], 1981. 253 p.

1559. Women, health and development in the Americas: an annotated bibliography. Washington, DC: Pan American Health Organization, 1984. 106 p.

1560. Zapata, Francisco. "Bibliografía sobre el sindicalismo en América Latina." Foro internacional, Ene-Mar 1983, 22 (3), 320-336.

1561. Zenzes Eisenbach, Carla, and Cristina Bernál García. "La familia (hemerografía)." Revista mexicana de ciencias políticas y sociales, Oct 1979-Mar 1980. (25-26), 179-208.

ANDES REGION

1562. Guillet, David. "The individual and the collectivity in Andean studies." Latin American Research Review, 1983, 18 (2), 240-251.

1563. Merlino, Rodolfo J. and Alicia C. Quereilhac. "Acerca de los estudios andinos en la Argentina." Revista andina, Jul 1984, 2 (1), 265-282.

BOLIVIA

1564. Albó, Victor. "Rural Bolivia: Do you speak English?; reseña de la literatura sobre el mundo rural boliviano en lenguas extranjeras." América indígena, Abr-Jun 1983, 43 (2), 397-412.

1565. Flores, Gonzalo. "Migraciones en Bolivia: bibliografía." Revista andina, 1983, 1, 143-150.

BRAZIL

1566. Almeida-Filho, Noamar de. "The psychosocial costs of development: labor migration and stress in Bahia, Brazil." Latin American Research Review, 1982, 17 (3), 91-118.

1567. "Bibliografia sobre recenseamento no Brasil [censos de 1872 a 1980]." Revista brasileira de estatística, Jul-Set 1980, 41 (163), 451-482.

1568. Catálogo bibliográfico sobre a formação do técnico industrial. São Paulo: Instituto Roberto Simonsen, 1981. 159 p.

1569. Estudos da administração pública paulista, 1979-1981. São Paulo: Fundação do Desenvolvimento Administrativo, 1983. 699 p.

1570. Fundação Carlos Chagas. Mulher brasileira: bibliografia anotada. v. 1-. São Paulo: Editora Brasileira, 1979-.

1571. Keremitsis, Eileen. "Immigrants in rural Brazil: some recent studies." Latin American Research Review, 1983, 18 (2), 190-200.

1572. Pereira, Luiz C. Bresser. "Seis interpretaciones sobre Brasil." Revista interamericana de planificación, Sept-Dic 1982, 16 (63-64), 19-47.

1573. Samara, Eni de Mesquita, and Iraci del Nero da Costa. Demografia histórica: bibliografia brasileira. São Paulo: Instituto de Pesquisas Econômicas, 1984. 75 p. (Série relatórios de pesquisa, 23).

1574. Zirker, Daniel. "Brazilian development: alternative approaches to an increasingly complex field." Latin American Research Review, 1983, 18 (2), 135-149.

CARIBBEAN AREA

1575. Brana-Shute, Rosemary, and Rosemarijn Hoefte. A bibliography of Caribbean immigrant communities. Gainesville: Reference and Bibliographic Department, University of Florida Libraries, in cooperation with the Center for Latin American Studies, University of Florida, 1983. 339 p. (Bibliographic series, 9).

1576. Jeffrey, Phillip, and Maureen Newton. Selected annotated bibliography of studies in the Caribbean Community. Georgetown, Guyana: Information and Documentation Section, Caribbean Community Secretariat, 1983. 17 p.

1577. Kempeneers, Marianne, and Raymond Massé. Les migrations antillaises: bibliographie sélective et annotée. [Montreal]: Centre de recherches caraïbes de l'Université de Montréal, c1981. 53 p.

1578. Newton, Velma. Civil rights with special reference to the Commonwealth Caribbean: a select bibliography. Cave Hill, Barbados: Institute of Social and Economic Research (Eastern Caribbean), University of the West Indies, 1981. 110 p.

1579. Ramesar, Marianne. A select bibliography of publications and studies relating to human resources in the Commonwealth Caribbean: material available in Trinidad and Tobago. St. Augustine, Trinidad: Institute of Social and Economic Research, University of the West Indies, 1981. 127 p. (Occasional Papers. Institute of Social and Economic research, University of the West Indies. Human resources, 3).

CENTRAL AMERICA

1580. Bibliografía anotada de obras de referencia sobre Centroamérica y Panamá de las ciencias sociales. San José, Instituto de Investigaciones Sociales, Universidad de Costa Rica: Friends Worlds College, Latin American Center, c1983. 2 vols.

1581. Fernández Vázquez, Rodrigo. "Poblamiento y ocupación territorial en Centro América, 1870-1940: informe bibliográfico, documental y cartográfico del proyecto de investigación 'Poblamiento y ocupación territorial en Centro América, 1870-1940.'" Estudios sociales centroamericanos, May-Ag 1981, 10 (29), 143-214.

CHILE

1582. "Chile: mujer y sociedad: notas bibliográficas." Boletín de planificación (Chile), Sept 1979, 3, 77-86.

COLOMBIA

1583. Barella, Adriana de, editor. Bibliografía anotada sobre planificación--Colombia. Bogotá: Asociación Colombiana para el Estudio de la Población: Corporación Centro Regional de Población, [1984]. 284 p.

1584. "Bibliografía sobre desarrollo regional en Colombia." Cámara de Comercio de Bogotá. Revista, Jun 1982, 13, 117-164.

1585. Castillo Sandoval, Stella. "Bibliografía del plan de integración nacional." Revista de planeación y desarrollo, Ene-Abr 1982, 14 (1), 113-141.

1586. Colombia. Departamento Nacional de Planeación. Bibliografía sobre el plan de integración nacional. [Bogotá, 1980]. 24 p.

1587. Hartwig, Richard. Transportation policy and administrative responsibility in Colombian government: a selected bibliography. Monticello, IL: Vance Bibliographies, 1980. 18 p.

1588. Naranjo de González, Livia. Inventario de estudios e informes. Vol. 2. Bogotá: Instituto de Fomento Industrial, [1982-].

1589. Parada Caicedo, Jorge Humberto. Bibliografía comentada sobre migraciones en Colombia. Bogotá: Instituto Colombiano para el Fomento de la Educación Superior, División de Documentación e Información, Centro de Documentación, 1980. 86 p. (Serie bibliográfica, v. 5, no. 1).

CUBA

1590. Oberg, Larry R. Human services in postrevolutionary Cuba: an annotated international bibliography. Westport, CT: Greenwood Press, c1984. 433 p.

1591. Santos Quilez, Aleida de los. El campesinado cubano: breve bibliografía. La Habana: Editora Política, 1980. 148 p.

JAMAICA

1592. Pottinger, L G. A bibliography of reports and studies, 1965-1981: a subject index of reports and studies prepared in government industries, departments and other bodies. Kingston: Jamaica National Investment Company, 1981. 3 vols.

MEXICO

1593. "Bibliografía seleccionada sobre migración mexicana a Estados Unidos." A: revista de ciencias sociales y humanidades, Ene-Abr 1983, 4 (8), 245-253.

1594. Forsyth, Elizabeth R., and Gilberto Ramírez, editors.

Development and equity in Mexico: an annotated bibliography. Austin: Mexico-United States Border Research Program, University of Texas at Austin: Distributed by University of Texas Press, c1981. 182 p.

1595. Huerta, María Teresa, et al. Balance y perspectivas de la historiografía social en México; Seminario de Historiografía Social, Departamento de Investigaciones Históricas, DEH-INAH. México: SEP, Instituto Nacional de Antropología e Historia, 1980. 2 vols. (Colección científica; 84. Fuentes. Historia social)

1596. Parcero López, María de la Luz. Mujer en el siglo XIX, en México. México: Instituto Nacional de Antropología e Historia, 1982. 111 p.

1597. Ruiz Dueñas, Jorge. "Bibliografía sobre recursos humanos en las empresas públicas." A; revista de ciencias sociales y humanidades, Ene-Abr 1981, 2 (2), 209-218.

1598. Sánchez Gutiérrez, Arturo, and Luis Angel Domínguez Brito. "Bibliografía sobre el movimiento obrero en México, 1940-1980." A; revista de ciencias sociales y humanidades, Sept-Dic 1980, 1 (1), 109-122.

PARAGUAY

1599. Aguilera de Zarza, Yenny. La mujer rural en el Paraguay: resumen bibliográfico. San José, Costa Rica: Instituto Interamericano de Ciencias Agrícolas, 1982. 41 p.

1600. Campos Ruiz Díaz, Daniel. "Economía, modernización agraria, diferenciación social y lucha por la tierra en el contexto paraguayo." Pensamiento iberoamericano; revista de economía política, Jul-Dic 1983. (4), 252-256.

1601. CEDOCPLAN resúmenes: datos básicos y situaciones existentes a nivel nacional, Paraguay, Presidencia de la República, Secretaría Técnica de Planificación, Centro de Documentación en Población y Desarrollo. Asunción: El Centro, 1984. 40 leaves.

1602. Kaufman, Edy. "Authoritarianism in Paraguay: the lesser evil?" Latin American Research Review, 1984, 19 (2), 193-207.

PERU

1603. Bonfiglio. Giovanni. Desarrollo de la comunidad y trabajo social. Ensayo bibliográfico. Lima: Celats Ediciones, 1982. 269 p.

1604. Deustua, José. "Sobre movimientos campesinos e historia regional en el Perú moderno: un comentario bibliográfico." Revista andina, 1983, 1, 219-240.

1605. Gibaja Vargas Prada, Pedro. Movimiento campesino peruano, 1945-1964: algunos elementos de análisis preliminares y una aproximación bibliográfica. Lima: Centro Peruano de Estudios Sociales, 1983. 79 p.

1606. León, Federico R. "Tipos de investigación de publicaciones en la psicología industrial peruana." Apuntes, 1983. (13), 37-46.

1607. Martínez, Héctor. Migraciones internas en el Perú: aproximación crítica y bibliografía. Lima: Instituto de Estudios Peruanos, 1980. 188 p. (Guías bibliográficas, 3).

1608. Pásara, Luis. "Diagnosing Peru." Latin American Research Review, 1982, 17 (1), 235-243.

1609. Peirano Falconi, Luis, and Tokihiro Kudo. La investigación en comunicación en el Perú. Lima: DESCO, Centro de Estudios y Promoción del Desarrollo, 1981. 400 p.

1610. Pérez-Rosas Cáceres, Augusto. Fuentes bibliográficas peruanas en las ciencias sociales: 1879-1979. Lima: DESCO, Centro de Estudios y Promoción del Desarrollo, 1981. 400 p.

1611. Salas Sánchez, Margarita, et al. Bibliografía sobre identidad cultural en el Perú. Lima: Instituto Indigenista Peruano, 1982. 128 p. (Serie bibliográfica, 2).

1612. Salas Sánchez, Margarita, et al. Bibliografía sobre formas tradicionales de organización social y actividad económica en el medio indígena. Lima: Instituto Indigenista Peruano, 1982. 185 p. (Serie bibliográfica, 3).

1613. Uribe, Maruja; Margarita Hernández; and Ligia O. de Carriazo. Bibliografía selectiva sobre desarrollo rural en el Perú. Bogotá: Instituto Interamericano de Cooperación para la Agricultura, 1981. 232 p.

PUERTO RICO

1614. Earnhardt, Kent C. Population research, policy and related studies in Puerto Rico: an inventory. Río Piedras, PR: Editorial de la Universidad de Puerto Rico, 1984. 132 p.

1615. Vivó, Paquita, compiler. Puerto Rican migration: the return flow. La migración puertorriqueña: el reflujo a la isla. Washington, DC: National Institute of Education, 1982. 45 p.

UNITED STATES

1616. Anson, Roberto, compiler. Projections and forecasts on U.S. Hispanic population: a selected annotated bibliography. [n.p.], 1980. 3 leaves.

1617. Poyo, Gerald E.; Lynda De la Viña; and Edna A. Olivo. Hispanic workers in the United states labor market: employment issues, problems and programs, 1960-1980: a bibliography. San Antonio: Human Resources Management and Development Program, College of Business, University of Texas at San Antonio, 1981. 53 p. (Center for the Study of Human Resources bibliography series, 8-81).

1618. Sahai, Hardeo. Studies on sociocultural issues involving Hispanics in the military: an annotated bibliography. Fort Sheridan, IL: Research and Studies Division, Program Analysis and Evaluation Directorate, U.S. Army Recruiting Command, 1984-. (USAREC research memorandum, 84-2).

URUGUAY

1619. Sabelli de Louzao, Martha, and Ricardo Rodríguez Pereyra, compilers. La vivienda en el Uruguay, 1960-1983: bibliografía. [Montevideo]: Centro de Informaciones y Estudios del Uruguay (CIESU), [1983 or 1984]. 49 p. (Serie bibliográfica/CIESU, Centro de Informaciones y Estudios del Uruguay, 5/83).

VENEZUELA

1620. Riera Encinoza, Argenis. Indice bibliográfico de la criminología venezolana: 1831-1975. Caracas: Dirección de Cultura, Universidad Central de Venezuela, 1980. (Colección humanismo y ciencia, 15).

STATISTICS

1621. Colombia. Departamento Administrativo Nacional de Estadística. Listado de publicaciones (disponibles para venta). Bogotá: Departamento Administrativo Nacional de Estadística, 1982. 31 p.

1622. La información estadística demográfica en México. México: Secretaría de Programación y Presupuesto, Instituto Nacional de Estadística, Geografía e Informática, 1983. 19 p. Note: Bibliographical essay based on a lecture given by Manuel Ordorica Mellado.

1623. Loh, Eudora, and Roberta Medford. Statistical sources on the California Hispanic population, 1984: a preliminary survey. Oakland [Los Angeles]: California Spanish Language Data Base; Chicano Studies Research Center, University of California, Los Angeles, c1984. 210 p.

URBANIZATION

1624. Aguilera Mier, María de los Angeles, and Federico Torres A. Bibliografía sobre desarrollo regional y urbano de México. Azcapotzalco, México: Centro de Estudios del Medio Ambiente, Universidad Autónoma Metropolitana, UAM-Azcapotzalco, 1978. 446 p.

1625. Blitzer, Silvia. Las ciudades intermedias y pequeñas an América Latina: Una bibliografía comentada. Buenos Aires: Centro de Estudios Urbanos, 1983. 137 p.

1626. Casper, Dale E. The urban environment of Latin America: recent writings, 1977-1983. Monticello, IL: Vance Bibliographies, [1984]. 14 p.

1627. Cela, Jorge. "El estudio de la ciudad: notas bibliográficas sobre sociología urbana." Estudios sociales (Dom. Rep.), Sept-Nov 1983, 16 (53), 55-66.

1628. Chance, John K. "Recent trends in Latin American urban studies." Latin American Research Review, 1980, 15 (1), 183-188.

1629. Galindo Cáceres, Jesús. "Bibliografía sobre antropología, sociología y cuestión urbana: cien títulos en español sobre el asunto." Nueva antropología, Jun 1984, 6 (24), 99-107.

1630. Kuznesof, Elizabeth Anne. "Brazilian urban history: an evaluation." Latin American Research Review, 1982, 17 (1), 263-275.

1631. U.S. Department of Housing and Urban Development Office of International Affairs. Housing and urban development planning in Mexico: a bibliography. Washington, DC, 1980. 54 p.

1632. Valladares, Lîcia do Prado, and Ademir Figueiredo. "Housing in Brazil: an introduction to recent literature (translated by David Hathaway)." Bulletin of Latin American Research, May 1983, 2 (2), 69-91.

1633. White, Sylvia. A bibliography of sources relating to urban and regional planning in Costa Rica. Monticello, IL: Vance Bibliographies, [1982]. 26 p. (Public administration series--bibliography, P-1014).

SUBJECT INDEX

Academia de la Historia, Madrid
  Catalogs 1295
Academia Nacional de la Historia, Caracas 1469
Academia Venezolana de la Lengua 1109
Academia Venezolana de la Lengua. Boletín 862
Acre, Brazil 87
Africa
  Foreign relations--Cuba 942
  Relations (General)--Caribbean area 945
African-Caribbean Institute of Jamaica 307
African studies
  Brazil 349
Afro-Americans
  Music 1364
Agave 198
Aged 1512
Agricultural laborers
  Cuba 1591
Agriculture
  Barbados 231
  Bolivia 207
  Brazil 209-210, 213, 225, 227
  Central America 232
  Chile 233, 1471
  Colombia 234, 237
  Cuba 242
  Dissertations 533
  Experimentation--Brazil 216
  Jamaica 230
  Latin America 197
  Paraguay 555
  Periodicals 1379, 1401, 1414
  Tropics--Periodicals 1376
  Peru 248-249
Agriculture and state
  Costa Rica 604
Agriculture, Economic aspects 202, 1177
  Bolivia 202
  Brazil 588

Costa Rica 604
Honduras 245
Latin America 1524
Peru 250
Agronomy 1150
Aguirre, Amado
Archives 1213
Alegría, Fernando 429
Alternativa 954
Alvear, Torcuato de
Archives--Catalogs 736
Amazon Valley 9, 54-57
America
Discovery and exploration 16
History--Manuscripts 1295
América indígena 851
American Federationist 1126
Anarchism and anarchists
Brazil 144
Mexico 807
Andes region 58-60, 262, 1563
Economic conditions 583
History 731
Industry 583
Social conditions 1562
Andrade, Mário de 1036
Anguilla 104
Animal nutrition 226
Anthropo-geography
Brazil 705
Anthropologists 286
Anthropology
Argentina 256, 1563
Bolivia 255, 277
Brazil 548, 947
Costa Rica 258
Ecuador 259, 268
Latin America 263, 272, 287, 1629
Mexico 270, 273, 786, 1472
Panama 261
Peru 1476
Venezuela 289-291
Antioquía, Colombia
History--Sources 1173
Antonio, Nicolás 402
Antropología e historia de Guatemala 863
Anuario de estudios americanos 864
Anuario de Historia (Mexico) 865
Anuario indigenista 851
Arce Araya, Guillermo 430
Archaeology

Central America 296
Chile 304
Ecuador 297
Guatemala 298
Mexico 270, 296
Mexico--Yucatan 294
Peru 295, 303
Architecture
Brazil 325
Chile 315
Cuba 321
Latin America 496, 967
Mexico 324, 329
Mexico--History 314
New Mexico 337
South America 330
West Indies 328
Architecture, Tropical 341
Archives
Austria--Catalogs 808
Bolivia--Oruro 1148
Bolivia--Sources 1149
Brazil 1157
Central America 1197
Chile 1165-1166, 1169-1171
Colombia--Pamplona 1174
Cuba 1180
Ecuador 1182
Europe 804
France 1191
Guatemala 1196
Latin America 1139
Martinique 1199
Mexico 1201-1203, 1210-1212, 1214, 1222, 1235, 1504
Mexico--Ahuacatlán 1216
Mexico--Mexico City 1204
Mexico--Rosamorada 1217
Mexico--Ruiz 1218
Mexico--Santa María del Oro 1219
Mexico--Santiago Ixcuintla 1220
Mexico--Xocchel 1215
Mexico--Zacatecas 1205
Mexico--Zacualpan de Amilpas 1200
Peru 1249
Peru--Arequipa 1250-1251
Archivo Carlos Fonseca 1246
Archivo de Buscas (Mexico)
Catalogs 802
Archivo de Notarias de Puebla (Mexico)
Catalogs 790
Archivo del Convento de Santo Domingo, Santiago 1168

Archivo del Monasterio de Santa Catalina del Cusco (Peru) 1249
Archivo General de Guatemala 1195
Archivo General de Indias (Spain) 1257
Catalogs 738, 746, 1254
Archivo General de la Orden Franciscana del Ecuador 1495
Archivo General de Notarías (Mexico)
Catalogs 1240-1241
Archivo General de Puerto Rico
Catalogs 173
Archivo Histórico de Hacienda (Mexico) 1243
Archivo Nacional de Historia (Ecuador) 1181
Catalogs 775
Argentina 70
Archival resources--France 1445
Bio-bibliography 412
Description and travel 73
Economic conditions 62, 584
Foreign relations--Brazil 938
Foreign relations--France 733
Foreign relations--Great Britain 936
History 739-741, 814
History--Sources 733, 738
History, Military 735
Imprints 367
Imprints--Catalogs 1142
Maps 269
Politics and government 1445-1446
Population 62
Social conditions 62
Argentina. Estado Mayor Conjunto. Biblioteca y Centro de Documentación 1388
Arid regions agriculture
Brazil 208
Arquivo Histórico do Rio Grande do Sul
Catalogs 1151
Art
Andean 334-335
Brazilian 325
Caribbean 338
Colombian 343
Cuban 319
Latin American 309, 322-323, 326, 496
Mexican 306, 473
Mexican--Catalogs 1230
Peruvian 313
Art industry and trade
Brazil 342
Chile 320
Ecuador 318
Artes de México 866

Artists
  Venezuela 520
Augier, Angel 471, 486
Authors, Argentine 428
  Biobibliography 408, 416
  Tucumán 404
Authors, Black 974
Authors, Bolivian 414, 422
Authors, Brazilian 411, 424
  Rio Grande do Sul 409
Authors, Chilean
  Biobibliography 1046
Authors, Colombian 395
Authors, Cuban
  United States 410
Authors, Latin American 407
Authors, Mexican 393
  Jalisco 152
Authors, Mexican-American 1088-1089
  Biobibliography 1087
Authors, Nicaraguan 1090
Authors, Paraguayan 162, 398
Authors, Peruvian 1093, 1252
Authors, Spanish 415
Authors, Venezuelan
  Falcón 189
Aymará Indians 255, 257
Aztec language 1074
Aztec literature 1074
Aztecs 284

Bahamas 1147
Bahía Blanca, Argentina 63
Baja California, Mexico 141
  History 782, 1229
Banco Central de la República Dominicana. Biblioteca 606
Banco Central del Ecuador. Archivo Histórico 1183-1189
Banco de la República (Colombia) 1481
Barbados 77
  Economic conditions 586
  History--Sources 78, 79
  Imprints 368
Barbosa, Ruy 1159
Barley 220
Barlow, Robert Hayward 431
Barragán, Luis 324
Barreda, Gabino 1434
Barreto, Paulo (João de Rio) 432
<u>Barricada</u> 867-868

Batres, Montufar, José 433
Bayamón, Puerto Rico
  History 173
Belize 80
Bello, Andrés 434-436
Benson Latin American Collection 1263, 1265, 1267, 1314
  Catalogs 1264
Bibliography 1280
  Bolivia 365
  Caribbean area 352
  Chile 374
  Ecuador 378
  Guatemala 379
  Haiti 381
  Honduras 382-383
  Jamaica 384
  Latin America 29, 33, 350-351, 353-354, 359-363
  Literature--Latin American 364
  Mexican Americans 356
  Nicaragua 386
  Peru 355, 358
  Philippines 350
  Puerto Rico 388
  Venezuela 391-392
  West Indies, British 352
Biblioteca Agropecuaria de Colombia 1379
Biblioteca de Martín Ferreyra. Sección historia, genealogía y heráldica 1140
Biblioteca Dr. Juan José Nissen 1141
Biblioteca Manuel Orozco y Barra 1206
Biblioteca Marco Fidel Suárez 1176
Biblioteca Mário de Andrade 1158
Biblioteca Nacional de Antropología e Historia (Mexico) 1207
Biblioteca Nacional José Martî 1178, 1288
  Catalogs 1179
Biblioteca Presidente Carlos A. López
  Catalogs 1248
Biblioteca Roosevelt
  Catalogs 159
Bibliothèque Nationale (Paris) 1192
Bilingualism 644, 646, 648, 652
Birth control
  Colombia 1583
Blacks
  Brazil 92
  Caribbean area 945
  Cuba 92, 114
  Latin America 25
  Music 1364
  Venezuela 190, 280-281
Bogotá, Colombia

Industries 600
Boletín de la Academia Hondureña de la Lengua 1460
Boletín de legislación nacional 869
Boletín de Resúmenes Analíticos en Educación 858
Boletín indigenista 851-852
Boletín interamericano de archivos 1164
Boletín Titikaka 870
Bolívar, Simón 437-443
Bolivia 82
Biography 397
Historiography 747
History 744, 746
Imprints 81, 83, 369-371
Rural conditions 1564
Bolivia. Biblioteca y Archivo Nacionales
Catalogs 745
Book reviews 39
Borges, Jorge Luis 444-445
Boturini Benaducci, Lorenzo 787
Manuscripts 1296
Manuscripts--Catalogs 1266
Brandão, Theo 446
Brazil 84, 89, 91, 526, 1192, 1290
Armed forces 755
Bio-bibliography 426
Census 1567
Church history 1501
Dictionaries 948
Economic conditions 594
Economic policy 587, 589, 593, 1574
Foreign relations--Argentina 938
Government publications 28
History 522, 750-751, 753-754, 756-757, 759, 904, 1298
History--Sources 749, 758
Imprints 88, 90, 372
Maps 702-703
Mato Grosso--Economic conditions 211
Microform catalogs 1317
Pernambuco--Economic policy 1477
Politics and government 522, 753, 1447-1449
Population--History 1573
Social policy 587, 1574
Superintendência do Desenvolvimento do Nordeste 1478
Brazil, Northeast
Maps 710
Brazil. Biblioteca Nacional 312, 372, 1293-1294
Catalogs 959, 1312
Brazil. Biblioteca Nacional. Coleção Teresa Cristina María 340
Brazil. Ministério das Relações Exteriores. Arquivo Histórico 1154
Brazil. Ministerio de Fazenda. Biblioteca 1292
Brazil. Ministério de Justiça. Biblioteca 1291

Brazil nut 218
Briceño Iragorry, Mario 447
Brigham Young University. Library 23
Brull, Mariano 1061
Buenos Aires, Argentina 66, 75
History 737
Politics and government 736
Buenos Aires, Arg. Biblioteca Nacional 743
Buenos Aires, Arg. Universidad. Biblioteca
Catalogs 1143
Buenos Aires, Costa Rica 112
Bulletin de l'Institut français d'Études andines 871
Business
Information services 566

Caballero de Rodas, Antonio
Archives--Catalogs 1258
Cahiers du monde hispanique et luso-brésilien
Indexes 994
Caillet-Bois, Ricardo R. 448
California
History 1229
History--Sources 829
Callahuaya Indians 257
Campeche, Mexico
History 145
Capitalism 1545
Caribbean area 19, 42, 44, 93-96, 98-100, 103, 539, 707, 1557
Economic conditions 1576
Economic policy 595
Emigration and immigration 102
History 761
History--Sources 97, 1191
Imprints 101, 373
Politics and government 1534
Relations (General)--Africa 945
Social conditions 1579
Caribbean Community 1576
Caro, José Eusebio 449
Carpentier, Alejo 450, 1057
Carrizal archives 1275
Casa de las Américas 1063
Cassava
Brazil 223
Catalogs, Union
Australia 1375
Bolivia 1389
Brazil--Piaui 1282
Colombia 1401
Costa Rica 111, 1401-1402

Dominican Republic 1407
Germany (West)--Hamburg 645
Guyana 1410
New Zealand 1375
Uruguay 1422
Catholic Church
Brazil 1501
Chile-History--Sources 1166
Mexico--History 1498, 1500
Catholic church in Latin America 1488
Caycedo Acosta, Bernardo J. 451
Central America 40, 42, 105-108, 1260, 1580
Economic conditions 596-597
Economic integration 598
Politics and government 1450-1451
Population 1581
Religion 1503
Social life and customs 1503
Central American Resource Center (Minneapolis)
Catalogs 1260
Centro de Documentación en Población y Desarrollo (Paraguay) 1601
Centro de Informaciones y Estudios del Uruguay (CIESU) 1485
Centro de Investigaciones Agrícolas del Noroeste (Mexico) 1414
Centro de Investigaciones y Estudios Superiores en Antropología Social 1472
Centro de Publicaciones de Organismos Internacionales (Mexico) 1473
Centro Latinoamericano de Demografía (Chile) 1474
Centro Nacional de Microfilm (Spain) 1322
CEPAL Review 872
Chaco, Argentina 68
Chaco War 814
Chacón, José María 452
Chávez, Angelino 453
Chicano Periodical Indexing Project 1329
Child welfare 1337
Children
Legal status, laws etc. 1125
Children of migrant laborers
Education--United States 689
Children's literature 965, 968, 979, 993, 1001-1002, 1009, 1355
Latin America 998, 1011
Chile 109
Economic conditions 599
Foreign relations 932, 943
History 766-768, 1162-1163, 1168
History--Sources 1164
Politics and government 1452
Social life and customs 696
China
Relations--Latin America 34

Chinese
  Latin America 1347
  Peru 1330, 1346
Chipaya Indians 257
Chiquimula, Guatemala 1194
Choco Indians 279
Choy, Emilio 454
Christianity
  Caribbean area 1491
Church and social problems
  Brazil 1487
  Latin America--Catholic Church 1520
Church archives
  Mexico--Catalogs 1492
Church records and registers
  Latin America--History 1508
  Mexico 1211-1212, 1242
CIAT (Central Internacional de Agricultura Tropical) 237
Cine cubano 873
Cities and towns
  Dominican Republic 115
  Latin America 1552, 1625
  Puerto Rico 169
City planning
  Costa Rica 1633
  Latin America 1626
  Mexico 1624
Civil rights
  Caribbean area 1578
  Latin America 1533, 1537
Civilization, Hispanic 1140
  Catalogs 1193
  Periodicals 1375
Classification
  Books--Paraguay 1284
Clergy
  Brazil 1497
Cochabamba (Bolivia: Dept.)
  Rural conditions 206
Coffee 196
  Colombia 236
Cofiño López, Manuel 455
Cojo ilustrado 874
Coleção Lamego 1298
Colegio San Ildefonso de Chillán (Chile)
  History--Sources 1170
Collective behavior 1522
College of the Bahamas. Library 1147
Colombia
  Bio-bibliography 401, 422
  Cauca River Valley 110

Economic conditions 544, 1583
Economic policy 1585-1586
Emigration and immigration 1589
History 769
Imprints 375
Industries 601, 1588
Libraries 1176
Politics and government 1587
Population 1583
Presidents--Biography 396
Statistics 1621
Colombia. Departamento Administrativo Nacional de Estadística 1621
Colombia. Departamento Nacional de Planeación 1586
Colombia. Instituto de Fomento Industiral 1588
Columbus, Christopher 456
Columbus Memorial Library 1054, 1262
Comisión Económica para América Latina y el Caribe (CEPAL) 1470
Committee for the Development of Subject Access to Chicano Literature 1328
Communication
Social aspects--Peru 1609
Communications 1307
Communism
Brazil 1448
Community development 1603
Compañía de Minas de Real del Monte y Pachuca
Archives 1234
Comparative education 651
Conferência Nacional dos Bispos do Brasil 1489
Conjunto 875
Constitutional law
Uruguay 1123
Convento de San Francisco de Santiago de Chile
History--Sources 1171
Convento Máximo de Santiago (Chile)
History--Sources 1169
Coordinación General de Estadística, Geografía e Informática (Mexico) 1479
Córdoba, Argentina 76
Biobibliography 1022
Córdoba. Universidad Nacional. Biblioteca Mayor 1144-1145
Corporación de los Andes (Venezuela) 1486
Correo del domingo 876
Cortázar, Julio 457
Costa Rica
Economic conditions 602-603
Education 858
Foreign relations 926
Imprints 111
Politics and government 1453
Costa Rica. Oficina de Planificación Nacional y Política Económica 1400

Cotton 204, 222
Courts
  Latin America 1137
Creole dialects 951
Crime and criminals
  Venezuela 1620
Criminology
  Latin America 1133
Croix, Carlos Francisco de Croix, marqués de
  Manuscripts--Catalogs 792
Crusade bulls
  Mexico 1496
Cruz Santos, Abel 458
Cuadernos dominicanos de cultura 877
Cuadernos políticos 878
Cuadernos republicanos 879
Cuadra, Pablo Antonio 459-460
Cuba 178
  City planning 321
  Economic policy 1455
  Foreign relations--Africa 942
  Historiography 771
  History 770, 1258
  History--Revolution 113
  Imprints 376
  Politics and government 1454, 1456
  Population 1269
  Rural conditions 1591
Cuba. Consulado (Key West, Fla.) 1271
Cuba internacional 880
Cuban Americans 1342
Cubans
  Florida--Key West 1271
  United States 1342
Cubberley Library
  Catalogs 671

Debate (Peru) 881
Dedications (in books) 1036
Democracy 1440
  Latin America 1442
  Peru 1465
Demography 1474
Díaz, Porfirio
  Archives--Catalogs 1244
Dissertations, Academic
  Argentina 529-530, 532
  Bolivia 542
  Brazil 531, 533, 536, 544, 547-549, 553-554, 1279

Canada 539, 551
Caribbean area 535
Chile 552
Colombia 540
France 526
France--on Latin America 537, 550, 556
Guatemala 557
Haiti 134
Jamaica 707
Mexico 541
Paraguay 555
Peru 543, 546
United States 528, 534, 538-539, 551, 558, 691
Domestic relations courts 1125
Dominican Republic 115
Economic conditions 606
Imprints 116, 377
Treaties 929
Drama
Argentine--20th century 428
Brazilian 912, 1025
Cuban 1053, 1059
Latin American 875, 973
Latin American--History and criticism 961-962
Puerto Rican 1105
Venezuelan 1115
Drug abuse 1526

East Indians in the West Indies 102
Eça de Queiroz, José María de 1024
Ecology 1548
Economic development 562, 582
Economics 544, 552, 1545
Ecuador 118
Aerial photographs 117
Church history 1495
History--Sources 775, 1181, 1183-1189
Maps 117, 701
Politics and government 1458
Education 650, 654
Brazil 536, 664
Brazil--Finance 663
Chile 636, 665
Colombia 666
Colombia--History 667
Costa Rica 668-670
Cuba 671, 1590
Dominican Republic 673
Dominican Republic--Periodicals 672
Economic aspects--Trinidad and Tobago 630

Latin America 632, 637, 649
Latin America--History 667
Latin America--Union lists 645
Mexican Americans 689, 1325, 1343, 1356
Mexico 674, 676, 680-682, 1480
Mexico--History 677, 683
Paraguay 684-687
Periodicals 655-656
Peru 688
Research--Latin America 653
Uruguay 692
Education, Bilingual 646, 647, 690-691
Education, Higher 633-634, 640-643, 657
Latin America 638
Mexico 675
United States 659
Education, Pre-school 647
Education, Rural
Mexico 678
Education technology 661
Education research
Brazil 664
Egaña, Mariano 1167
El Progreso, Guatemala 1194
El Salvador 119-121
Politics and government 122-124, 1459
Elections
Mexico 1463
United States 1467
EMBRAPA (Empresa Brasileira de Pesquisa Agropecuaria) 209, 212-213, 216, 219, 222, 229, 348, 1390
Emigration and immigration
Bolivia 1565
Brazil 1571
Caribbean area 1575
Mexico 1593
Environmental law
Caribbean area 1131
Errázuriz, Crescente 461
Espinosa de los Monteros, Samuel 1237
Espírito Santo (Brazil: State)
History 748
Estudios sociales centroamericanos 882
Ethnology
Andes region 283, 288
Brazil 253, 267, 694
Ecuador 259
Guatemala 271
Latin America 1509
Mexico 252
Peru 303

Trinidad 264
United States 1547
Venezuela 280
Exceptional children 1556
Eyzaguirre, Jaime 462

Falcón, Venezuela 184, 189
Falkland Islands 61, 64-65, 67, 69, 71, 732, 734, 936
Family 1561
Fantastic literature 984
Federación Latinoamericana de Sociedades de Sexología y Educación Sexual 1528
Federación Nacional de Cafeteros de Colombia 236
Felipe, León 463
Felipe Herrera Library 844
Feminism
Brazil 1570
Fernández de Larraín, Sergio 1163
Fertilizers 203
Festschriften
Venezuela--Indexes 842
Fiber plants
Brazil 214
Finance 579
Finance, Public
Latin America 577
Mexico--History 1226, 1231
Flamenco music 1363
Flax
Brazil 229
Folk art
Caribbean area 338
Chile 320
Ecuador 318
Folk literature
Argentina 698
Folk medicine
Mexico 282
Folk music
Bolivia 1361
Latin America 1371
Folklore
Argentina 698
Brazil 694, 697, 699-700
Chile 696
Guatemala 695
Fondo bibliográfico Armando Samper Gnecco 1177
Fondo Simón Bolívar 1524
Fonseca, Carlos 464, 1246
Forests and forestry

Argentina 68, 205
Colombia 238, 240
Paraguay 555
Peru 247
France
Foreign relations--Argentina 733
Franciscans 347
History--Ecuador 1495
Mexico--History 1492
Francisco Madero collection 1221
Freira, Maria Ines Aragão 1150
Fruit culture
Brazil 224
Venezuela 251
Fuentes, Carlos 465
Fundação Instituto Brasileiro de Geografia e Estatística 703
Fundação Nacional do Indio 957
Fundación Mariano Ospina Pérez, Bogotá 1475
Fundación para el Desarrollo de la Región Centro Occidental de Venezuela 631

Gabaldoni, Luis E. 466
Gaceta, La. Diario Oficial (Nicaragua) 883
Galvão, Clidenor Coelho 1150
García Bossa, Antonio 585
García Márquez, Gabriel 467, 954
Genealogical Society of the Church of Jesus Christ of Latter Day Saints 1242
Genealogical Society of Utah. Manuscript Collection 1261
Genealogy
Argentina 743
Guatemala 1261
Geography 35
Andes region 704
Argentina 708
Brazil 705
Latin America 712
Mexico 1479
Geography, Economic
Andes region 704
Geopolitics
Latin America 1437
Glass 300
Godwin-Ternbach Museum 310
Goethe, Johann Wolfgang von 959
Gómez Carrillo, Enrique 468
Gómez de la Serna, Ramón 469
González Antias, Antonio 514
González Ortega, Jesús 1245
Gottschalk, Louis Moreau 1365

Goveia, Elsa 400
Government publications 109
Goya, Argentina 416
Great Britain
  Foreign relations--Argentina 936
Grenada 125, 193
Guaranía 884
Guatemala 126
  History 776-777
  History--Sources 1194-1195, 1198, 1267
Guaymi Indians 261
Guerrillas
  Latin America 770
Guillén, Nicolás 470-471
Guyana
  Boundaries--Venezuela 127
  Imprints 380
Guzmán Brito, Alejandro 472

Haciendas
  Ecuador 701
Haiti 129, 132-134
  Economic conditions 607
  Economic policy 607
  History 778
  Imprints 130-131
Haitians
  Intellectual life 128
Handicapped 1507
Handicraft
  Brazil 342, 344
Haydn, Joseph 1368
Hemeroteca Luis López de Mesa
  Catalogs 1175
Henry Raup Wagner Collection
  Catalogs 1272
Heraldry
  Argentina 743
Hispania 885
Hispanic American aged 1512, 1547
Hispanic American historical review 886
Hispanic American women
  Employment 1521
Hispanic Americans 15, 1306, 1348, 1507, 1539, 1618
  Culture 1522
  Education 647, 660
  Employment 1617
  Medical care 1540
  Mental health 1516
  Michigan 1353

Middle West 1353
Minnesota 1350
Population 1616
Population--Statistics 1623
Statistics--Catalogs 1331
Wisconsin 1324
Historia (Chile) 887
Historians
Latin America--Biography 425
Historic sites
New Mexico--Conservation and restoration 317
Historiography
Mexico 1595
Hogar, El 445
Honduras 135-136
History 779-780
Politics and government 1460-1461
Housing
Brazil 1632
Mexico 1631
Howard University. Moorland-Spingarn Research Center 1270
Hueso húmero 888
Human resources
Mexico 1597
Humboldt 889
Humorists
Latin American 1004
Venezuelan 1111

ICA (Colombia) 890
Identity (Psychology) 1611
Iglesia Cristiana Evangélica
Argentina 1490
Ilustración musical hispano-americana 1370
Income distribution
Paraguay 626
Indians 266
Argentina 269
Bolivia 255, 260
Bolivia--Wars 745
Brazil--Education 662
Caribbean area--Art 332
Central America 276
Central America--Antiquities 301
Central America--Art 331-332
Central America--Languages 1005
Central America--Manuscripts 1207
Central America--Painting 327
Central America--Religion and mythology 1503
Central America--Textiles and fabrics 278

Chile 269
Chile--Legal status, laws, etc. 1130
Ecuador 297
Ecuador--Languages 1068
Latin America--Literature 981
Mexico 265, 276, 284, 1074
Mexico--Antiquities 299, 301, 305, 431
Mexico--Architecture 345
Mexico--Art 331-332, 336
Mexico--Education 678
Mexico--Government relations 793
Mexico--History 790, 1266, 1296-1297
Mexico--Languages 1080-1081
Mexico--Manuscripts 1207
Mexico--Medicine 282
Mexico--Missions 1499
Mexico--Oaxaca 285
Mexico--Painting 327
North America--New Mexico 302
Panama 261
Peru 1604
Peru--Art 333
Peru--Languages 1097
Peru--Religion and mythology 1494
South America 257, 279, 292
South America--Art 334-335
South America--Languages 975, 1096, 1114
South America--Legends 275
South America--Peru 546
South America--Religion and mythology 275
Venezuela 280
Indians in literature 971
Industries
Latin America 573
Industry and education
Brazil 1568
Industry and state
Mexico 621
Inflation (Finance)
Brazil 591
Information science 1279, 1282
Chile 1281
INRA (Instituto Nacional de Reforma Agraria) 880
Institute of Jamaica, Kingston. West India Reference Library
Catalogs 1278
Instituto Argentino del Petroleo 1146
Instituto de Antropología e Historia (Guatemala) 1198
Instituto de Desenvolvimento de Pernambuco 1477
Instituto de Investigaciones Agropecuarias (Chile) 233, 1471
Instituto Histórico de la Ciudad de Buenos Aires. Archivo Histórico 736

Instituto Indigenista Peruano 1476
Instituto Literario del Estado de México
  Archives--Catalogs 1209
Instituto Nacional de Antropología e Historia (Mexico) 786, 1210
Instituto Roberto Simonsen (Brazil) 1568
Inter-American Center for Documentation and Agriculture Information 1401
Interamerican Development Bank 1135
International agencies 48
International business enterprises 565, 570
  Latin America 572
International economic relations 575
International relations
  Research--Caribbean area 939
  Research--Latin America 939
Interpersonal communication 1348
Investments, Foreign
  Latin America 568-569
  Mexico 617
Irrigation
  Brazil, Northeast 219
  Cuba 242
Ixtacamaxitlán, Mexico 1212

Jalisco, Mexico 151-152
  Biobibliography 393, 427
Jamaica 137
  Government publications 1592
Japanese
  Bolivia 1352
  Brazil 1352
Jesuits
  Paraguay 1505
Jews
  Latin America 1333-1334
Jiménez Berguecio, Julio 1161
Jivaro Indians 292, 1097
Journalism 1034, 1303
Judicial power
  Latin America 1137
Jute 200
Juvenile courts 1125
Juvenile literature 993, 1002
  Hispanic American 1000, 1003
  Latin American 999
  West Indian 968, 1122

Kahlo, Frida 473
Klumb, Henrique 340

Labor and laboring classes
Brazil 590, 1566
Caribbean area 1579
Latin America 561, 580, 1483
Mexico 623, 1598
Peru 1605
Labor disputes
Mexico--History 1233
Labor laws and legislation
Chile 1130
Lacerda de Moura, María 474
Land grants
New Mexico 828
Land reform 1530
Cuba 605
Latin America 201
Mexico 246
Peru 248
Land tenure 1530
Mexico (State)--History 803
Mexico 618
Land titles
Registration and transfer--Mexico 1224
Languages
Brazil 957, 1035
Mixed 951
Venezuela 1114
Láscaris, Constantino 475
Latin America 4, 12, 19, 21, 24, 27, 35, 37, 41, 46, 539, 558, 730, 1276
Biography 417
Census 1535
Commerce 721
Commerce--Information services 578
Description and travel 53
Economic conditions 560, 564-565, 567, 571, 576, 578-579, 844, 1523
Economic integration 559, 575
Economic policy 564
Emigration and immigration 1510-1511, 1552
Ethnic relations 1334, 1543
Foreign economic relations 574
Foreign relations 933
Foreign relations--United States 935, 946
Government publications 357, 1513
Historiography 425
History 6, 717-718, 723-724, 729
History, Military 1273
History--20th century 716
History--Sources 1191, 1254, 1255-1256, 1300, 1314
Imprints 13, 36

Manuscripts--Catalogs 804
Mental health 1517
Microform catalogs 1317
Notaries 1544
Officials and employees 1544
Politics and government 1136, 1437, 1441, 1443, 1523, 1532, 1534, 1542
Population 1554
Population--History 1508
Race relations 1543
Relations--China 34
Social change 1532
Social conditions 1509, 1523, 1542
Social security 1546
Latin American Centre for Economic and Social Documentation 1551
Latin American Institute for Economic and Social Planning 1551
Latin American studies 11, 38
Brazil 84
Canada 45
Germany 5, 26, 32, 593
Hungary 49
Italy 1, 7, 8, 47
Poland 10
Sources 1518
Soviet Union 720, 1550
Spain 3, 30, 31
Sweden 20
USSR 52
Latin Americanists
Directory 40
Italy 394
United States 413
Lauricocha, Peru 59
Law 1125-1126, 1133, 1137-1138
Argentina 1127
Caribbean area 1132
Colombia 1128
Latin America 1136
Mexico 1129
Puerto Rico--Indexes 1126
United States 1124
Venezuela 1138
Legal research 1283
Puerto Rico 1134
Leisure
Brazil 85
León, Carlos Augusto 476
León, Mexico 1211
Levaggi, Abelardo 399
Lewis, Sir Arthur 477
Liberation theology 1487

Libraries
Automation 1285
Brazil--Automation 1285
Brazil--Curitiba 1156
Brazil--Florianopolis 1152
Brazil--Paraná 1153
France 1192
Mexico 1206
Libraries and minorities
United States 1335
Library of Congress 1269
Library of Congress. Geography and Map Division
Catalogs 711
Library of Congress. Law Library 1124
Library resources on
Caribbean area 1270
Lilly Library (Indiana University)
Catalogs 1300
Lima Barreto, Afonso H. 478
Linguistic analysis (Literature) 997
Linguistics 956, 1062
Brazil 957
Mexico 1076
Peru 1094
Liquor traffic
Mexico 1225
Lisboa, Antônio Francisco 325
Lispector, Clarice 479-481
Literacy
Mexico 678
Literary prizes 1063
Literature
African--Black authors 419
American--Afro-American authors 419
Argentine 404, 502, 1019-1021
Argentine--Biobibliography 421, 1022
Argentine--Mendoza 1017
Argentine--Tucumán 1018
Bolivian--Biobibliography 414
Brazilian 409, 1026-1027, 1033, 1037
Brazilian--Biobibliography 411, 418
Brazilian--Dictionaries 1032
Brazilian--Espírito Santo 748
Caribbean area 346, 527, 1038-1040
Caribbean area--Black authors 419
Chilean 497, 538, 1045, 1047-1048, 1172, 1262, 1397
Chilean--Biobibliography 1049
Chilean--in the United States 1041-1043
Colombian 1052
Cuban 1054, 1056, 1061
Cuban--History and criticism 1055, 1057, 1060

Dominican 1064
Ecuadorian 1067
Gallegan--Biobibliography 418
Guatemalan 1070
Guatemalan--Biobibliography 1069
Haitian--History and criticism 1071
Latin American 263, 366, 963, 967, 972, 980, 982, 985, 988, 990, 992, 1004, 1006-1008, 1012
Latin American--20th century 716
Latin American--Biobibliography 953
Latin American--Dissertations 545
Latin American--History and criticism 39, 976, 978, 983, 995, 1016
Latin American--Translations 963
Latin American--Translations into Danish 976
Latin American--Translations into English 964, 991
Latin American--Women authors 964
Mexican 498-499, 513
Mexican--History and criticism 1073
Mexican-American 1077, 1079, 1082-1089
Mexican-American--History and criticism 1082
Paraguayan 1092
Peruvian 1098-1099
Peruvian--Biobibliography 1093
Portuguese--Biobibliography 418
Puerto Rican 1104
Spanish 366, 1006
Spanish American 974
Trinidad and Tobago 1106
Uruguayan--Tacuarembo 420
Venezuelan 1111
Venezuelan--History and criticism 1110
Venezuelan--Lara 1113
West Indian 1118-1120
West Indian--History and criticism 1117, 1121
Literature and society 955
Logos (Argentina) 891
Loja, Ecuador
History 772-774
Lópes Cançado, Maura 482
Lozier Almazón, Bernardo F. 743

Macadamia nut 217
Machado de Assis, Joaquim Maria 1023
Malva 214
Malvinas Islands 61, 63, 65, 67, 69, 71, 732, 734, 936
Mañach, Jorge 483
Manuscripts
Brazil 1293-1294, 1298
Mexico 1288

Mexico--Mexico City 1297
Spain 1295
Maranhão, Brazil
Social life and customs 700
Mariátegui, José Carlos 484
Marley, Bob 1374
Marques, René 485
Martí, José 486
Martínez Baeza, Sergio 487
Martinique 194-195
History--Sources 1199
Marxism 1444
Mass media
Caribbean area 1308
Venezuela 1309
Maule, Chile
Biobibliography 1046
Mayas 254
Antiquities 274
Architecture 345
Languages 1010, 1013
Medical care
United States 1539
Medicine
Latin America--History 1190
Meneses, Guillermo 488
Mercado Común Centroamericano 598
Meriño, Fernando Arturo de 489
Merino Reyes, Luis 490
Mestre, Antonio 491
Mexican Americans 148, 928, 1274, 1323, 1326, 1335-1336, 1340-1341, 1345, 1349, 1351, 1355, 1356-1357
Ethnic identity 1311
Film catalogs 1327
History 1339, 1344
History--Sources 1263, 1264
Minnesota 1350
Periodicals--Indexes 1328-1329
Politics and suffrage 1332
Services for 1337
Statistics--Catalogs 1331
Mexican-American Border Region
Economic conditions 614
Industries 621
Mexico 42, 142, 146-148, 1276
Antiquities 305, 431
Archivo General de la Nación 1226
Azcapotzalco 143
Boundaries--United States 149
Census 1622
Church history 1496, 1500, 1504

Church history--Sources 1492, 1499
Commerce 624-625
Commerce--History 1231
Diplomatic and consular services--Archives 1238
Economic conditions 608-609, 612-613, 616, 622, 1594
Economic conditions--History 615
Economic conditions--Sources 1243
Economic policy 610
Foreign economic relations--United States 614, 934
Foreign relations 944
Foreign relations--United States 931, 937, 940, 1462
Genealogy 1240-1242
Government publications 28, 620
Historiography 799, 809
History 541, 616, 784, 789, 801, 805, 865
History--Archival resources 788, 804
History--Manuscripts 1289, 1301
History--Revolution 785
History--Sources 783, 787, 791-792, 795-797, 802, 808, 1213, 1223, 1227, 1236, 1239, 1244-1245, 1265, 1277, 1297, 1313
History--War with the United States 806, 1313
History, Local--Sources 794
History, Military--Sources 791, 1208, 1228
Imprints 138, 144, 150, 385
Industries 611, 619
Maps--Catalogs 1230
Periodicals 1416
Politics and government 800, 1462, 1594
Politics and government--Sources 1237
Population--Statistics 1622
Relations (General) with the United States 928
Social conditions 1594-1595
Social conditions--History 615
Statistics 1479
Women in mass media 1412-1413
Mexico. Archivo General de la Nación 791-797, 1221, 1223-1225, 1229-1230, 1232, 1234-1236, 1238, 1297, 1417, 1496, 1498-1500
Mexico. Archivo General de Notarías 1239
Mexico. Archivo Histórico de Hacienda
Catalogs 622
Mexico. Secretaría de Educación Pública 1480
México. Secretaría de Programación y Presupuesto 620
Mexico (City). Universidad Nacional. Instituto de Investigaciones Sociales 141
Mexico City, Mexico
History 781
History--Sources 798, 1204
Microfilming projects newsletter [SALALM] 892
Migrant labor
Latin America 1347
Migration

Puerto Rico 1615
Migration, Internal
Colombia 1589
Peru 1607
Migration, Rural 1530
Military
Argentina 735
Central America 765
Latin America 713, 725
Paraguay 813
Military art and science 813
Milla y Vidaurre, José 492
Mines and mining
Mexico--History 1234
Minorities
Education--United States 1354
United States--Psychology 1338
Miranda, Venezuela 191
Mistral, Gabriela 1172
Monagas, Venezuela 183
Montevideo, Uruguay 182
Mossoró, Brazil
Imprints 1160
Moving pictures 1327
Brazil 1029
Chile 1044
Latin America 960, 1014
Venezuela 1112
<u>Mundo universitario</u> 893
Mural painting and decoration
Mexico 327
Museo de América. Biblioteca del Ultramar (Madrid) 1256
Museo Nacional de Historia (Mexico) 1237
Museo Social Argentino (Buenos Aires) 74
Museu do Rio de Janeiro 957
Museums
Argentina 74
Music
Bolivia 1360
Brazil 1366
Caribbean area 1358, 1362
Cuba--19th century 1369
Ecuador 1367
Latin America 1370-1371
Nicaragua 1359
Puerto Rico 1373
Venezuela 1372
Music, Popular
Jamaica 1374

Nabuco, Joaquim 1287
Nación, La (Chile) 1048
Nahuatl language 1080-1081
Nahuatl literature 1080-1081
Names, Geographical
  Brazil 709, 1035
National Chicano Research Network 1331
Natural resources
  Amazon Valley 55
  Brazil--Mato Grosso 211
  Caribbean area--Management 595
  Latin America 1548
  Virgin Islands of the United States--Management 595
Navarro, Desiderio 493
Neme, Mário 494
Netherlands Antilles
  History 760
New Mexico 176
  Antiquities 302
  History 824
  History--Sources 827, 1275
New West Indian Guide 894
New York City. Office of Bilingual Education 690
New York Times 125, 895
Newspapers
  Brazilian 1394
  Costa Rican--Indexes 847
  Cuban 1404
  Mexican 1417
  Mexican--San Luis Potosí (State) 1418
  Puerto Rican 1373
  Puerto Rican--Indexes 854
  Virgin Islands 1427
Nicaragua 157
  Atlantic Coast 154-155
  Atlantic Coast--History 153
  Atlantic Coast--Literature 153
  Bio-bibliography 1090
  History 156, 810-812
Notaries
  Mexico 1239
  Mexico--History 1232, 1240-1241
  Zacatecas, Mexico 1205
Noticias indigenistas de América 851-852
Noticias sobre el libro y bibliografía 896
Nouvelle revue française 995
Nuevo Mercurio 897

O, Genovevo de la
  Archives 1223

Oaxaca 285
Occupational training 639
Olmecs
  Culture 265
Olmos, Andrés de 1075
Organization of American States 1482, 1484
Ortiz, Abelardo 495
Ortiz Fernández, Fernando 114

Painting
  Latin American--Exhibitions 310
  Nicaraguan 308
Palabra y el hombre 898
Palau y Dulcet, Antonio. Manual del libero hispanoamericano 899
Palm, Erwin Walter 496
Panama 158
  History--Sources 1247
Panama. Archivo Nacional 1247
Pano languages 1096
Panoan Indians 975
Paraguay 159-161, 163, 1092, 1284
  Description and travel 164
  Economic conditions 1600-1601
  Foreign relations 1602
  History 814, 884
  History--Sources 815
  Imprints 162, 1248
  Politics and government 1602
  Social conditions 1601
Parra, Nicanor 497
Paz, Octavio 498-499
Peach
  Brazil 224
Peasantry
  Peru 628
Periodicals
  Agriculture--Brazil 1390
  Argentina 1388
  Argentina--Indexes 1387
  Bolivia 1389
  Brazil 1312, 1391, 1394-1395
  Caribbean area 1396
  Chile--Indexes 1397
  Colombia--Antioquia 1399
  Colombia--History 1398
  Costa Rica 905
  Costa Rica--Indexes 847
  Criminology--Indexes 845
  Cuba 1403-1406
  Dominican Republic 1408-1409

Education--Brazil 1392
Geography 1393
Guyana 1410
Humanities--Indexes 846
Land reform--Nicaragua 1420
Latin America 1382, 1384, 1385-1386
Latin America--Indexes 840-841, 843-845, 850-852, 855-856, 859-861, 1377-1378
Mexican-American 1383
Mexico 1411-1415, 1417, 1419
Mexico-San Luis Potosí (State) 1418
Mexico--Yucatan 1259
Paraguay--Indexes 848
Penology--Indexes 845
Peru 1421
Puerto Rico 1373
Puerto Rico--Indexes 901
Social sciences--Indexes 846
Spanish-American 1381
Statistics 1393
Union lists 1422
Venezuela 1423-1426
Perón, Eva 500
Perón, Juan 500
Peru 166, 1276
Biobibliography 402
Economic conditions 165, 168, 629, 1608
Economic policy 1612
Emigration and immigration 1346
History 816-818
History--Archival resources 788
History--Insurrection of Tupac-Amaru, 1780-1781 745
History--Sources 1253
Imprints 387
Industries 627
Politics and government 168, 1464, 1465, 1608
Religious life and customs 1494
Rural conditions 1604
Social conditions 168, 543, 546, 1604, 1608
Peru. Dirección de Archivo Colonial
Catalogs 1253
Perú indigena 900
Perú integral 900
Peru. Real Aduana
Archives--Catalogs 1253
Peruvian Collection. National Library of Peru 1252
Petroleum 581
Information sources 1146
Petroleum industry and trade
Legal aspects 1135
Pharmacy

Latin America 1257
Philology
Portuguese 534
Spanish 534
Philosophy
Argentine 501, 1433
Brazilian 1436
Chilean--Biobibliography 1429
Ecuadorian 1428, 1431
Latin American 1430, 1432, 1435
Mexican 1434
Photography
Brazil 340
Caribbean 307
Photography, Artistic
Latin America 316
Physicians as authors 412
Picaresque literature 977
Pineapple
Diseases and pests 212
Pinzón, Fernando
Archives 1301
Piper nigrum 215
Piranesi, Giovanni Battista 312
Plácido 1056
Plerus 901
Poetry
Brazilian 1030-1031
Colombian 1050
Jamaican 1072
Latin American 996
Peruvian 1095, 1101-1103
Venezuelan--Zulia 1108
Poisonous plants
Brazil 226
Political parties
Latin America 1310
Political rights
Latin America 1537
Political science 1438
Latin America 1439
Periodicals 1400
Politics in literature 970
Pontificia Universidad Católica del Ecuador. Revista 902
Popoloca Indians
History--Sources 790
Population
Caribbean area 1531
Latin America 1531
Population forecasting
United States 1616

Population research
  Puerto Rico 1614
Portugal
  History 6
  History--Sources 758
Portuguese language
  Brazil 1028
  Dictionaries 948
  Etymology--Names 949
Positivism
  Mexico 809
Poverty
  Latin America 1552
Power resources 1514
Prensa (New York)
  Indexes 853
Presidents
  Colombia 401
Press
  Costa Rica 1304
Prints
  Cuban 319
Prisma 857
Proa 857
Programa Regional del Empleo para América Latina y el Caribe (PREALC) 1483
Progreso de Quilmes 903
Proverbs
  Mexican-American 1078
Provincia de São Paulo 904
Psychology, Industrial
  Research--Peru 1606
Public administration 1440
Public health
  Brazil 547
  Brazil--São Paulo (State) 1569
  Cuba 1590
  Latin America 1559
Pucciarelli, Eugenio 501
Puerto Ricans 1323
  New York (N.Y.)--Indexes 853
  United States--Indexes 895
Puerto Rico 170-171, 174
  Economic conditions 169
  Emigration and immigration 854
  History 172, 819-823
  Indexes 853, 895
  Politics and government 1466
  Population 1614
  Social conditions 169
Puig, Manuel 502
Puquino Indians 257

Quechua language 1068
Quiles, Samuel 503
Quintana, Mário 504
Quintana Roo, Mexico 139
Quirarte Ruiz, Martín 505

Radio broadcasting
  Panama 1305
Rama, Angel 506
Ramírez Rivera, Hugo Rodolfo 1162
Ramírez Vázquez, Pedro 507
Rape (Plant) 221
Rare books
  Brazil 1290-1292
  Cuba--Santiago de Cuba 1302
Real Academia de la Historia (Spain) 1258
Real Expedición Botánica del Nuevo Reyno de Granada
  Bibliography 2
Reference books 14, 27, 982, 1156, 1357
  Central America 1580
  Latin America 17-18, 22-23, 51, 730
  Linguistics--Hispanic 958
  Literature--Hispanic 958
  Mexican Americans 1336
Refugees
  United States 1536
Refugees, Political
  Spain 415
Regional planning
  Costa Rica 1633
  Latin America 563, 1551
  Mexico 1624
  Peru 1613
Religion
  Argentina 1490
  Brazil 1489
  Caribbean area 1491, 1493
  Latin America 1542
  Peru 1502
Repertorio americano 905
Repositorio Nacional (Bolivia) 1149
Research
  Brazil 1572
  Mexico 140
  Venezuela 693
Restrepo Canal, Carlos 509
Restrepo, José Manuel 508
Revista bimestre cubana 906
Revista brasileira de estatística 907
Revista de ciência política (Brazil) 908

Revista de derecho puertorriqueño 849
Revista de Indias 909
Revista de la Biblioteca Nacional José Martí 910
Revista de Legislación y Documentación en Derecho y Ciencias Sociales 869
Revista de planeación y desarrollo 911
Revista de teatro (Brazil) 912
Revista del Colegio de Abogados de Puerto Rico 849
Revista del Instituto Paraguayo 913, 914
Revista interamericana de bibliografía 915
Revista jurídica de la Universidad de Puerto Rico 849
Revista jurídica de la Universidad Interamericana de Puerto Rico 849
Revista nacional de letras y ciencias 916
Revista paraguaya de sociología 917
Revista Puerto Rico Ilustrado 918
Revolución y cultura 919
Revolutions
  Central America 764
Reyes, Bernardo
  Archives 1237
Rio, João de 432
Rio Branco, José Maria da Silva Paranhos, visconde do
  Archives 1154
Rio de Janeiro, Brazil 1293
  Description 86
Río de la Plata 742
Rio Grande do Sul, Brazil 1294
  Politics and government--Sources 1151
Robles Domínguez, Alfredo
  Archives--Catalogs 1227
Rocafuerte, Vicente 510
Rock painting
  Caribbean area 339
Rodney, Walter 400
Rojas, Gonzalo 511
Rojas, Manuel 512
Rosa, João Guimarães 1157
Rosenbach Museum and Library
  Catalogs 1289, 1301
Rosenberg Library
  Catalogs 1299
Rulfo, Juan 513
Rum 1225
Rural development
  Colombia 241, 1584
  Latin America 1524
  Peru 628, 1613
Rural-urban migration
  Brazil 1566
  Peru 1607

St. Kitts-Nevis 104
SALALM Microfilming Projects Newsletter 1320-1321
SALALM Newsletter 920
Salazar y Castro, Luis de
  Library--Catalogs 1255
Salom, Bartolomé 514
San Diego State University. Library 1272
San Marcos de Arica (Peru) 706
Sánchez, Luis Alberto--Correspondence 1268
Santiago, Chile
  History--Sources 1165
São Paulo (State), Brazil
  Economic conditions 1569
  Politics and government 1569
São Paulo. Universidade. Centro de Estudos Africanos 349
Sarmiento, Domingo Faustino 515
Scientific expeditions
  Latin America 714
Sculpture
  Nicaraguan 308, 311
Selective dissemination of information 1549
Seler, Eduard
  Catalogs 276
Selvon, Samuel 516-517
Semiotics 1094
Sex customs
  Latin America 1528
Shepherds
  Andes region 262
Signo (Bolivia) 921
Silveira, Aluaro Ferdinando Sousa da 518
Sinaloa, Mexico
  History 1229
Sisal 239
Slavery 722, 726
  Caribbean area 727, 763
  Latin America 1557
Slums
  Brazil 1632
Small business
  Colombia 601
Social classes
  Latin America 1515
Social problems 1526
Social sciences 543, 1529
  Argentina 585
  Information services 1558
  Periodicals 1400
  Peru 1610
Social services
  Cuba 1590
  Peru 1603

Socialism
  Cuba 1454-1457
  Latin America 1442
Sociolinguistics 1015
Sociology, Urban 1629
  Dominican Republic 1627
Soils 203, 235
Sonora, Mexico
  History 782, 1229
South America 43
  History 16
  Population 1525
Southwest, New 149
  Antiquities 293
  History 826, 1272
  History--Sources 783, 1313
Spain
  History 6
  Politics and government 721
Spanish language 997
  Colombia 1051
  Cuba 1058, 1060
  Dialects--Argentina 966
  Dialects--Uruguay 966
  Dictionaries 952
  Etymology--Names 949
  Grammar 987
  Morphology 986
  Nicaragua 1091
  Periodicals 1380
  Phonology 986, 989
  Technical Spanish--Dictionaries 952
Spanish philology
  Biobibliography 394
Speeches
  Venezuelan 1109
Suárez, Federico González 519
Subject headings
  Paraguay 1284
Sugar industry and trade
  Caribbean area 762
  Cuba 243
Summer Institute of Linguistics 260, 1005
Suplemento antropológico del Ateneo paraguayo 922
Surinam 175
  History 760
Szuchman, Mark D. 399

Tacanan languages 1096

Tandil, Argentina 72
Taxation
  Mexico--History 1231
Teatro Esperanza Iris 1214
Technical education
  Mexico 679
Technology 582
  Dictionaries--Spanish 969
Tehuacán, Mexico
  History--Sources 790
Teología y vida 923
Texas 180
  History 177, 825
  History--Manuscripts 1299
  History--Sources 1299
Textbooks
  Paraguay 686
Theater
  Cuba 1059
  Ecuador 1065-1066
  Peru 1100
Theology
  Latin American 1435
Tobacco 199
Tourist trade
  Brazil 85
Tovar y Tovar, Martín 520
Trade unions
  Latin America 1553, 1560
  Mexico--History 1233
Transportation and state
  Colombia 1587
Travelers
  Argentina 73
Tres Américas 924
Trinidad and Tobago
  Economic conditions 630
  Imprints 389
Tucumán, Argentina
  Bio-bibliography 404
Tulane University. Howard-Tilton Memorial Library 326
Turner, Ethel Duffy 521

United Nations. Economic commission for Latin America 1551
United States 178-179
  Armed forces--Military life 1618
  Boundaries--Mexico 149
  Foreign economic relations--Mexico 614, 934
  Foreign relations 946, 1356
  Foreign relations--El Salvador 1459

Foreign relations--Latin America 935
Foreign relations--Mexico 931, 937, 940
History--War with Mexico 806
Imprints--Translations into Spanish 50
Maps 711
Politics and government 1443
Relations (General) with Mexico 928
United States Military History Institute 1273
Universidad de Antioquia. Biblioteca Central
Catalogs 1398
Universidad de Córdoba (Argentina)
Students 406
Universidad de Oriente (Santiago de Cuba)
Catalogs 1302
Universidad de Puerto Rico. Biblioteca de Derecho 1466
Universidad Iberoamericana
Archives--Catalogs 1244
Universidade de São Paulo. Faculdade de Saúde Pública 547
Universidade Federal de Goiás. Biblioteca Central
Catalogs 1395
Universidade Federal do Rio Grande do Norte. Biblioteca. 1155
Université de Paris IV: Paris-Sorbonne. Institute d'Études Hispaniques 1193
Universities and colleges 658
Venezuela--Graduate work 693
University of Arizona. Library 1274
University of California, Berkeley. Library
Catalogs 51
University of Puerto Rico. Centro de Investigaciones Históricas 172
University of Texas, Arlington. Library. Center for Mesoamerican Studies 1259
University of Texas at El Paso. Library. Special Collections Dept. 1313
University of the West Indies 93
University of Wisconsin--Madison. Library
Microform catalogs 1317
Urbanization
Brazil 1630
Latin America 1625-1626, 1628
Uruguay
Constitutional law 181
Economic conditions 1485
Foreign relations 830, 930
Historiography 834
History 831-833, 835
Imprints 390
Social conditions 1485, 1619

Valdés, Gabriel de la Concepción 1056

Vargas, Getulio 522
Vasconcelos, José 523
Veja 1467
Venezuela 185, 187
  Boundaries--Guyana 127
  Civilization--African influences 281
  Economic conditions 631
  History 715, 836-837
  History--Sources 514
  Imprints 186
  Politics and government 836, 1468
Venezuela. Universidad de Oriente
  Catalogs 1426
Venezuelan studies
  USSR 188
Vidaurreta, Alicia 399
Viganti, Milcíades Alejo 524
Violence 1526
Virgin Islands (U.S.)
  Economic policy 595
  Languages 1116
Vitier, Cintio 525
Vocational education 635, 639
  Brazil 1568
Voyages and travels 728
Voyages around the world 752

Wages
  Brazil 592
Walker, William 812
Weaving 278
Wellcome Institute for the History of Medicine. Library 1190
West Indies 95, 192-193, 1278
  Census 1535
  Emigration and immigration 1577
  History--Sources 97
  Maps 711
West Indies, French 195
  History 838-839
Wheat
  Brazil 228
Williams, Eric 400
Wisconsin
  Ethnic relations 1324
Women 728, 1406, 1541, 1561
  Argentina--Biography 423
  Brazil--Rio de Janeiro 752
  Brazil--Social conditions 1570
  Chile 1582
  Cuba 405

Employment--Latin America 1527
Latin America 405, 719, 1506, 1555, 1559
Latin America--Social conditions 1538
Mexico 405, 1596
New Mexico 176
Paraguay 1599
Puerto Rico 405
Women authors 947, 991
Argentina 1020
Caribbean area 1040
Spanish-American 403
Venezuela 1108
Women in literature 950, 1024, 1027, 1033, 1367
Women in rural development
Latin America 1538

Xochimilco (Distrito Federal, Mexico)
History--Sources 803

Yale University. Library. Latin American Pamphlet Collection
Catalogs 1276-1277
Youth
Employment 1519
Yucatan, Mexico 254
History 145

Zacapa, Guatemala 1194
Zona franca 925

AUTHOR INDEX

Abalo, Carlos 584
Abrams, H. Leon, Jr. 431
Academia Nacional de la Historia, Caracas. Departamento de Publicaciones 1469
Acevedo, Esther 306
Adot, Juan C. 503
African-Caribbean Institute of Jamaica 307, 1358
Agraz García de Alba, Gabriel 393
Aguilar Zarandona, Irene 1200
Aguilera de Zarza, Yenny 1599
Aguilera Mier, María de los Angeles 1624
Aguirre, Carlos 781
Alanís Boyso, José Luis 1201-1203
Alarcón, Norma 947
Albán, María Elena 1428
Albizúrez Palma, Francisco 1069
Albó, Victor 1564
Albonico, Aldo 1
Albuquerque, Fernando Carneiro 215
Ales, Oreste Carlos 903
Alexander, Robert J. 1468
Alfaro Bolaños, Flor de M. 632, 669
Aljure Chalela, Simón 437, 449, 769
Allis, Jeannette B. 1117
Almeida, Horácio de 948
Almeida-Filho, Noamar de 1566
Alvarez, Jesús 1398
Alvarez, Victor 1173
Alvarez de Péz, Graciela 638
Alvarez Rudolph, Inés 690
Alves, Ephraim Ferreira 1487
Amaral, Raúl 161
Amaya, José Antonio 2
Anderson, Frank G. 293
Anderson, Victor D. 169
Andrade, Ana Isabel de Souza Leão 1287
Andrade, Diva Carrero de 526
Andrade Aguiar, Paulo Anselmo 208
Anrup, Roland 1506
Anson, Roberto 1616
Anzaldúa, Mike 1077
Aragão Dias Freire, Maria Ines 1150
Aramayo Santa Cruz, Carlos 81
Aranguren, Willy 520
Araujo, María Celina Soares d' 522
Araya Incera, Manuel E. 926
Arbeláez B, Leda Inés 600
Archer, Christon I. 713
Archives de Martinique 194
Archivo General de Indias 1254
Archivo Nacional de Historia (Ecuador) 1181
Ardilla, Hector M. 395
Ardissone, Elena 857, 1387
Arellano, Jorge Eduardo 153-154, 308, 386, 459, 1090-1091, 1359
Argentina. Estado Mayor Conjunto. Biblioteca y Centro de Documentación 61
Argüelles Espinosa, Luis Angel 1288
Argueta, Mario 382, 779
Arguez, Samuel 898
Arias Divito, Juan C 714
Ariza Viguera, Manuel 949
Arizmendi Posada, Ignacio 396

Arnold, Bill R. 1507
Arnold, Linda 1204
Arora, Shirley L. 1078
Arquivo Histórico do Rio Grande do Sul 1151
Arretx, Carmen 1508
Arriaga Weiss, Davis 252, 955, 1509
Arrigunaga Coello, Maritza 1259
Arriola Grande, Maurilio 1093
Arrue Rius, Susana 692
Arteaga Sáenz, Juan José 181, 1123
Arujo, Marta Maria Alencar 1390
Arze, José Roberto 397
Asdrúbal Silva, Hernán 1510
Associação Catarinense de Bibliotecarios. Grupo de Bibliotecarios em Informação e Documentação em Processos Técnicos 1152
Associação dos Bibliotecários de Minas Gerais. Grupo de Bibliotecários de Ciências Sociais e Humanidades 694
Astorquiza Pizarro, Fernando 1429
Atondo Rodríguez, Ana María 782, 1229
Augel, Johannes 84
Auro, María Adela d' 1146
Auza, Néstor Tomás 876
Averbuck, Lígia 950
Avilés, Jorge M. 732
Axline, W. Andrew 559
Ayala Espino, José 608
Azevedo, Thales de 253
Azocar, Jesús Napoleón 183

Bagby, Albert Ian, Jr. 1023
Bagu, Sergio 62
Bahamón, Sundary de 239
Bailey, Joyce Waddell 309
Bailey, Juan P. 1511
Baird, Keith E. 951
Baklanoff, Eric N. 560
Ballón, Enrique 1094
Bamat, Thomas 1488
Banco Central de la República Dominicana. Biblioteca 606
Banco Central de Nicaragua. Biblioteca y Servicios de Información 155
Banco de la República, Bogotá 1175
Banco de México 609
Bandara, Samuel B. 346, 527, 1038
Baptiste, Fitzroy André 93
Barberena Blásquez, Elsa 866
Barcala de Moyano, Graciela G. 448
Barcelo Sifontes, Lyll 862
Barella, Adriana de 1583
Barker, G.H. 230
Barnadas, Josep 744
Barnes, Catherine A. 1289
Barnes, Thomas Charles 783
Barnitz, Jacqueline 310
Barrera Vázquez, Alfredo 294
Barrios Pintos, Anibal 952
Barrios Valdés, Marciano 923, 1161
Barros Mott, María Lucía de 752
Bastarrachea Mansano, Juan Ramón 254
Bastien, Joseph W. 255
Bazant, Jan 1205, 1239-1241
Becco, Horacio Jorge 4, 438, 953, 1430
Becerra, Rosina M. 1512
Becker, David G. 1464
Becker, Félix 5
Beckers, Frances López 689
Behar, D. 6
Behar, R. 6
Bellegarde-Smith, Patrick 128
Bellini, Giuseppe 7, 8
Beltrán González, Ignacio 1206
Bencomo de León, Guadalupe 476
Bendfeldt Rojas, Lourdes 776
Benjamin, Thomas 784
Benseler, David P. 528
Benson, John 954
Berberian, Eduardo E. 256
Bercht, Domitila María 85
Berg, Hans van den 257

Berger, Paulo 86
Bergquist, Charles 561
Bernal, Marie-Louise H. 1124
Bernal García, Cristina 955, 1561
Berrini, Beatriz 1024
Berry-Cabán, Cristóbal 1324
Bertrand, Jean Wilfrid 381
Beshers, Olga Espejo 479
Best, Carlyle 77, 94
Bettiol, Eugénia Maranhão 225
Biava, María de Lourdes 87, 216
Biblioteca Dr. Juan José Nissen 1141
Biblioteca de Martín Ferreyra. Sección Historia, Genealogía y Heráldica 1140
Biblioteca Nacional (Brazil) 372
Biblioteca Nacional de Antropología e Historia. Archivo Histórico 1207
Biblioteca Nacional José Martí. Departamento de Investigaciones Bibliográficas 376
Biblioteca Presidente Carlos A. López 1248
Biblioteca Pública do Estado (Santa Catarina, Brazil) 1391
Biblioteca Pública do Paraná. Divisão de Documentacão Paranaense 1153
Biblioteca Roosevelt 159
Bilsky, Edgardo 1445
Bisio, Carlos A. 1490
Bittencourt, Gabriel Augusto de Mello 748
Blanes Jiménez, José 206
Bleznick, Donald W. 958
Blitzer, Silvia 1625
Bloch, Thomas 596, 1513
Bloomfield, Valerie 96
Bohdziewicz, Jorge C. 733
Boisier, Sergio 563
Boland, Roy 1375
Bonfiglio, Giovanni 1603
Bonilla, Heraclio 816
Booth, John A. 810
Borba de Moraes, Rubens Borba de 1290
Borges de Carvalho, María de Lourdes 749
Bosque Paz, Gisela 842
Botasso, Juan 292
Boucher, Philip 838
Boultbee, Paul G. 1147
Bozzoli de Willie, María 258
Braem, Martin 113
Brana-Shute, Rosemary 1575
Brathwaite, Edward Kamau 1072
Bravo M., Veronica 233
Brazil. Biblioteca Nacional 439, 959, 1312
Brazil. Congresso. Senado Federal 90
Brazil. Ministério da Fazenda. Biblioteca 1292
Brazil. Ministério da Justiça. Biblioteca 1291
Brazil. Ministério das Relações Exteriores. Arquivo Histórico 1154
Brem, Walter B., Jr. 1514
Bribiesca Sumano, María Elena 792, 795, 1208, 1231
Britto Pereira, Cecilia Duprat de 312
Browar, Lisa 1276, 1277
Brown, Larissa V. 722
Bruna V., Alicia 1471
Bryant, Melrose M. 65
Bueno, Luis Alfonso 184
Bueno, Newton 203
Buenos Aires. Universidad 1143
Buenos Aires. Universidad. Biblioteca 1142
Buenos Aires. Universidad. Facultad de Derecho y Ciencias Sociales 530
Buenos Aires. Universidad. Instituto Bibliotecológico 529
Buntinx, Gustavo 313
Burns, Ada 356
Burton, Julianne 960
Bustamente, Jorge A. 928
Bustillos Vallejo, Freddy 1361
Butler, Erwin 13-14, 116, 138
Buve, Raymond Th. J. 760

Caballero, César 1313
Cabel, Jesús 1095
Cáceres Carísimo, Cirilo 813
Cáceres Castro, Elías 1516-1517
Cáceres Freyre, Julián 524
Caillavet, Chantal 259, 701, 772-773, 1182
Calazans, Maria Julieta Costa 664
Caldeira, Paulo da Terra 749
Callender, Jean A. 77, 1491
Camino, Alejandro 295
Campillo Celado, Rosa C. 929
Campos, Héctor 963
Campos Ruiz Díaz, Daniel 1600
Canak, William L. 1515
Canedo, Lino Gómez 1492
Cano-Sánchez, Beatriz 610
Cárdenas Timoteo, Clara 900
Cardich, Augusto 59
Cardona, Luis Antonio 171
Cardozo, Lubio 185-186, 715, 1115
Careaga Viliesid, Lorena 139
Caribbean Archives Conference (2nd: 1975: Guadeloupe and Martinique) 97
Cariola, Patricio 637
Cariola Sutter, Carmen 599
Carnegie, Jenipher 94, 400, 1119
Carpenter, Charles A 961-962
Carrera de Mangiola, Silvia 1388
Carriazo, Ligia O. de 1613
Carrillo Viveros, Jorge 611
Carrizosa Argaez, Enrique 401
Carvalho, Eliezita Romcy de 225
Casas, Jesús Manuel 1325
Casper, Dale E. 1626
Castañon Barrientos, Carlos 369
Castellanos, Rafael Ramón 440, 447
Castellón Covarrubias, Alvaro 462
Castells Montero, Carlos A. 830, 930
Castillo, Homero 1041-1043
Castillo López, Victor 433, 468
Castillo Sandoval, Stella 1585
Castro, Manuel de 347
Castro, María de los Angeles 172
Castro Arroyo, María de los Angeles 822
Castro Campillo, Galia 1516-1517
Castro de Salmerón, Alicia 638
Castro Feinberg, Rosa 660
Castro-Klarén, Sara 963
Castro Rodríguez, Napoleón 247
Cattarossi Arana, Nelly 1017
Cavalcanti, Sylvia Pereira de Holanda 344
Cavanagh, Jonathan 165
Ceará, Brasil (State). Universidade Federal. Centro de Ciencias Agrárias 533
Ceballos, Jorge 612
Cela, Jorge 1627
Center for U.S.-Mexican Studies. University of California, San Diego 140
Central America Resource Center (Minneapolis). Library 1260
Centro de Documentación Antropológica 260
Centro de Documentación e Información Agrícola (Honduras) 245
Centro de Estudios Puertorriqueños, New York 1126
Centro de Informacion Científica y Tecnológica 1407
Centro de Investigaciones y Estudios Superiores en Antropología Social 1472
Centro de Investigaciones Históricas UNAM-UABC 141
Centro de Pesquisas e Desenvolvimento 348
Centro de Publicaciones de Organismos Internacionales 1473
Centro Internacional de Agricultura Tropical. Unidad de Servicios de Documentación

1376
Centro Latinoamericano de Demografía 1474
Centro Nacional de Documentación Científica y Tecnológica 82
Centro Paraguayo de Documentación Social 684
Centro Paraguayo de Estudios Sociológicos 160
Cerezo Dardón, Hugo 379
Cervo, Amado Luis 750
Céspedes de Reynaga, Alicia 546, 900
Chabrán, Richard 1329, 1335
Chaffee, Wilber A. 886
Chagas, Lujan N. 217
Chamberlain, Bobby J. 1026
Chambers, Frances 129
Chamorro Abadie, María Victoria 879
Chance, John K. 1628
Chandler, Michael J. 231
Chapetón de Ortiz, Gloria 55, 1128
Chapman, David L. 197
Chatham, James R. 534
Chauleau, Liliane 1199
Chavaría, Elvira 1326-1327
Chavarría Mendoza, María C. 1096
Chilcote, Ronald H. 1448
Child, John 933
Church of Jesus Christ of Latter-day Saints. Genealogical Department 1261
Cibes Viadé, Alberto 819
Cipoletti, María Susana 698
Ciria, Alberto 500
Clark, Carter Blue 824
Clarke, Colin C. 761
Clinton, Richard Lee 817
Cobo, Eugenio 1363
Cobo Borda, J.G. 1050
Cobos, Ana María 859
Coddou, Marcelo 511
Coelho, Nelly Novaes 1027
Collado Ardón, Rolando 1516-1517
Colombia. Departamento Administrativo Nacional de Estadística 1621
Colombia. Departamento Nacional de Planeación 1586
Colombia. Ministerio de Educación, Dirección General de Capacitación y Perfeccionamiento Docente, Currículo y Medios Educativos 666
Colombia. Ministerio de Relaciones Exteriores. Biblioteca 1176
Colon Jiménez, Elvira 918
Coloquio Latinoamericano de Fotografía (2nd: 1981: Mexico City, Mexico) 316
Colston, Stephen A. 1272
Columbus Memorial Library 843, 1262
Comissiong, Barbara 352
Commonwealth Agricultural Bureau, Slough 232
Contreras, Remedios 1255, 1295
Cook, Michael 100
Cooney, Jerry W. 815
Coppa & Avery Consultants 317
Coppens, Walter 289-291
Corbatta, Jorgelina 502
Corbera Mori, Angel 1097
Cordero, Luis Agustín 402
Cordero Iñíguez, Juan 318
Córdoba. Universidad Nacional. Biblioteca Mayor 1144-1145
Cordova, César Ramón 1476
Córdova, Gilbert Benito 1340
Cornejo, Atilio 1127
Coronado Rodríguez, José 1414
Correa, Franklin Riet 226
Cortés, Darío A. 512
Cortina, Lynn 403
Corvalán, Graciela N.V. 964
Corvalán-Vásquez, Oscar 1519
Costa, Iraci del Nero da 1573
Costa, Silvio Leopoldo Lima 218
Costa Rica. Oficina de Planificación Nacional y Política Económica. Centro de Documentación 1400
Costilla, María Isabel 404, 1018
Cotera, Martha 405, 1263

Covington, Paula 1377-1378
CRESALC-UNESCO 640-643
Cruz, Alberto 825
Cuenca, Pilar de 690
Cuesta Domingo, Mariano 1256
Cueto, Emilio C. 319
Cuevas, Miriam 277
Cunha, Isabel María Ferin 349
Cunha, Paulo Vieira da 592

Dahlin, Terry 1493
Dahlin, Therrin C. 1520
Dale, Doris Cruger 644, 965
Danby, Colin 135
Dannemann Rothstein, Manuel 320
Dantas, Tereza Cristina de Souza 1287
Daumas de Poncho, Ana María 406
Daus, Federico A. 67
Davidson, Russ 519
Davies, Thomas M., Jr. 818
Dávila, Carlos 295
Davis, Jack Emory 966
Debien, Gabriel 839
De Courtivron, Isabelle 991
De la Viña, Lynda 1617
Delepiani, Oscar E. 187
De Lerma, Dominique-René 1364
Delgado, Elizabeth 442
Delgado, Melvin 1522
Delgado, Susana 1313
Delorme, Robert 1523
Derpich Gallo, Wilma 1330
Deustua, José 1604
Díaz, Marco 967
Díaz, Marta 1331
Díaz Acosta, América 716
Díaz Díaz, Gonzalo 1432
Díaz Gámez, María E. 1058
Díaz Mellán, Mafalda Victoria 913
Díaz Pérez, Viriato 161
Diehl, Richard A. 296
Dietrich, Wolf 1028
Dietz, James L. 820
Di Genio de Carlomagno, Ana M. 182
Domínguez Brito, Luis Angel 623, 1598
Domínguez Camacho, A. 1257
Domschke, Elaine 1531
Donahue, Mary Kaye 1332
Dorn, Georgette Magassy 1280
Doyle, John Godfrey 1365
Drake, Paul W. 1525
Duarte de Bogadjian, Elis 182
Dunkerley, James 764
Duport, Claude 537
Du Pouget, Françoise 630
Durand, Francisco 583, 627
Durango de Martínez Almudever, Norma 408
Durón, Jorge Fidel 383
Dutra, Francis A. 751
Dyal, Donald H. 197

Earnhardt, Kent C. 1614
Echevarría, Israel 1178-1179
Echeverría C., Evelio 905
Edelman, Marc 602
Eger, Ernestina 1079
Eguren, Fernando 248
Eisenhood, Elizabeth D. 1366
Elkin, Judith Laikin 968, 1333-1334
Elso G., Sonia 233
Emery, Sarah Snell 676-679
Epple, Juan Armando 430, 538
Equipo del Centro de Información y Documentación (CIDOC) 261
Espinosa Domínguez, Carlos 1053
Espinosa Elerick, María Luz 969
Estévez, Irma I. 441
Estrada de Asensio, Gloria 600
Estupiñan, Argentina Ch. de 1367
Etchepareborda, Roberto 734-735
Eyzaguirre, Juan 1164-1165
Eyzaguirre, Luis B. 467
Ezquerra Abadia, Ramón 456

F. de Zamora, Rosa María 143

Fahmel Beyer, Bernd 270
Falch Frey, Jorge 1166
Faraco, Sergio 409, 504
Fauroux, Emmanuel 774
Federación Nacional de Cafeteros de Colombia. Centro de Documentación 236
Feijoó, María del Carmen 1527
Feldman, Lawrence H. 1194-1195
Felipe Herrera Library 844
Fernandes, Antônia Régia Mendonça 1392
Fernández, Antonio A. 321
Fernández, David W. 1423
Fernández, Herbene M.V.R. 223
Fernández, José B. 410
Fernández, Maximino 497
Fernández Baca L., José 60
Fernández-Kelly, María Patricia 931
Fernández P., María Angélica 932
Fernández Vázquez, Rodrigo 1581
Fernicola, Anna 1276-1277
Ferrari, Gustavo 1446
Ferreira, Carmosina N. 587
Ferreira, Gloria Isabel Sattamini 1286
Ferreira, Nadir Duarte 1154
Ferreira, Sonia Campos 1155
Ferreira da Costa, Rosa Amarilla de 1284
Ferrer Andrade, Guadalupe 970, 1509
Ferry de Moraes, Alice 1159
Figueiredo, Ademir 1632
Figueras, Myriam 53, 1054
Figueroa, Mercedes 1247
Finan, John J. 933
Finch, Mark S. 1039
Findlay, James A. 322
Fischer de Figueroa, Marie Claire 934
Fisher, Darien 1336
Fitch, J. Samuel 1458
Fitz, Earl F. 480
Fitzgerald, E.V.K. 613
Fleak, Kenneth 1045
Flores, Ana María 442
Flores, Gonzalo 206, 1565
Flores, María G. 1264
Flores Colombino, Andrés 1528
Flores Ochoa, Jorge A. 262
Florescano, Enrique 142, 612
Foote, Cheryl J. 176, 827
Forsyth, Elizabeth R. 1594
Fortes, Helvia de Luces 663
Foster, David William 15, 263, 411, 444, 484, 515, 523, 971, 972, 1019, 1055, 1073, 1098, 1104
Foster, Stephenie 614
France. Archives Nationales 1191
Franco, Isete Cordeiro 54
Franco, Rolando 1440
Franklin, Woodman B 126
Freudenthal, Juan R. 1281
Fuhrmann, Joyce 320
Fundação Carlos Chagas 1570
Fundação Instituto Brasileiro de Geografia e Estatística 1393
Fundação Instituto Brasileiro de Geografia e Estatística. Biblioteca Central 703
Fundación Ecuatoriana de Estudios Sociales 1529
Fundación Mariano Ospina Pérez 1475
Fundación Mariano Ospina Pérez. Servicio de Documentación e Información 1177
Fundación para el Desarrollo de la Región Centro Occidental de Venezuela 631
Funes, Antonieta del Valle 1144
Fustinoni, Osvaldo 412

Gade, Daniel 704
Galindo Cáceres, Jesús 1629
Galloway, J.H. 705
Galván, Max 646
Galván de Terrazas, Luz Elena 681, 683
García, Enildo Alberto 1056
García, Gervasio Luis 172

García, Rupert 473
García-Ayvens, Francisco 1329, 1335-1336
García Blasquez, Raúl 1476
García Carranza, Araceli 525, 910, 1057
García Carranza, Josefina 470, 525
García González, José 1058
García Losada, Matilde Isabel 1433
García Moll, Roberto 786, 1210
García Riera, Gladys 488
García Saucedo, Jaime 1305
Garibay Alvarez, Jorge 1211-1212
Garner, Jane 1271, 1314
Garritz Ruiz, Amaya 1213
Geggus, David P. 778
Gerber, Raquel 1029
Gertz, René E. 904
Ghosh, Pradip K. 564
Gibaja Vargas Prada, Pedro 1605
Gibbs, Donald 1265
Gilbert, Dennis 811
Gillum, Gary P. 1520
Giraldo Isaza, Martha Helena 55
Girbal de Blacha, Noemí M. 68, 74
Gladden, Earle M. 130-131
Glass, John B. 787, 1266, 1296
Glazier, Stephen 264
Gomes, Eduardo Rodrigues 754
Gómez de Matos, Patricia 1282
Gómez Fuentes, Héctor 1281
Gómez Pérez, Griselda 143
Gómez S., Magdalena 793
Gómez V., Stella 237
Gonçalves, Neuma Pinheiro Salomão 1291
González, Ansón 1106
González, Nelly S. 539, 1530
González, Rosa María 491
González Cícero, Stella María 1214-1220
González de Arellano, Josefina 1237
González de Olarte, Efraín 628
González Echenique, Javier 1167
González Echevarría, Roberto 450
González Flores, Abel 1232
González Martínez, José Luis 1494
González Petit, Elena Richer 162
Gonzalo de Giles, Doris 408
Goodman, Edward Julius 16
Goodman, Louis Wolf 565
Gormly, Mary 17-18
Goslinga, Marian 19, 125
Gotlib, Nádia Battella 481
Goyer, Doreen S. 1531
Graciarena, Jorge 1532
Granmer, Jan 20
Graupera Arango, Elena 1059
Gray, Silvia Sims 1337
Greaves, Cecilia 541
Greenfield, Richard 1533
Gregg, Kathleen 1427
Griffith, William J. 21
Grijalva Cobo, Adriana 510
Grindle, Merilee 935, 1462
Grossi, María Clara 665
Grothey, Mina Jane 22
Grover, Mark L. 23, 1520
Guarda, Gabriel 706
Gudmundson, Lowell 1453
Guerra Bravo, Samuel 510
Guevara de Bejarano, Martha 1379
Guillet, David 1562
Guimarães, Anarcila Ma. C. 54
Guimarães, Pedro Jose 211
Guittard, Jean-Michel 1193
Guthrie, Kathryn 1350
Gutiérrez, Zenaida 452
Gutiérrez de la Solana, Alberto 1060
Gutiérrez Solana, Nelly 265
Gutiérrez-Witt, Laura 323, 1264
Guttentag Tichauer, Werner 370-371
Guyot, Mireille 266
Guzmán, Augusto 414

Haddad G., Oscar 251
Haines, David W. 1536
Hall-Alleyne, Beverley 100
Hallewell, Laurence 25
Hancock, Susan B. 1507
Handelman, Howard 118
Handler, Jerome 78-79
Hanisch Espíndola, Walter 434
Hanke, Lewis 788
Harmon, Robert Bartlett 324
Hart, John M. 789
Hartmann, Roswith 26
Hartmann, Thekla 267
Hartness Graham, Ann 27
Hartness-Kane, Ann 28, 566-567, 1267
Hartwig, Richard 1587
Haugse, Vera Lúcia Oliveira de Araujo 649
Headlam, Freya 1511
Hébert, John R. 29
Heeter, Carrie 1306
Henderson, Donald C. 864, 1268
Hennessy, Alistair 1339
Heredia Herrera, Antonia 1254
Hernández, Luis Guillermo 1108
Hernández, Margarita 1613
Hernández, María Magdalena 110
Hernández de Caldas, Angela 55, 110, 238, 1128
Hernández Díaz, Mayda 243
Hernández G., María Magdalena 601
Hernández Hernández, Alberto 611
Hernández Ruigómez, Manuel 936
Herstein, Sheila 147, 157
Hickmann, Blasio 504
Híjar de Suárez, Rose 543
Hilton, Sylvia L. 30-31, 350
Hirst, Monica 753
Hodgman, Suzanne 892, 1315-1317
Hoefte, Rosemarijn 1575
Hoffman, Herbert H. 973
Hoffman, Léon-François 1071
Hogan, James E. 325
Holm, Olaf 268
Hough, Samuel 78-79
Howe, Robert 357, 568-569
Hoy, Don R. 106
Huerta, María Teresa 1595
Huneeus, Carlos 32
Hurtado Mánguez, Eugenio 1129
Hux, Meinrado 269

Ibarra, Hernán 244
Inch, Marcela 83
Ingram, Kenneth E. 137, 192
Institute of Jamaica, Kingston. West India Reference Library 1278
Instituto Argentino del Petroleo. Comisión de Biblioteca 1146
Instituto Costarricense de Electricidad 112
Instituto de Desenvolvimento de Pernambuco 1477
Instituto de Estudos Avançados em Educação 664
Instituto Histórico de la Ciudad de Buenos Aires. Archivo Histórico 736
Instituto Histórico de la Ciudad de Buenos Aires. Equipo Técnico 737
InterAmerica Research Associates 647
Inter-American Center for Documentation and Agriculture Information 1538
Inter-American Center for Documentation and Agriculture Information. Biblioteca y Terminal de Servicios 1401
International Institute for Educational Planning. Library 630
Irby, James Arthur 825
Itzstein, Gertraud 297

Jackson, Loraine 77
Jackson, Richard L. 974
Jackson, William Vernon 1192,

1196
Jara, Alvaro 1130
Jaramillo, Phillip 1539
Jáuregui Cordero, Juan Heriberto 745
Jeffrey, Phillip 1576
Jenkins, John H. 177
Jenkins Company 33
Jibaja, Pedro 1465
Jiménez, Dina 604
John F. Kennedy Library, Guyana 1307
Johnson, Peter T. 351
Jordan, Alma 352
Jordan, Anne H. 1099
Jungo, M.E. 648
Juzyn, Olga 498, 513

Kallsen, Margarita 814, 884, 914
Kauffmann Appenzeller, Bertha 752
Kaufman, Debra 937
Kaufman, Edy 1602
Kempeneers, Marianne 1577
Kenamore, Jane A. 1299
Kennedy, Patricia 1003
Kennedy Troya, Alexandra 1495
Kensinger, Kenneth M. 975
Kenton, Charlotte 1540
Kenwood, Alun 1375
Keremitsis, Eileen 1571
Kerr, Lucille 457
Khorramzadeh, Heshmatallah 1415
Kim, Vivian C. 1338
Klaczko, J. 834
Klein, Dennis A. 885
Klementeva, N.M. 34
Knight, Franklin W. 762
Köppen, Elke 1463
Kossmar, Sylvia 947
Kozhjevnikov, Emil 188
Kruse, David Samuel 121
Kuczynski, Pedro Pablo 166
Kudo, Tokihiro 1609
Kügelgen Kropfinger, Helga von 496
Kupfer, Monica E. 326
Kuznesof, Elizabeth Anne 1630

Lafourcade V., Pedro 668
La France, David G. 1221
Laguerre, Michel S. 132
Langstaff, Eleanor De Selms 158
Lapique Becali, Zoila 1369
Laporte Molina, Juan Pedro 298
Lara Tenorio, Blanca 790
Larbi, Kaye 102
Larouche, Irma 717-718
Larraga, Ricardo 1061
Larsen, Jurgen Ingemann 976
Larson, Everette E. 69
Láscaris Comneno, Constantino 475
Lastarría del Alamo, Aida 850
Lauerhass, Ludwig 649
Laurenti, Joseph L. 977
Lavrin, Asunción 719, 1541
Lavrov, Nikolai 720
Layera, Ramón 875
Leal, Luis 1085
Leal, Maria Antonieta Oliveira de Barros 1478
Leão, Carmen Lúcia de Souza 1287
Lechuga Barrios, Carmen 1222
Lee, Thomas A. 299
Leite, Miriam Lifchitz Moreira 474, 752
Leiva, Imelda 258
Lemoine, Ernesto 505
Lent, John A. 1308
LeoGrande, William M. 1454
Leon, Federico R. 1606
León, René 114
León Pinelo, Antonio de 35
León-Portilla, Ascención H. de 1074, 1080-1081
León (Swadesh) Quintana, Frances 1340
Leonel, Maria Célia de Moraes 1157
Lertora Mendoza, Celia Ana 1433
Levine, Daniel H. 1542

Levine, Robert M. 91, 1543
Levistre de Ruiz, Jeanine 56
Levy, Daniel C. 650
Lewald, H. Ernest 1020
Lewinski, Liliana 1148
Leyva Franco, Clemencia 667
Liberalli Bellotto, Heloisa 1298
Library of Congress. Hispanic Division 69
Lifschitz, Edgardo 570
Likins, John R. 122
Lima, Francisca Dantas de 54
Lima, Maria Cristina Pedrinha de 1291
Lima, María Regina Soares de 938
Lindstrom, Naomi 978
Litvak King, Jaime 270
Llanos de Ramírez, Emperatriz 110
Lluberes, Antonio 489
Loh, Eudora 1623
Lombardo de Ruiz, Sonia 327, 798
Lomeli, Francisco A. 1082
López Cervantes, Gonzalo 300
López de Valdivieso, Miriam 1109
López Díaz, María T. 1257
López Iñiguez, Iraida 1062
López M. de Badilla, María del Rocío 1402
López Rosado, Diego G. 615-616
Lorini, Irma 1149
Loroña, Lionel V. 353-354
Losada, Alejandro 980
Lostaunau Rubio, Gabriel 355, 688
Lotchin, Roger W. 1341
Lotis, Howard 1371
Louie de Irizarry, Florita Z. 328-330, 507, 1521
Lovera de Sola, Roberto J. 435, 1110
Lowder Stella 37
Lowenthal, Abraham F. 939
Lozano, Eduardo 331-336, 981, 1403
Lucero M., Miguel Angel 617
Lucero Nieto, Teodoro 466
Luján Muñoz, Jorge 271, 1544
Lulat, Y. 651
Luna, Laurentino 1223
Luna Marez, Patricia 1224-1226
Luna Tamayo, Milton 1185
Lundahl, Mats 571, 607
Luque de Sánchez, María Dolores 172
Lutz, Cristóbal H. 1197
Luyten, Joseph Maria 1030
Luzuriaga, Gerardo 1065-1066

MacCorkle, Lyn 1342
Mace, Carroll Edward 1416
Macfie, Samuel 106
Machado, Nadia Dorian 212
Mackey, William F. 652
Maffei Hunter, Lucy 1298
Magalhães, Alencar D'Avila 588
Magee, Susan Fortson 301
Málaga Medina, Alejandro 1250-1251
Malagamba A., Francisco 928
Malish, Basil 1318-1319
Manigat, Max 133
Manrique Castañeda, Leonardo 1075
Manrique P., Myriam 600
Mansutti Rodríguez, Alejandro 1496
Mantillo, Martha Eugenia 544
Marecki, Sofía 685
Marichal, Carlos 1545
Marín, Lucas 123-124
Marín de Sandoval, Concepción 686
Marinho, Luiz Claudio 572
Marino Flores, Anselmo 272
Marquez, Esther M. 660
Martí, Oscar R. 1434
Martin, Cheryl English 721
Martin, Dolores Moyano 38
Martin de Acuña, Carmen 199
Martínez, Héctor 1607
Martínez, Julio A. 356, 1082
Martínez, Manuela O. 1283
Martínez Bribiesca, Gilberto

1228
Martínez Paulino, Marcos Antonio 1408
Martínez Ríos, Jorge 618
Martínez Rizo, Felipe 682
Marting, Diane 1040
Martinique. Archives 1199
Martins, Miriam Dalva Lima 213
Marván Laborde, Ignacio 1553
Masferrer K., Elio 851-852
Masias Q., Lorena 60
Masiello, Francine R. 1021
Massé, Raymond 1577
Massone, Juan Antonio 1397
Matos, Antonio 39
Matos Mar, José 249
Matte Varas, José Joaquín 461
Maxwell, Simón 207
Mayaweski, Teresa 1195
Mayman, Valerie 982
Mazzetti Gardiol, Rita 469
McClendon, Carmen Chaves 545
McGowan, Gerald L. 1417
McKinnon, Linda T. 1343
McLachlan, Ross W. 1274
McMurray, George R. 983
McWatt, Mark 1120
Mead, Robert G., Jr. 144
Medeiros, Ana Ligia Silva 522, 753
Medford, Roberta 1623
Medina, Rubens 1124
Medina Mondragón, Celia 1236
Meehan, Thomas C. 984
Meier, Matt S. 1344
Meireles, Mário M. 1497
Mejía, José M. 249
Mellafe, Rolando 1508
Mendes, Evelyse Maria Freire 1449
Méndez, M.A. 242
Méndez-Domínguez, Alfredo 40
Méndez N., Eloína 619
Mendoza Deleon, Arely 441
Menton, Seymour 1070
Mercader Martínez, Yolanda 940
Merlino, Rodolfo J. 1563
Merubia, Sonia 70, 739
Mesa, Rosa Q. 357
Mesa-Lago, Carmelo 1546
Mesa Nápoles, Angel 243
Metress, Eileen S. 1547
Metress, Seamus 1547
Mexico. Archivo General de la Nación 791-797, 1227-1236, 1498-1500
México. Instituto Nacional de Antropología e Historia 273
Mexico. Secretaría de Educación Pública 1480
México. Secretaría de Programación y Presupuesto 620
México. Secretaría de Programación y Presupuesto. Coordinación General de Estadística, Geografía e Informática 1479
Miceli, Sergio 1501
Milanca Guzmán, Mario 874
Miller, Eugene Willard 41-43
Miller, Joseph C. 722, 763
Miller, Ruby M. 41-43
Millones, Luis 1502
Miranda, Altagracia 1466
Miranda Cárabes, Celia 916
Miranda E., Mirza 869
Moe, Annette T. 302
Moe, Christine 337
Moisés, Massaud 1032
Montejano y Aguiñaga, Rafael 1418
Montes, Toby 1349
Montes Huidobro, Matías 985
Monzon, Susana 266
Moore, Wenceslao 416
Mora Gutiérrez, Dominga Venancia 922
Morais da Cruz, Ana María 1282
Morales, Phyllis S. 453
Morales Padrón, Francisco 723
Moreira, Cecília 1549
Morel Solaeche, Rubén Eugenio 162, 917
Moreno, M.A. 1435
Moreno Toscano, Alejandro 798
Moriya de Freundorfer, Yoshiko 1284
Morles Sánchez, Victor 693
Morley, Sylvanus Griswold 274

Mörner, Magnus 724
Moseley, Edward H. 294
Mosquera, Martha 1548
Moss, Alan 44
Moss, Sylvia 1131-1132
Moura, Gerson 938
Mucharraz de Díaz, Olga 865
Mulcansingh, Vernon C. 707
Mulet de Cerezo, María Luisa 777
Müller, Klaus 5
Müller-Bergh, Klaus 450
Müller de Ceballos, Ingrid 667
Mundo Lo, Sara de 71, 417
Muñoz, Heraldo 941
Muñoz de Linares, Elba 546, 900
Murchie, Anita 258
Museo Nacional de Historia (Mexico) 1237
Musso Ambrosi, Luis Alberto 740, 831-833

Nagelkerke, Gerard A. 175
Naranjo de González, Livia 1588
Nassar, Nazira Leita 200, 214-215
Nasta, Susheila 516-517
Natal, Carmelo Rosario 821
Natella, Arthur A., Jr. 1100
National Library (Guyana) 338
Nauman, Ann Keith 1139
Naylor, Thomas H. 783
Nazario, Olga 1467
Nazoa, Aquiles 1111
Nef, J. 45
Nef, Jorge 1452
Nelson, Reed 1493
Newman, Bud 1313
Newton, Maureen 1576
Newton, Velma 1132, 1578
Neymeyer, Robert J. 95
Nicaragua. Centro de Investigaciones y Estudios de la Reforma Agraria. Biblioteca 1420
Nieschulz de Stockhausen, Elke 1424
Niles, Susan A. 275
Nilsen, Kirsti 101
Nilsson, Maj-Britt 860
Nocetti, Milton A. 1285, 1549
Nodal, Roberto 92, 195, 942
Nogueira, Norma Maria Fernandes 549
Nolff, Max 573
Noronha, Daisy Pires 547
Nostrand, Richard L. 149
Novo, Palmira Costa 203
Nuessel, Frank H., Jr. 986-987
Nunn, Frederick M. 725

Oberbeck, Charles D. 626
Oberg, Larry R. 671, 1590
Oberti R., Italo 303
Ocasio-Meléndez, Marcial 784
Oczon, Annabelle M. 828
Ojeda Díaz, María de los Angeles 276, 1207
Olazagasti, Ignacio 173
Oliveira, Américo Lópes de 418
Oliveira, Edilson Batista de 216
Oliveira, Francisco de 589
Oliveira, Joanyr de 1031
Oliveira, Lúcia Lippi 754
Oliveira, Silas Marques de 217
Olivera, Otto 1064
Olivo, Edna A. 1617
Olmo, Rosa del 1133
Olson, Nadine 545
Oniki, Kazuko 548
Oporto, Luis 260, 277
Oqueli, Ramón 1460-1461
Ordoñez, Elizabeth J. 1083
Ordoñez Chiriboga, Patricio 1185
Organization of American States 1482
Orihuela, Augusto Germán 924
Orlandi, Alberto 574
Ortal, José Casimiro 178
Ortega, Emiliano 201
Ortiz de López, María del Pilar 1177
Osorio Tejeda, Nelson 988
Ospina, Miryam A. 1276-1277

Padilha da Luz, María Cira 219
Padrón, Nicolasa 605
Paes, José Paulo 1032
Pagán Perdomo, Dato 339
Pagani, Estela 736
Page, James Allen 419
Paim, Antonio 1436
Painter, Michael 250
Palau Claveras, Agustín 899
Palen, Roberta R. 278
Palmer, Colin A. 726
Panama. Archivo Nacional 1247
Paniagua, Cándida S. de 863
Paolucci, Gabriella 1503
Papkov, Oleg 1550
Parada Caicedo, Jorge Humberto 1589
Parcero López, María de la Luz 799-800, 1596
Pardo, Mauricio 279
Parejas Moreno, Alcides J. 746
Parfait, Blanca H. 501
Parodi, Claudia 1076
Pásara, Luis 1608
Patiño, Beatriz 1173
Patterson, Orlando 727
Paulino, José C. 463
Payne, Aldeen 586
Paz, Miguel Angel 189, 1425
Pedrique, Vilma 1112
Peirano Falconi, Luis 1609
Pellitero, Antonio 72
Pellón Caballero, Marcela 1200
Peña, Devon Gerardo 621
Peña, Guillermo de la 683
Peñín, José 1372
Peraza Zarausa, Norma T. 906
Perdomo Correa, Omar 486
Perdomo, Omar 471
Peregrino, Umberto 755
Pereira, Isanira Coutinho Vaz 218
Pereira, Luiz C. Bresser 756, 1572
Pereira, Marília Mesquita Guedes 549
Pérez, Grace R. 1268
Pérez, Lisandro 1269
Pérez, Louis A. 770-771, 1180
Pérez de Zapata, Amarilis 653, 672-673
Pérez Herrero, Pedro 1238
Pérez López, Jorge F. 1455
Pérez Martínez, Hector 145
Pérez-Rosas Cáceres, Augusto 582, 1610
Pérez Stable, Marifeli 1456
Pérez Zevallos, Juan M. 803
Pergola, Federico 412
Perú. Biblioteca Nacional 387, 1252
Perú. Dirección de Archivo Colonial 1253
Perú. Instituto Nacional de Cultura. Biblioteca Nacional 358
Phillips, Beverly 168
Phillips, Glenn O. 1270
Phipps, Shelley F. 1274
Piedracueva, Haydée 359-363
Pierre, Guy 1545
Pinto, Regina Pahin 1033
Pinto, Sonia 1130
Pinzás García, Teobaldo 629
Pio del Corro, Gaspar 1022
Pluto, Joseph A. 1051
Podestá, Bruno 47
Pollak-Eltz, Angelina 280-281
Polzer, Charles W. 783
Poppe, René 83
Porras Barrenechea, Raúl 57
Portales, Carlos 943
Portantiero, Juan Carlos 1442
Portes, Alejandro 1552
Porto, Everaldo Rocha 219
Portocarrero, Felipe 1465
Post, Edite E. 220-221, 228
Potash, Robert A. 1239-1241
Pottinger, L.G. 1592
Poyo, Gerald E. 1271, 1617
Pozo, Melvin 207
Presidencia de Quito 775
Price, Robin 1190
Programa Regional del Empleo para América Latina y el Caribe 1483
Provincia Franciscana de Chile 1169-1171
Prümers, Heiko 297
Puentes de Oyenard, Sylvia 420, 1107

Quamina, Lynda 102
Quemel, Maria Angélica Rodrigues 526
Querales, Juandemaro 1113
Quereilhac, Alicia C. 1563
Quilis, Antonio 989

Raat, William Dirk 801
Rafide, Matías 1046
Ramesar, Marianne 1579
Ramírez, Axel 282
Ramírez, Gilberto 1594
Ramírez, Rafael L. 174
Ramírez de Díaz, María 1177
Ramírez de Díaz, María Teresa 239
Ramírez R, Rubén 944
Ramírez Rivera, Hugo Rodolfo 887
Ramos Guédez, José Marcial 190-191, 837
Rauls, Martina 945
Redonet Cook, Salvador Pedro 493
Reeve, Richard M. 465
Reeves, Rosa E. 429
Reich, Peter L. 1504
Reis, Roberto 411
Rela, Walter 990
Resnick, Margery 991
Restrepo Manrique, Daniel 508
Revista interamericana de bibliografía. Interamerican review of bibliography 915
Rey Balmaceda, Raúl 67, 708
Reyes, Silvia 181, 1123
Reyes García, Cayetano 793, 802, 1297
Reyna, José Luis 1553
Rial, Juan 834
Ricardo García, Ismaela 1302
Riera Encinoza, Argenis 1620
Rieznik, Pablo Héctor 577
Rieznik, Rodolfo 577
Río, Carmen Del 661
Río, Martha del 655-656
Rios, María E. 76
Rivarola I., Mirtha María 687
Rivas, Rafael Angel 1114
Rivas Dugarte, Rafael Angel 436
Rivera, Mario A. 304
Rivera de Alvarez, Josefina 1105
Rivera de Baryón, Vilma 1134
Rivera de Figueroa, Carmen A. 341
Rivero, Eliana 1084
Robbins, Naomi C. 147
Robinson, Barbara J. 1345
Robinson, David James 1242
Robinson, Joy Cordell 1345
Rocard, Marcienne 992
Rocha Nogueira, Arlinda 1298
Rodríguez, Andrés 1086
Rodríguez, Humberto 1346
Rodríguez, Rita de Cassia 1034
Rodríguez, Selma C. 1135
Rodríguez Castelo, Hernán 993
Rodríguez Chaurnet, Dinah 202
Rodríguez Chávez, Pedro 1206
Rodríguez de Baliero, Haydée 835
Rodríguez de Lebríja, Esperanza 622, 1243
Rodríguez Pastor, Humberto 1347
Rodríguez Pereyra, Ricardo 1619
Rodríguez Ramos, Esther 485
Rodríguez Rea, Miguel Angel 355, 454, 688, 870, 888, 1101-1103
Rodríguez Tamay, Julia 850
Rodríguez Vicente, Encarnación 1258
Roh, Jae Min 419
Rojas, Ana Cecilia 1112
Rojas Gutiérrez, Angel M. 240
Rojas R., Teresa 803
Rojas Uzcátegui, José de la Cruz 1115
Rolland, Denis 48
Román-Lagunas, Jorge 994-995, 1047
Romero, Cira 455
Romero Rojas, Francisco José 375, 890
Rondinelli, Roseli Curi 1159
Ronzelen, Teresa María van

1494
Rosa, Ottoni de Sousa 228
Roscoe, Lori A. 1348
Rosenberg, Mark B. 107
Rosenberg Library 1299
Ross, Stanley Robert 886
Rosso, Hespéria Zuma de 709
Rovirosa, Dolores 483
Roy, Joaquín 179, 996
Rubiales Torrejón, Javier 1254
Rubio de Lertora, Patricio 1048
Ruhl, J. Mark 1450
Ruiz, Amarilis 1112
Ruiz Dueñas, Jorge 1597
Ruiz-Fornells, Enrique 534, 1381
Ruiz y Blanco, Emilio R. 891
Russell-Wood, A.J.R 757

Sabelli de Louzao, Martha 1485, 1619
Sabino, Robin 1116
Sacerio-Garí, Enrique 445
Sacoto, Antonio 1067
Sáenz, Gracia, Nieves 1256
Sáez-Godoy, Leopoldo 997
Sahai, Hardeo 1618
Saint, William S. 590
Saínz Chávez, Luis 1356
Salas Sánchez, Margarita 1611-1612
Salazar Alonso, Francisco A. 1379
Salisbury, Lutishoor 1410
Salles, Vicente 342
Salmito, Adeilda Rigaud 710
Salom, Bartolomé 514
Salomon, Frank 283, 1068
Salvador, Nélida 857
Samara, Eni de Mesquita 1573
San Diego State University. Library. Department of Special Collections 1272
Sánchez, Efraín 343
Sánchez, María Elsa B. 555
Sánchez, Sara M. 443
Sánchez Gutiérrez, Arturo 623, 1598
Sánchez López, Luis María 422
Sánchez M., Esther 425
Sánchez Moya Zaida 632, 668-669, 858
Sandos, James 1273
Sant' Ana, Moacir Medeiros de 446
Santley, Robert S. 284
Santos, María 1349
Santos, Walda Correa dos 203
Santos, Yolanda Lhullier dos 728
Santos Escudero, Ceferino 1432
Santos Gómez, Susana 73
Santos Quilez, Aleida de los 1591
Saucedo Lugo, Elena 638
Saupe, Barbara 168
Sayad, João 591
Scarano Fiol, Francisco 821
Schaffer, Ellen G. 578, 598
Schavelzon, Daniel G. 265
Scheidesser, Elisabeth 1554
Schiefelbein, Ernesto 665
Schkolnik, Susana 657
Schmidt, Steffen W. 1555
Schon, Isabel 148, 998-1003
Schultz, Rosario A. 1556
Schwartzmann, Simon 658
Seckinger, Ron 765
Seiferhels, Alfredo M. 163
Selinsky, Cheryl 1350
Sellers, John R. 711
Senra, Angela 482
Sensano Zárate, Rosa María 81
Serbín, Andrés 103
Serrano, Elisabeth de Oliveria 204, 222
Seybolt, Richard A. 1016
Shaw, Bradley A. 364
Shaw, David 1512
Sheahan, John 579
Sheetz de Eherd, Pamela 1005
Shimose, Pedro 407
Siles Guevara, Juan 365
Silva, Maximiliano de Carvalho e 518
Silva, Sergio 181, 1123
Silveira Santos, Daury Da 1035
Silvestre, Inalda Monteiro 344
Silvestrini Pacheco, Blanca 822

Simões, Neusa Quirino 1036
Simón Díaz, José 1006
Simón Palmer, María del Carmen 1007-1008
Singh, Sydney 1121
Sipkov, Ivan 1124
Sisson, Edward B. 305
Slater, William F. 741, 768
Sloan, John W. 946
Smith, John David 1557
Smith, Paul Christopher 1063
Smith, Ronna 495
Snyder, Frederick E. 1136
Socolow, Susan M. 742
Sofer, Eugene F. 580
Solano Navarro, Yamileth 670
Solís, Miguel de J. 729
Solveira de Báez, Beatriz Rosario 74
Somoshegyi-Szokol, Gaston 51
Somoza, Jorge L. 1508
Sonntag, Iliana L. 1274, 1310, 1382-1283
Sosa de Macial, Ramona 1248
Sosa de Newton, Lily 423
Souza, Maria da Conceição 424
Souza, Maria da P.N. de 223
Souza, Maria Helena de 223
Souza, Paulo Renato de 592
Souza Silva, Aderaldo de 219
Spain. Centro Nacional de Microfilm 1322
Sperry, Suzana 224
Stark, Greg 1350
Stark O., María del Valle 932
Stemplowski, Ryszard 1443
Stenzel, Norma 1286
Stern, Irwin 1037
Sternberg, Rolf 712
Stoddard, Ellwyn R. 149
Storni, Hugo 1505
Stratta, María Eugenia 1146
Streeter, Thomas Winthrop 180
Stuart, George E. 1010
Stultz, Modeena 305
Suárez, Angeles 1233
Suárez, Ida L. 425
Suárez Díaz, Osvaldo 243
Sullivan, LeRoy L. 659
Sunkel, Osvaldo 599
Swedberg, Richard 135
Szewczyk, David M. 1289, 1301
Szmulewicz, Efraín 1049

Tamayo Rodríguez, Carlos 1405
Tardieu, Patrick 134, 381
Tatum, Charles 1351
Tausch, Arno 593
Taylor, Alexander Smith 829
Teixeira, João Batista 225
Teja Angeles, Ileana de la 1311, 1356
Tentle J., Hortencia 802
Tepaske, John J. 731
Terrazos Contreras, Máximo 1558
Terry, Edward D. 294
Tesler, Mario 75
Teytaud, A. Robert 595
Thompson, Annie Figueroa 1373
Tigner, James L. 1352
Tobar Cruz, Pedro 1198
Topete, María de la Luz 285
Torre-Rivas, Edelberto 1451
Torre Villar, Ernesto de la 804
Torres A., Federico 1624
Torres Soarez, Ronaldo 222
Tosstorff, Reiner 1459
Tóth, Agnes 49
Towle, Edward L. 595
Trujillo, Roberto G. 1085-1087
Tuleskyu, Sueli A. 699
Turner, Mary C. 50
Tutino, John 805
Tutorow, Norman E. 806
Tyler, Daniel 1275

U.S. Department of Housing and Urban Development. Office of International Affairs 1631
Ugalde de Chudina, María Dolores 743
Universidad de Antioquía. Departamento de Bibliotecas, Medellín 1052
Universidad de Oriente (Cumaná, Venezuela). Dirección de

Bibliotecas 1426
Universidad de Oriente (Santiago de Cuba) 1302
Universidad Iberoamericana. Centro de Información Académica 1244
Universidad Nacional Autónoma de México. Instituto de Investigaciones Sociales 1419
Universidade Federal de Goiás. Biblioteca Central. Seção de Periódicos 1395
Université de Haute Bretagne. Centre d'études portugaises, brésiliennes et de l'Afrique lusophone 758
Université de Paris IV: Paris-Sorbonne. Institute d'Études Hispaniques. Bibliothèque 1193
University of California, Berkeley. Library 51, 1384
University of Kansas. Libraries 108
University of the West Indies. Library 193
Uribe, Maruja 241, 1613
Uribe de H., María Teresa 1398

Valadés, José C. 807
Valdés, Dennis Nodin 1353
Valdés, Nelson P. 1406
Valdez Escalera, Martha 76
Valentino Ramírez, Pablo 940, 1245
Valenzuela de Garay, Carmen 492
Valis, Noel 1012
Valjalo, David 490
Valk, Barbara G. 859-860, 920
Valladares, Lícia do Prado 1632
Valle, Rafael Heliodoro 136, 780
Valle Prieto, María Eugenia 286
Valois, Eliana Candeira 226
Valverde, Leonard A. 660
Van den Berg, Hans 747
Van Ee, Patricia Molen 711
Vanden, Harry E 1444
Vandenburgh, Anne 1317
Vargas Zúñiga, María Dolores 1254
Vasconcelos, Sandra Guardini Teixeira 1157
Vasque, Josetine 1160
Vásquez, James A. 1354
Vázquez, Josefina Z. 1239-1241
Veerkamp, Verónica 624, 625
Velasco, Ana María 1088
Velasco Barraza, Carlos R. 661
Velázquez, Gonzalo 388
Velázquez Chávez, María del Carmen 808
Véliz, Vito 287
Ventur, Pierre 1013
Ventura, Jose Aires 212
Verani, Hugo J. 499
Verner, Joel G. 1137
Versiani, Flávio Ravelo 594
Vickers, William T. 288
Vidaurreta, Alicia 164
Vieira, Dirceu Justiniano 204
Vieira, Francisca Terezinha Batista 227
Vieira, Nelson H. 426
Vieira Filho, Domingos 700
Vigil Batista, Alejandro 1200
Vila Vilar, Enriqueta 823
Villacis V., Eduardo 1186-1189
Villalobos Vázquez, Miguel Angel 151
Villareal, René 581
Villarreal, Hilda 1336
Villaseñor y Villaseñor, Ramiro 152, 427
Villasmil de Losada, Helen 1138
Villegas, Carmen 199
Vinci, Liliana F. 76
Vinh, Augustine Ha T. 1536
Vivó, Paquita 1615
Von dem Bussche, Gastón 1172
Vorobeva, Z.G. 52
Voss, Stuart F. 809

Wagenaar Hummdicks, P. 894
Wagner, Erika 289-291
Wagoner, Shirley A. 1355
Walters, Marian C. 558
Weathers, Shirley A. 1261
Weber, David 1341
Webre, Stephen 1197
Weinstein, Barbara 759
Weiss, David 1356
Welch, Thomas L. 53, 1262
Werlich, David P. 730
Wessman, James W. 246
West, Dennis Deforest 1014
West, Jonathan P. 149
Whately, Maria Celina 754
Whigham, Thomas Lyle 815
White, Anthony G. 345
White, Garth 100, 1374
White, Sylvia 1633
Wiederhecker, Hilda de Sena Corrêa 1392
Wiggers, Maria Salete 221, 228-229
Wilkinson, Audine 104, 477
Williams, Gayle 1385, 1386
Williams, Maxine 586
Wilson, Lofton 1276
Wilson, Michael E. 1299
Wood, Richard E. 1015
Woodbridge, Hensley Charles 366
Woods, Richard D. 27, 1357
Woodward, Ralph Lee 80, 157
Woodward, Ralph Lee, Jr. 812
Worrell, De Lisle 586

Yale University. Library. Historical Manuscripts and Archives 1277

Zanutto, Juan Carlos (Karus Watink) 292
Zapata, Francisco 1560
Zapata, Megala de 1486
Zapata Cuéncar, Heriberto 1399
Zayas de Lima, Perla 428
Zeitz, Eileen 1016
Zenzes Eisenbach, Carla 1561
Zenzes Eisenbach, Ernestina 955, 970
Zevallos y Muñiz, Marco Aurelio 582
Zimmerman, Enid 1089
Zirker, Daniel 1574
Zubatsky, David S. 861
Zuleta, Ignacio M. 897